England and Scotland, 1286–1603

British History in Perspective

General Editor: Jeremy Black

Toby Barnard   *The Kingdom of Ireland, 1641–1760*
Eugenio Biagini   *Gladstone*
D. G. Boyce   *The Irish Question and British Politics, 1868–1996* (2nd edn)
Keith M. Brown   *Kingdom or Province? Scotland and the Regal Union, 1603–1715*
A. D. Carr   *Medieval Wales*
Gregory Claeys   *The French Revolution Debate in Britain*
Eveline Cruickshanks   *The Glorious Revolution*
Anne Curry   *The Hundred Years War* (2nd edn)
John Derry   *Politics in the Age of Fox, Pitt and Liverpool* (rev. edn)
Susan Doran   *England and Europe in the Sixteenth Century*
Seán Duffy   *Ireland in the Middle Ages*
Ian Gentles   *Oliver Cromwell: God's Warrior and the English Revolution*
David Gladstone   *The Twentieth-Century Welfare State*
Brian Golding   *Conquest and Colonisation: The Normans in Britain, 1066–1100* (2nd edn)
Sean Greenwood   *Britain and the Cold War, 1945–91*
Steven Gunn   *Early Tudor Government, 1485–1558*
Richard Harding   *The Evolution of the Sailing Navy 1509–1815*
David Harkness   *Ireland in the Twentieth Century: Divided Island*
Ann Hughes   *The Causes of the English Civil War* (2nd edn)
Kathryn Hurlock   *Britain, Ireland and the Crusades, c.1000–1300*
I. G. C. Hutchison   *Scottish Politics in the Twentieth Century*
Ronald Hutton   *The British Republic, 1649–1660* (2nd edn)
Kevin Jeffreys   *The Labour Party Since 1945*
T. A. Jenkins   *Disraeli and Victorian Conservatism*
T. A. Jenkins   *Sir Robert Peel*
J. Gwynfor Jones   *Early Modern Wales, c.1525–1640*
H. S. Jones   *Victorian Political Thought*
D. E. Kennedy   *The English Revolution, 1642–1649*
Christine Kinealy   *The Great Irish Famine*
Andy King & Claire Etty   *England and Scotland, 1286–1603*
David Loades   *The Mid-Tudor Crisis, 1545–1565*
Diarmaid MacCulloch   *Later Reformation in England, 1547–1603* (2nd edn)
John F. McCaffrey   *Scotland in the Nineteenth Century*
W. David McIntyre   *British Decolonisation, 1946–1997*
A. P. Martinich   *Thomas Hobbes*
Roger Middleton   *The British Economy Since 1945*
G. H. Murray   *Pittock Jacobitism*
G. H. Murray   *Pittock Scottish Nationality*
W. M. Ormrod   *Political Life in Medieval England, 1300–1450*
Richie Ovendale   *Anglo-American Relations in the Twentieth Century*
Ian Packer   *Lloyd George*
Anthony Page   *Britain and the Seventy Years War, 1744–1815*
Keith Perry   *British Politics and the American Revolution*
A. J. Pollard   *The Wars of the Roses* (3rd edn)

David Powell *British Politics and the Labour Question, 1868–1990*
David Powell *The Edwardian Crisis: Britain, 1901–1914*
Richard Rex *Henry VIII and the English Reformation* (2nd edn)
Matthew Roberts *Political Movements in Urban England, 1832–1914*
David Scott *Politics and War in the Three Stuart Kingdoms, 1637–49*
G. R. Searle *The Liberal Party: Triumph and Disintegration, 1886–1929* (2nd edn)
John Stuart Shaw *The Political History of Eighteenth-Century Scotland*
George Southcombe & Grant Tapsell *Restoration Politics, Religion and Culture: Britain and Ireland, 1600–1714*
W. M. Spellman *John Locke*
William Stafford *John Stuart Mill*
Robert Stewart *Party and Politics 1830–1852*
Alan Sykes *The Radical Right in Britain*
Bruce Webster *Medieval Scotland*
Ann Williams *Kingship and Government in Pre-Conquest England*
Ian S. Wood *Churchill*
John W. Young *Britain and European Unity, 1945–99* (2nd edn)
Michael B. Young *Charles I*
Paul Ziegler *Palmerston*

Please note that a sister series, Social History in Perspective, is available covering the key topics in social and cultural history.

England and Scotland, 1286–1603

Andy King and Claire Etty

BLOOMSBURY ACADEMIC
LONDON • NEW YORK • OXFORD • NEW DELHI • SYDNEY

BLOOMSBURY ACADEMIC
Bloomsbury Publishing Plc
50 Bedford Square, London, WC1B 3DP, UK
1385 Broadway, New York, NY 10018, USA
29 Earlsfort Terrace, Dublin 2, Ireland

BLOOMSBURY, BLOOMSBURY ACADEMIC and the Diana logo
are trademarks of Bloomsbury Publishing Plc

First published 2016 by PALGRAVE

Copyright © Andy King and Claire Etty 2016

Andy King and Claire Etty have asserted their rights under the Copyright,
Designs and Patents Act, 1988, to be identified as the authors of this work.

For legal purposes the Acknowledgements on p. xiv constitute
an extension of this copyright page.

All rights reserved. No part of this publication may be reproduced or
transmitted in any form or by any means, electronic or mechanical,
including photocopying, recording, or any information storage or retrieval
system, without prior permission in writing from the publishers.

Bloomsbury Publishing Plc does not have any control over, or responsibility for,
any third-party websites referred to or in this book. All internet addresses given
in this book were correct at the time of going to press. The author and publisher
regret any inconvenience caused if addresses have changed or sites have
ceased to exist, but can accept no responsibility for any such changes.

A catalogue record for this book is available from the British Library.

A catalog record for this book is available from the Library of Congress.

ISBN: PB: 978-0-2302-8233-9
ePDF: 978-1-1374-9155-8
ePub: 978-1-3503-0697-4

To find out more about our authors and books visit
www.bloomsbury.com and sign up for our newsletters.

To my parents, Beth King and Ted Hutchinson, with gratitude and love
A.K.

To Ally, without whom…
C.E.

Contents

Preface — xiii
Acknowledgements — xiv
Abbreviations — xv

Maps

i. England and Scotland — xvii
ii. The Anglo-Scottish Marches — xviii

Genealogical Tables

i. The Scottish Succession, 1286–1332 — xix
ii. The English Succession, 1509–1603 — xx

Introduction — 1
i. Historiography — 1
ii. Origins: England and Scotland to 1296 — 5

Part 1

1. Hammer of the Scots? Edward I and Scotland, 1286–1306 — 13
i. The Scottish Succession and the 'Great Cause', 1286–92 — 13
ii. English Conquest, 1292–1306 — 19

2. Scottish Civil Wars, 1306–37   29
i. Good King Robert, 1306–28   29
ii. Edward Balliol and the Disinherited, 1332–7   39

3. The Hundred Years War: War on Two Fronts, 1337–1453   47
i. Edward III and David II, 1337–71   47
ii. England at Bay, 1369–1406   55
iii. Stalemate, 1406–53   64

4. The Wars of the Roses, 1453–1502   73
i. English Civil Wars, 1453–80   73
ii. 'Rigorous and Cruel War' to Perpetual Peace, 1480–1502   79

5. Auld Alliance, New Europe, 1503–37   92
i. The End of the Perpetual Peace, 1503–13   92
ii. England *versus* France: Minority Regimes in Scotland, 1513–24   95
iii. France Eclipsed: 1524–37   102

6. Reformations and Rough Wooing, 1537–60   107
i. The Road to Solway Moss, 1537–42   107
ii. Overlordship or Union? 1542–51   109
iii. France Victorious, 1551–8   117
iv. Turning Point? 1558–60   120

7. Better Together? 1561–1603   123

Part 2

8. Armies and Warfare   137

9. The Marches   149
i. Border Society   149
ii. The March Laws   161

10. Relations between Peoples   170

11. National Identity and Propaganda: The Appeal to
History and Contemporary Views of the 'Other' 182
  i. National Identities 182
  ii. England, Scotland and 'Britain' 188

Conclusion 195

Notes 203

Select Bibliography 219

Glossary 226

Index 229

Preface

Endnotes have been used to provide additional information for further reading, and otherwise for referencing sources. References have not generally been given to works already listed in the **Select Bibliography**, except where a particular or controversial line of argument has been followed (and note that works listed in the **Select Bibliography** are referred to by an abbreviated title in the endnotes).

Quotations from contemporary texts are given in translation; those written in English have been modernized in both spelling and vocabulary, and those written in Scots have been 'Englished'. For the sake of consistency and familiarity (and due to the linguistic ignorance of the authors), anglicized forms of Gaelic names have been employed throughout. French monarchs have been referred to by their French names for the sake of clarity.

At many times throughout the period, many Scots were in the allegiance of the kings of England. However, for simplicity's sake, we have usually referred to supporters of the kings of Scots as 'the Scots', and supporters of the kings of England as 'the English', a practice which conforms with contemporary usage.

We have tried to be scrupulous in looking at events from both the English and Scottish perspectives. Sometimes, however, the weight of evidence; the course of events; or the locus of the factors driving relations, have demanded a closer focus on one side or the other. In particular, Anglo-Scottish relations often loomed larger in Scottish than in English politics (where France was the main concern for much of this period), and the book reflects this.

Acknowledgements

We would both like to thank the anonymous readers for their helpful comments; and Sonya Barker, Felicity Noble, Jenna Steventon, Rachel Bridgewater and Clarissa Sutherland at Palgrave for their saintly patience in the face of repeated delays.

Thanks also to Beth King and Bob Etty who read and commented on most of the book; to Liz and Janet Etty; to Katie Stevenson and David Simpkin who commented on particular chapters; and to Anne Curry who helped to launch it.

Various aspects of the book have been shaped by discussions over the years with Jeff Becker, Richard Britnell, Michael Brown, Robin Frame, Sandy Grant, Aly Macdonald, Cynthia Neville, Michael Penman, Tony Pollard, Michael Prestwich, Len Scales and Sarah Tebbit.

In addition, Andy would like to thank students at Southampton and the Department of Continuing Education at Oxford who have listened (or not) to his half-formed views on Anglo-Scottish relations.

We would both like to thank Lewis King for his unbridled enthusiasm; and Freya King, who tells us that without her, all this would not have been possible – and for being real horrorshow, as it might be.

Thanks, too, to W.T., B.S., U., E., T.W., G. and W.G. for keeping us sane.

Abbreviations

ASR	*Anglo-Scottish Relations, 1174–1328. Some Selected Documents*, ed. E.L.G. Stones (2nd edn, Oxford, 1970).
BP	*The Border Papers. Calendar of Letters and Papers Relating to the Affairs of the Borders of England and Scotland*, ed. J. Bain (2 vols, Edinburgh, 1894–6).
CDS	*Calendar of Documents Relating to Scotland*, ed. J. Bain (4 vols, Edinburgh, 1881–8).
CSP	*Calendar of State Papers.*
EHR	*English Historical Review.*
Fordun	*John of Fordun's Chronicle of the Scottish Nation*, tr. F.J.H. Skene (Edinburgh, 1872).
Hamilton Papers	*The Hamilton Papers. Letters and Papers Illustrating the Political Relations of England and Scotland in the XVIth Century*, ed. J. Bain (2 vols, Edinburgh, 1890–92).
JMH	*Journal of Medieval History.*
LP	*Letters and Papers, Foreign and Domestic, Henry VIII.*
NH	*Northern History.*
ODNB	*Oxford Dictionary of National Biography* (Oxford, 60 vols, 2004) – accessible online at: www.oxforddnb.com
PROME	*The Parliament Rolls of Medieval England*, eds. C. Given-Wilson, et al. (CD-Rom, Leicester 2005) – accessible online at: www.sd-editions.com/PROME/home.html

RS	Rolls Series.
Rot. Scot.	*Rotuli Scotiæ*, eds. D. Macpherson, et al. (2 vols, Record Commission, 1814–19).
RPS	*Records of the Parliaments of Scotland to 1707*, eds. K.M. Brown, et al. (St Andrews, 2007–11) – accessible online at: www.rps.ac.uk
Scalacronica	*Sir Thomas Gray: Scalacronica (1272–1363)*, ed. A. King, Surtees Society ccix (2005).
Scotichronicon	*Bower's Scotichronicon*, eds. D.E.R. Watt, et al. (9 vols, Aberdeen and Edinburgh, 1987–98).
SHR	*Scottish Historical Review*.

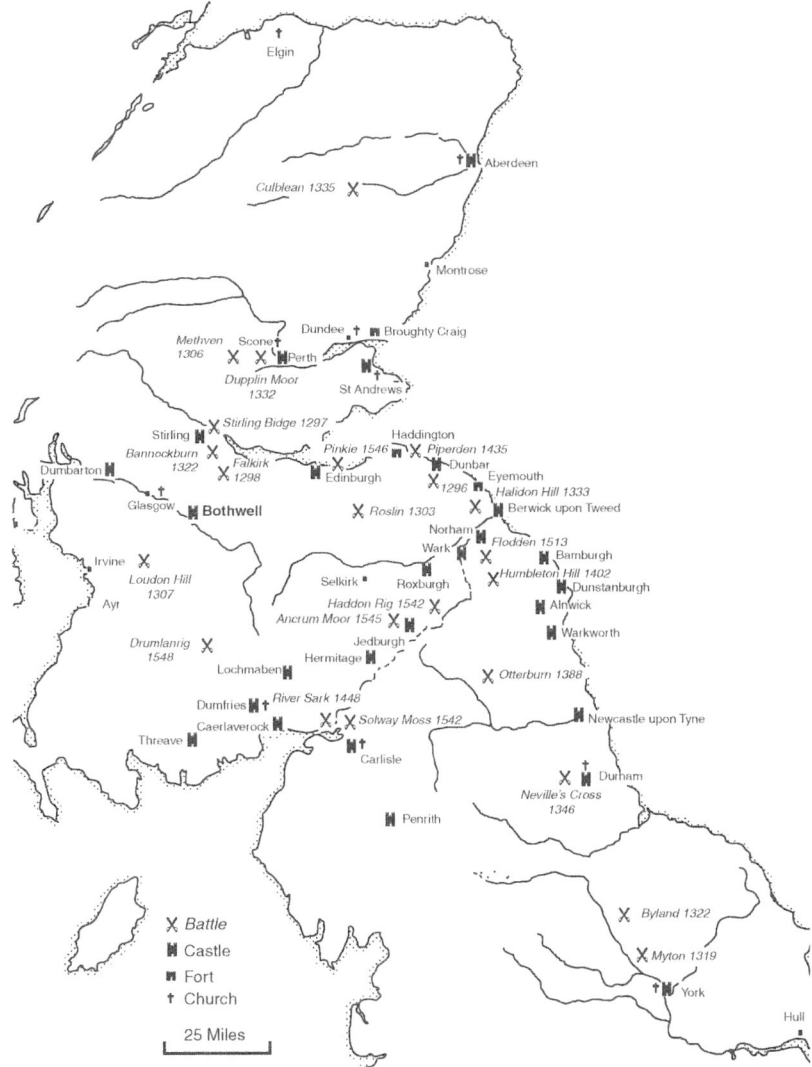

Map 1: England and Scotland

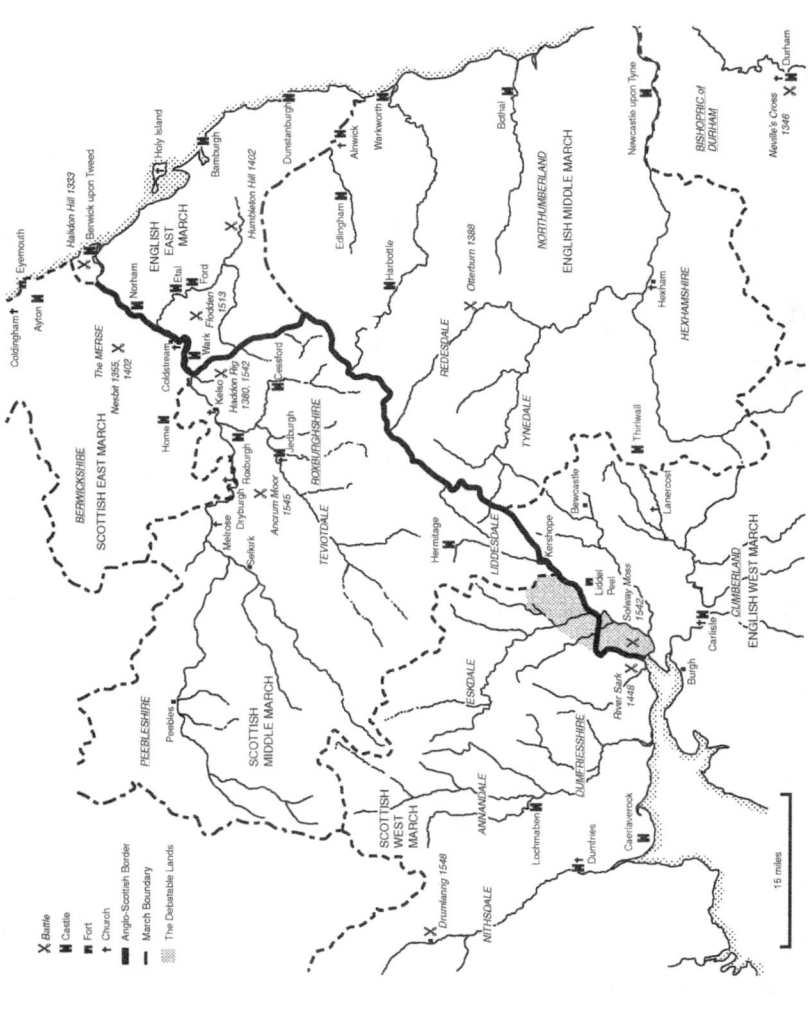

Map 2: The Anglo-Scottish Marches

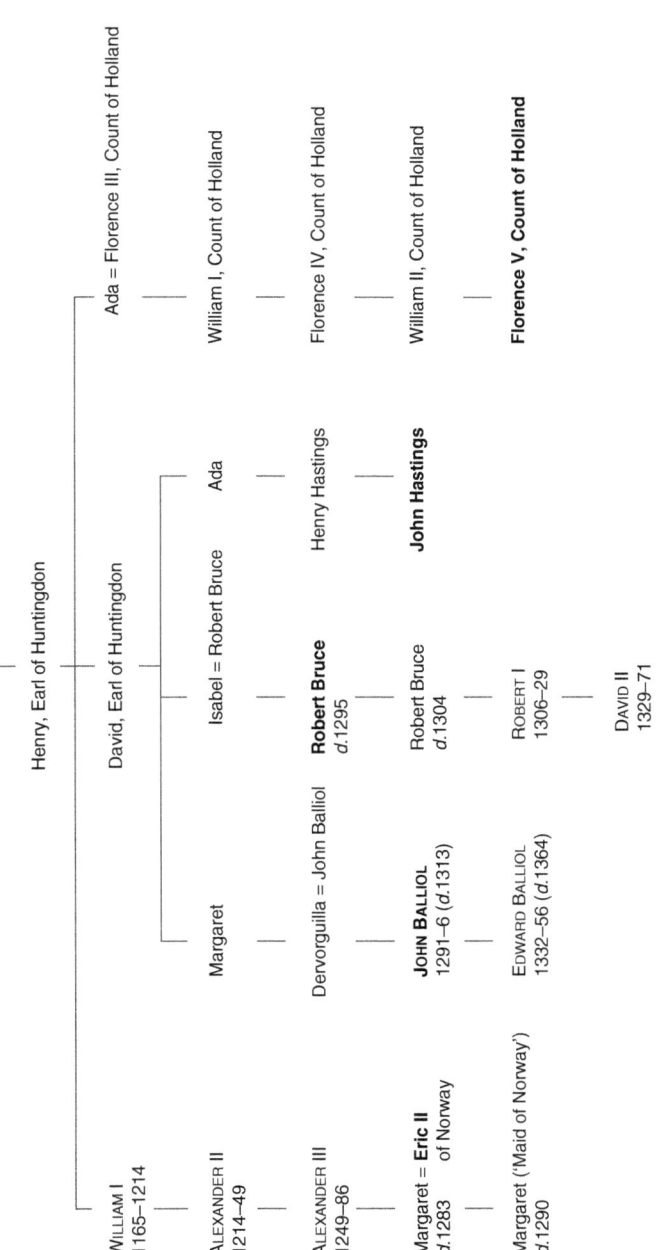

Table 1 The Scottish Succession, 1286–1332

Greatly simplified; claimants in 1291–2 are marked in **bold**; kings of Scots are named in CAPITALS (with dates of reigns). *d.* died.

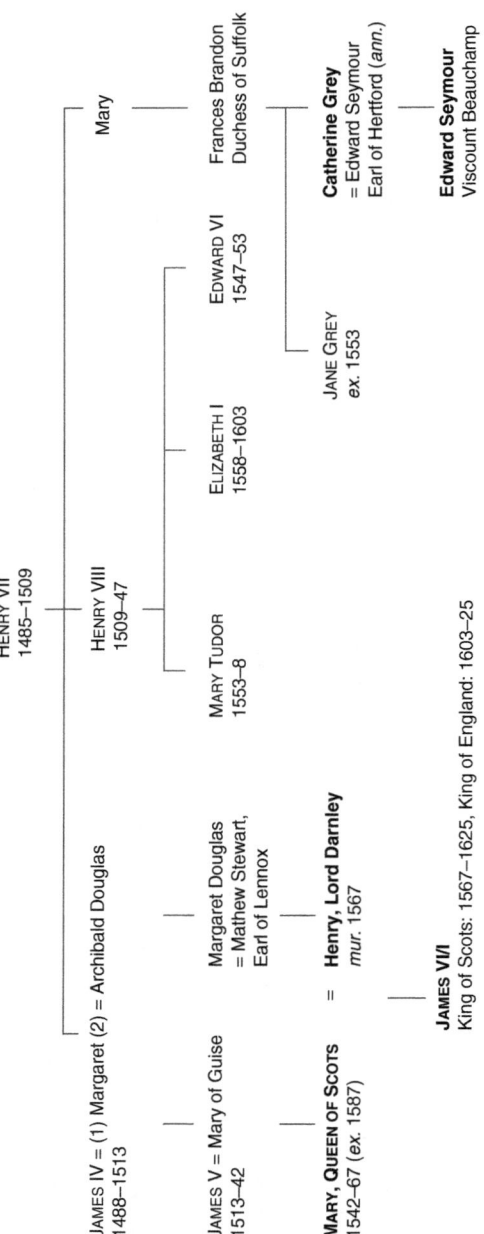

Table 2 The English Succession, 1509–1603

Introduction

i. Historiography

> As far as possible the public annals of the two countries [England and Scotland] should be revised. Errors and irritating expressions must be expunged ... and a new history of Britain should be written with the utmost regard for accuracy.[1]

So wrote the Scottish lawyer Thomas Craig in 1605, two years after James VI, King of Scots, had united the Crowns of England and Scotland. Yet, until the late twentieth century, Craig's call for a specifically 'Anglo-Scottish' history went largely unheeded. The writing of history across the two separate kingdoms presents certain problems, notably a considerable disparity of evidence. At the end of the thirteenth century, England was perhaps the most bureaucratically governed realm in Western Christendom, producing vast quantities of accounts and records, which were stored for possible future reference. Scottish government, on the other hand, wielded rather less bureaucratic authority, and so has left little by comparison with the acres of parchment generated and preserved by the English Crown.

Consequently, rather more evidence is available from England than from Scotland; and information about Scotland is frequently preserved only in English sources, leaving an unbalanced picture. There is, for instance, copious evidence of the damage wrought in England by invading Scottish armies, from financial accounts, taxation records and petitions for relief or aid. By contrast, there is rather less evidence to measure the devastation inflicted on Scotland by invading English armies (although the sources do improve greatly towards the end of the period – see Chapter 9, Section i). Indeed, for some campaigns, there is more evidence of the damage which English armies caused in England, on their way to Scotland, than of the damage they inflicted once they got there.

Fortunately, chronicles and other literary sources provide a vital complement to the records; and in the sixteenth century, the advent of printing enabled the mass production of pamphlets and tracts. Here there is much more parity between English and Scottish sources. However, these were influenced by – or sometimes specifically produced to – political agendas, which have in turn shaped later historical interpretations. For instance, Robert Bruce's seizure of the Scottish kingship in 1306 led to an immediate outbreak of war. Bruce and his followers successfully cast this as a national struggle against the English, although it was also a civil war fought against fellow Scots. Bruce's line was followed by Scottish chroniclers writing later in the fourteenth century. Subsequent historians have often taken this self-serving propaganda at face value, coloured in some cases with an additional layer of nationalist sentiment. Thus those Scots who opposed the English have been labelled 'patriots'.[2] But Bruce's Scottish opponents would also undoubtedly have considered themselves 'patriotic'; for them, his seizure of the kingship was unlawful, murderous – and 'unpatriotic' (Chapter 2, Section i). Similarly, the Scots who assured with the English in the 1540s (Chapter 6) have been labelled 'collaborators', a somewhat loaded term, carrying pejorative and anachronistic overtones.[3]

Conversely, some aspects of Anglo-Scottish relations have become almost de-politicized. For instance, the execution of Mary, Queen of Scots, provoked an outpouring of partisan tracts, ranging from the hagiographic 'The Martyrdom of the Queen of Scotland', to the rather less sympathetic 'An Excellent Ditty made as a General Rejoicing for the Cutting off of the Scottish Queen'. However, contemporary political and religious agendas have to be separated from the subsequent torrent of historical romanticism (and indeed, historical romances) arising from an enduring fascination with the lurid sex-and-violence scandals in which Mary became embroiled.[4]

When Thomas Craig made his plea for a reappraisal of the history of England and Scotland, a pioneering contribution had already been made by the Scottish historian John Mair (or Major), who published his *History of Greater Britain* in 1521 – although this was a parallel account of the histories of the two kingdoms, rather than an integrated work of Anglo-Scottish history.[5] Anglo-Scottish relations have continued, even to the present day, to feature rather more conspicuously in Scottish than in English historical writing. This reflects an English national consciousness in which the victories over the French at Crécy, Poitiers and Agincourt are better known than those over the Scots at Neville's Cross and Pinkie (though Flodden is perhaps an exception). This is itself partly a product of Anglo-Scottish relations. Agincourt, in particular, owes much of its fame to Shakespeare's *Henry V*. But Shakespeare wrote his history plays at a time when the succession of the Scottish James VI to the English throne was an imminent prospect; understandably therefore, Anglo-Scottish conflict is not prominent. *Macbeth*, written after James's accession, was set in the comfortably distant past, and featured the English co-operating with the Scots to remove a tyrannical usurper, reflecting England's interventions on the side of King James's party in Scotland in the 1570s (see Chapter 7).

Long before James's succession to the English throne, English historians had tended towards an Anglo-centric view which equated Britain with England (see Chapter 11, Section ii). Such habits were given an additional intellectual underpinning by their eighteenth- and nineteenth-century successors, who largely subsumed the history of Britain within the record of the majestic and unstoppable onward progress of English civilization (a teleological approach known irreverently to modern historians as the 'Whig interpretation of history'). From this viewpoint, three centuries of periodic Anglo-Scottish hostilities after 1296 represented an unfortunate misstep, serving merely to delay Scotland's participation in the unquestioned benefits of Union. This was not a view confined to the English alone, being endorsed by adherents of the 'Scottish Enlightenment' during the eighteenth century; the Scottish philosopher and historian David Hume described his country's attacks on England during the Middle Ages as 'invidious and unjust'.[6] And the tendency of Scottish Jacobites to portray themselves as successors to William Wallace and Robert Bruce only served to confirm such opinions.

An added twist was supplied by the nineteenth-century obsession with theories of race, which led to the characterization of Highlanders as 'Celts' and Lowlanders as 'Teutons'. As the English were also considered to be Teutonic, the Anglo-Scottish conflict came to be regarded by some Scottish commentators as – in the words of the Scottish jurist James Lorimer, writing in 1860 – an 'unhappy war', which served to divide two peoples who were 'kindred offshoots from the great Teutonic stem'.[7]

'Whig history' has cast a long shadow, continuing to influence accounts of Anglo-Scottish relations long after suffering the merciless lampooning of Sellars and Yeatman's immortal *1066 and All That* (first published in book form in 1930). As late as 1984, it was still possible for a popular history to describe Edward I's intervention in Scotland in terms of the natural extension of English authority throughout Britain. Sir Arthur Bryant introduced his account of the 'Great Cause' with the words: 'Wales was not the only part of the British *imperium* to which Edward wished to bring law and order'.[8] Another manifestation of this attitude is the habit of conflating England with Britain, which continues in popular – if not academic – tradition today. A notable example is the remark made by Simon Jenkins, author of *A Short History of England* (2011); in an interview discussing why he chose to write about England, rather than Britain, he commented that '[England] is an island and islands tend to be different'. In this, he was of course echoing Shakespeare's famous 'sceptred isle' speech (see Chapter 11).[9] It was partly this sort of attitude which prompted the development, from the late twentieth century, of new consciously 'British' schools of academic history, which take an integrated view of the histories of England, Scotland, Wales and Ireland, rather than operating within separate 'national' perspectives.[10]

Popular tradition has also been influenced by the 'Highlandization' of Scotland during the nineteenth century, a romanticizing tendency owing much to the storytelling of Sir Walter Scott, which propagated a tamed and sanitized version of Highland culture. The combination of an increasingly 'Highland' Scottish identity with Victorian racial theories led some historians to depict the Anglo-Scottish wars as a battle between Celtic Highlanders and the Teutonic English. Or as Evan Barron put it, in 1914: 'I may say that I claim to have proved beyond the possibility of doubt that the War of Independence was the achievement of Celtic Scotland … and that Teutonic Scotland – Lothian – had neither lot nor part in the Scots' long struggle for freedom.'[11]

Similarly, the attempts of Robert and Edward Bruce to enlist the Gaelic Irish and the Welsh in a common cause against the English (Chapter 11, Section ii) have been characterized as a 'Celtic Alliance'. But the usage of 'Celtic' as an umbrella term embracing the Welsh, Irish and Scots did not arise until the eighteenth century; and it was not a concept that would have been recognized by the Bruces. Indeed, the very term 'Celt' was not rescued from classical obscurity until the sixteenth century. While the Scots certainly claimed kinship to the Gaelic Irish, they did not generally make any claim to common descent with the Welsh (except when trying to gain their support against the English); rather, they claimed descent from Scota, daughter of the Pharaohs, whereas the Welsh claimed descent from the Trojan Brutus (Chapter 11, Section i).

Meanwhile, the pan-Celtic strand of Scottish historiography reached its popular apotheosis in the 1995 Hollywood epic *Braveheart*, with its wildly anachronistic depiction of 'Celtic' Scots sporting woad and tartan, supported by bands of Irish sympathizers, raring to throw off the oppression of the effete-but-wicked English. The film is, of course, replete with many other crass historical errors.[12] Nevertheless, *Braveheart* has had a significant impact on modern perceptions of Scotland's past; and it has been used to attempt to shape perceptions of Scotland's present or potential future.

And this points to another influence on perceptions of Anglo-Scottish relations in the Middle Ages: politics. The Jacobite espousal of Wallace and Bruce set an example which later political dissidents enthusiastically followed. Striking Scottish radicals in 1820 compared themselves to their medieval forebears: 'justice and humanity forbid us tamely to surrender that freedom which our gallant ancestors fought for and established on the glorious field of Bannockburn'.[13] And it was reported that the Scottish Nationalist Party wanted to hold the referendum on Scottish independence on the day of the 700th anniversary of Bannockburn, in 2014, 'to tap into nationalist fervour'.[14] Thus, Anglo-Scottish relations in the Middle Ages continue to have a political resonance in the twenty-first century.

ii. Origins: England and Scotland to 1296

In *c*.923, 'the king of Scots and the whole Scottish nation' (along with the Scandinavian king who ruled at York, the people of Northumbria, and the king of Strathclyde) accepted Edward, King of Wessex, as 'father and lord'.[15] This claim to what amounted to the overlordship of Britain (excluding Wales) could perhaps be taken as a starting point for relations between the kingdoms of England and Scotland – even if it did predate, by a few years, the reign of Athelstan as the first king of the whole of England.

Over the course of the next four centuries, the Wessex kings of England and the MacAlpin kings of Scots would eliminate all other kingships remaining within the British Isles. One of these was

Northumbria, which at its widest extent had stretched from the Humber to the Forth. By 921, it had already largely disintegrated, undermined by Scandinavian invasion, and both the kings of England and the kings of Scots moved to extend their authority into the resulting vacuum. By the end of the tenth century, Northumbria had effectively been partitioned along the Tweed, leaving a large region of English language and culture under the rule of the kings of Scots. By the end of the eleventh century, the kingship of Strathclyde and Cumbria in the west had similarly been partitioned at the Solway Firth, leaving the Anglo-Scottish border more or less as it is today.[16] Successive Scottish kings aimed at extending their authority further southwards, while, partly as a reaction to these ambitions, kings of England continued to attempt to impose their overlordship on Scotland.

These conflicting aims can be seen at work in the reign of Malcolm III. Between 1061 and 1091, he invaded England four times, prompting counter-invasions of Scotland by both William I and William II. Malcolm submitted on both occasions, recognizing their overlordship. At this stage, overlordship was a fluid concept, which Malcolm may have understood differently from the kings of England; at any rate, it did not prevent him invading again in 1093, when he met his death. His successors were prepared to accept overlordship as the price of English support against rival claimants to the Scottish kingship; thus, in 1095, King Edgar sealed a charter referring to himself as 'possessing the land of Lothian and the kingdom of Scotland by the gift of my lord William, King of the English' (i.e., William II).[17] Malcolm had married Margaret, who was descended from the English royal dynasty ousted in 1066. Their daughter Matilda was married to Henry I, and so the English and Scottish royal dynasties came to share a common descent from Margaret, who would be canonized in 1250 (Chapter 11, Section i). And this link would be reinforced by further marital ties, long before the marriage of Margaret Tudor and James IV in 1502 (Chapter 4, Section ii).

In 1114, Alexander I admitted English overlordship to the extent of serving Henry I in Wales. Alexander's younger brother, David, was brought up in Henry's household, acquiring the earldom of Huntingdon, through marriage to an English heiress; and he was allowed to retain it when he subsequently became king of Scots. The Scottish royal dynasty thus acquired a substantial landed estate south of the border, for which, however, they owed fealty to the kings of England.

When Stephen seized the English crown on Henry's death in 1135, David intervened in the resultant civil war, ostensibly on behalf of his niece Matilda, Henry's daughter. David's invasion of England in 1138 led to defeat at the battle of the Standard; nevertheless, Stephen had to buy him off with Cumberland, and the earldom of Northumbria. Though both were nominally held of the king of England, the border of Scotland had effectively moved to the Tyne. But Scottish authority south of the Tweed lasted only as long as the divisions within England. Stephen was succeeded unopposed by Henry II; and when a young Malcolm IV became king of Scots in 1157, he was forced to surrender Cumberland and Northumbria. He was, however, allowed the earldom of Huntingdon, and became Henry's man, 'as his grandfather [David] had been the man of the elder Henry [I], saving all his dignities', a phrasing sufficiently vague to avoid any troublesome precision of definition. In 1159, Malcolm took a contingent of men to serve Henry in France, service which earned him knighthood at Henry's hands, while provoking rebellion in Scotland.[18]

William, who succeeded Malcolm in 1165, was bent on recovering Northumbria and Cumberland, and once again, conflict in England offered an opportunity. Joining a French-backed rebellion against Henry II in 1173, William invaded northern England, but was captured the following year, near Alnwick. As Henry's prisoner, he had little choice but to accede to his terms. The treaty of Falaise of 1174 duly recorded that 'William, King of Scots, has become the liegeman of the lord king [Henry] against all men, for Scotland, and for all his other lands'.[19] This, the most definite statement of Scotland's subordination to England before 1292, would later be employed as one of the main planks of Edward I's justification of the English claim to overlordship (Chapter 1, Section i). However, Henry's successor, Richard I, was more concerned with funding his crusade than maintaining lordship over the king of Scots; and so in 1189, he sold William a charter releasing him from all obligations arising from his capture, and specifying that he 'shall do for us [i.e., Richard] ... whatever Malcolm, King of Scotland, did of right and ought to have done of right', a studiedly vague formulation which restored the *status quo*. Naturally, the Scots would make use of this release in denying Edward I's claims – while Edward himself passed over it in dignified silence (Chapter 1, Section i).[20]

Richard had even considered selling the earldom of Northumbria to William, who pursued these negotiations with King John. Nevertheless, in 1209, relations broke down almost to the point of war. The cause is obscure, but it may be that – as would so often be the case over the coming centuries – Scotland's relations with France aroused disquiet in England, for Philippe II of France seems to have been negotiating for a marriage alliance between himself and William's daughter, aimed against John. However, after his experience in 1174, William was unwilling to risk war. He therefore conceded the treaty of Norham, granting his daughter's? marriage to John, and thus effectively ending any prospect of a Franco-Scottish alliance.[21]

By the time Alexander II succeeded in 1214, the balance of power had shifted in Scotland's favour, for John was facing rebellion. Alexander took the opportunity to invade, gaining the allegiance of rebel northern English barons (many of whom held lands from him in Scotland). This prompted John to mount the first royal expedition to Scotland since 1072, though – like so many subsequent royal expeditions to Scotland – it succeeded in deterring the Scots only briefly. However, John's death in 1216, and the succession of the nine-year-old Henry III, removed the main cause of the civil war; Alexander was left isolated, and was obliged to do homage to Henry for his English lands. Nevertheless, the council which ruled England during Henry's minority was anxious to conciliate him, and arranged for his marriage to Henry's sister, Joan, at York, in 1221. From then on, until the death of Margaret of Norway in 1290, these familial links helped to foster a greater degree of amity and goodwill on both sides. This found formal expression in the treaty of York of 1237, by which Alexander gave up all claim to Northumberland, Cumberland and Westmorland.

The treaty did not resolve every issue between England and Scotland. Alexander II's marriage to Marie de Coucy of France in 1239 again raised English fears of a Franco-Scottish alliance, and in 1244, armies were mustered on both sides of the border. But the dispute was settled peaceably; under the treaty of Newcastle, the treaty of York was reaffirmed, and Alexander's son and heir was betrothed to Henry's eldest daughter, Margaret. When this son succeeded as Alexander III in 1249, at the age of seven, factional squabbling led to an appeal from Scotland for Henry to intervene. A new royal council was appointed which included two of Henry's barons, who held lands in Scotland. Alexander was knighted by Henry, and married to Margaret, at York, in 1251, but Henry's continuing efforts to exert his influence led to further disputes, particularly over calls for Scottish military service in Gascony. Mounting political crisis in England after 1257 precluded further involvement in Scottish affairs; however, Henry's interventions would provide a clear precedent for Edward I.

Relations between the English and Scottish Crowns were shaped by growing links between their peoples. The Norman, Breton and French adventurers who invaded England under William I soon came to identify with their adopted homeland, seeing themselves as English. Many went on to seize estates for themselves in Wales; and after 1169, their successors established themselves in Ireland. The first Normans had already arrived in Scotland as early as 1052, expelled from the court of Edward the Confessor in a palace *coup*, and finding refuge as mercenaries in the service of Macbeth. Many more came north in the decades after the death of Malcolm III, and were settled with landed estates, so they could serve as knights in Scottish armies. Crucially, these incoming Norman-English were absorbed into the existing power structure of Scotland, rather than setting themselves up in opposition to native rulers, as happened in Wales and Ireland. This was because Scotland was an established kingdom, compared with the fragmented and fluid multiple kingships of Wales and Ireland. Nevertheless, the process of assimilation was greatly eased by cultural factors.

From about the mid-twelfth century, there was an increasing tendency for English commentators to dismiss the Welsh and Irish as primitive and uncivilized savages, because their morals, laws and social habits did not conform to the cultural norms of Francophile Western Christendom.[22] The attitude to Scotland was rather more ambivalent. Gaelic-speaking Scots, too, were considered barbarians, especially the men of Galloway, the closest Gaelic region to England. English-speaking Scots, however, were a different matter, for culturally they had more in common with their English neighbours than with their Gaelic-speaking fellow countrymen (see Chapters 9 and 10). The influences of English incomers, contacts with France, and the Church, were pushing Scotland towards the overbearing mainstream of European culture. David I, who spent much of his youth at the English court, was highly regarded by contemporary English chroniclers, who saw him as a civilizing force. By 1286, lowland Scotland – though not the Highlands – had been heavily 'anglicized'.[23] Scottish common law was derived in large part from the English model, and Scottish royal government had adopted many of the forms of its English counterpart, though it remained very much less centralized and pervasive.

Many of the English who settled in Scotland in the twelfth century retained estates in England, and cross-border marriages led to more cross-border landholding. By 1296, many landowners held lands in both countries (see Chapter 9, Section i).[24] These included the Bruces and the Balliols, the main contenders for the Scottish kingship in 1291–2.[25] Both families were of French origin, and had been established in England after 1066, before acquiring lands in Scotland. At the time of the 'Great

Cause', both held extensive estates in northern England; the Bruces held Hartness in the bishopric of Durham, and the Balliols Barnard Castle in Durham and Bywell in Northumberland. Robert Bruce, the claimant of 1290–91, was married to the sister of the earl of Gloucester (one of the most powerful magnates in Britain, who held lands across England, Wales and Ireland). Bruce chose to be buried at Guisborough priory, Yorkshire, which had been founded by his ancestors; his like-named son (the father of King Robert) who died in 1304, chose to be buried at Holm Cultram abbey in Cumberland, to which the family had granted lands. John Balliol, who became king of Scots in 1292, was schooled at Durham priory, and his father had founded Balliol College at Oxford; the college also benefited from the patronage of his mother, Dervorguilla of Galloway.

The Anglo-Saxon kings of England had harboured ambitions to extend their authority across all of Britain. Meanwhile, successive kings of Scots were bent on extending their authority southwards. The Norman kings who ruled England after 1066 were more concerned with their lands in France, and overlordship of Scotland was perhaps primarily pursued as a means of reducing the Scottish threat to northern England. Anglo-Scottish relations would thus be characterized by fitfully pursued English claims to overlordship, and opportunistic Scottish invasions, played out against a background of Anglo-French hostilities. After the loss of Normandy in 1204, however, kings of England began again to take a greater interest in extending English dominion in Britain. At the same time, across Western Christendom, developing legal and political theories of kingship and government were emphasizing the overarching authority of sovereign rulers. Consequently, relationships of power which had been expressed only vaguely and flexibly came to be defined much more narrowly, with increasing emphasis on the legal rights which overlordship entailed.

In England's dealings with its neighbours in Britain, these developments were, to an extent, masked by the weakness of Henry III's government. This would change under his successor, Edward I, for Edward was set on establishing and enforcing to the maximum those royal rights which he considered had been lost during the civil wars of Henry's reign, both within England and beyond. Alexander III did homage to Edward in a ceremony at Westminster in 1278. The exact terms of his homage were subsequently disputed, though English commentators were convinced of its significance; one chronicler wrote, rather hyperbolically, that 'the triumph of so great a surrender should not be hidden from our countrymen for the future'.[26] As would soon become clear, it was not hidden from Edward.

Part 1

Chapter 1: Hammer of the Scots? Edward I and Scotland, 1286–1306

i. The Scottish Succession and the 'Great Cause', 1286–92

On a stormy night in March 1286, a man fell off his horse and broke his neck. This unfortunate accident was to set in train a series of events leading to nearly three centuries of hostilities between Scotland and England. The man was Alexander III, King of Scots, and his unexpected death left Scotland in a state of uncertainty, for his two sons and his daughter were already dead. This left as his prospective heir his three-year-old granddaughter Margaret, daughter of King Eric of Norway, and now the only living descendant of the Scottish royal line as far back as William the Lion (1165–1214). Norwegian law excluded women from the succession, but no such rule applied in Scotland, although there was no precedent for the reign of a queen of Scots. Following the death of the second of Alexander's sons, the kingdom's magnates had sealed an undertaking recognizing the young Margaret as heir, should Alexander die without leaving a son or daughter. Scotland was now faced with the prospect of a long minority.

In the meantime, the country had to be governed; and a committee of six guardians 'was chosen by the clergy and estates of the whole kingdom of Scotland, in a parliament held at Scone'.[1] Despite this show of consensus, and although the guardians were carefully selected to represent a broad cross-section of the kingdom's political elite, there remained the threat of factional dispute.

For much of the thirteenth century, Scottish politics had been dominated by the Comyns, the kingdom's most powerful magnate family, and their allies. Their dominance left a number of rival magnates excluded; one of these was Robert Bruce of Annandale, who had a claim to the kingship. Despite having put his seal to the undertaking of 1284, Bruce now refused to accept Margaret as the heir. Together with his son, the earl of Carrick, he seized royal castles in Galloway, along with others belonging to John Balliol. The latter was singled out for attack because his claim to the kingship was as strong, or stronger, than Bruce's; and because he was the brother-in-law of John Comyn of Badenoch, one of the leaders of the Comyn faction. Both Bruce and Balliol were descended from daughters of David, Earl of Huntingdon (d.1219), William the Lion's younger brother. Balliol was the grandson of David's eldest daughter; Bruce the son of his second daughter. Bruce argued that his claim was superior because, as David's grandson, he was a nearer relative than Balliol, David's great-grandson; and as a male he had a better right than Margaret. Nevertheless, his rebellion gained little support, and was subdued by early 1287, although the guardians lacked the power to punish him for it.

It was in these difficult circumstances that the guardians decided to approach Edward I of England for help and advice. With the benefit of hindsight, it may seem naïve of the Scots to have expected him to act disinterestedly, especially given that he had recently conquered Wales – another region of Britain over which the English had long claimed overlordship. Yet the Scots would not have recognized this as a precedent. Unlike Wales, Scotland was a long-established kingdom, whose kings and nobles shared England's Francophile chivalric culture. Indeed, some Scottish nobles (including Bruce) had fought in Wales in their capacity as lords of English estates. Moreover, Edward had an international reputation as an arbiter of disputes; and he had a family connection, for he was Alexander III's brother-in-law, and Margaret of Norway was his grandniece. Furthermore, Edward's father, Henry III, had intervened in Scottish politics to protect the interests of the young Alexander III during his minority, and had conceded that this should not be taken as a precedent for English overlordship. Nor had Edward pressed the issue of overlordship in 1278, when Alexander had done homage for his English lands. And, like their king, many of the Scottish nobility held extensive lands in England, and were familiar with Edward as their lord (see Introduction, Section ii and Chapter 9, Section i).

In the event, Edward was more concerned with his own affairs than with Scotland's difficulties; he left for France in May and did not return until 1289. It was then that negotiations began for the marriage of Margaret and Edward's five-year-old heir, Edward of Caernarvon (the future

Edward II). Who first proposed the match is not clear, but the initial negotiations seem to have been conducted between Edward and Eric of Norway. This presented the Scots with something of a dilemma. The continued absence of a king exacerbated disputes among the Scottish political community; however, the guardians were still maintaining a functioning government. Indeed, Margaret was generally referred to by the Scots only as their 'lady' and/or 'heir', rather than their 'queen', a reflection of the fact that a young girl could wield no real authority. There was therefore no pressing reason for them to bring her over from Norway, nor to invite further foreign interference by arranging her marriage.[2] Nevertheless, a marriage alliance with England was by no means unacceptable to the Scots *per se*; both Alexander II and Alexander III had married English princesses.

Inevitably, the marriage of Margaret to the future king of England would open Scotland to English political influence, and the Scots demanded guarantees of their liberty. These demands were met by the treaty of Birgham (also known as the treaty of Northampton), a unilateral grant of terms to the Scots, ratified by Edward in August 1290.[3] Among other concessions, Edward promised that the laws and customs of Scotland should be preserved; that no Scot should be tried outside Scotland for offences committed within that realm; and that no taxes or military service should be imposed on Scotland beyond those customarily imposed by previous kings of Scots for the needs of that realm. Crucially, the treaty included the promise that Scotland would remain 'separated and divided and free in itself, without subjection, from the kingdom of England'. Nor were these concessions presented as contingent on the marriage. The Scots therefore believed they had been granted an unequivocal guarantee of Scotland's independence from English overlordship.

Had the marriage gone ahead, and assuming that Edward and Margaret had produced an heir, then the union of the English and Scottish Crowns would have come about in the early fourteenth century, some three centuries before the accession of James VI, King of Scots, as King James I of England. But it all came to nothing, for the unfortunate Margaret died on her way to Scotland, in September 1290. For the Scots, the succession was now a straightforward dispute between Balliol and Bruce. Given the friction between the Comyns, who backed Balliol, and Bruce, who had his own partisans, they had little choice but to approach someone outside of Scotland with the necessary standing to arrange an authoritative settlement of the dispute. And Edward I of

England was the only practical candidate, with the treaty of Birgham an apparent guarantee of his probity. But Edward had an agenda of his own. He had not raised the issue of English overlordship in the negotiations for Margaret's marriage, for it had offered the prospect of the succession of a king of England as king of Scots, rendering the issue largely redundant. But while Margaret's death had removed this prospect, the disputed succession offered a once-in-a-lifetime opportunity to realize a suzerainty which the English had claimed for centuries. As for the treaty of Birgham, Edward chose to regard it as irrelevant.

Edward was offered some encouragement in his ambitions by Bruce, in a letter which promised the obedience of both himself and his followers, and requested that Edward grant him his 'right'. In effect, he was offering to recognize Edward's overlordship in return for support for his claim to the kingship. At the same time, Florence, Count of Holland, arrived at Edward's court, along with his son, who was betrothed to one of Edward's daughters. Florence, who was descended from Ada, a sister of King William, put forward a claim to the kingship as Ada's heir. In the event, he would fail to substantiate his claim; but by further complicating an already intractable dispute, he would strengthen Edward's hand.[4] Edward also commissioned some historical research. Various prominent English abbeys, priories and cathedrals were hurriedly ordered to search their chronicles for material relating to English overlordship, and to send relevant extracts to the king. The more pertinent – and favourable – were compiled into a dossier, to serve as precedents.[5]

Having prepared his ground, Edward summoned the Scots to a parliament to be held on 6 May 1291 at Norham castle, on the English bank of the Tweed. The Scots were reluctant to cross the river, concerned that appearing before Edward in his own realm might be construed as an admission of superior lordship. And their concern proved fully justified; when a delegation finally went to Norham on the 10th, it was informed that Edward desired 'to do right to all those who can make any claim to the inheritance of the kingdom of Scotland'. To this end, he now requested recognition of this overlordship.[6] The Scots, unaware of Florence's claim, had expected that Edward would arbitrate between Balliol and Bruce; but Edward was offering judgement in court for all claims to the kingship which might be entered. The difference between arbitration and judgement was hugely significant. In legal terms, arbitration required an impartial arbitrator to arrange a settlement between two (and no more than two) disputing parties. Judgement, on the other hand, required the disputing parties to recognize the jurisdiction and authority of the judge, who would then impose a settlement. An arbitration was politically neutral; but a judgement was an exercise of lordship.

Unsurprisingly, the Scots were appalled, and only after an adjournment of three weeks did they make a reply. Addressing Edward in conciliatory terms, they argued that they had no authority to accept his demands, and that only 'he who shall be king' could consider them.[7] This was a perfectly valid response according to contemporary legal theory, which held that guardians did not have the authority to grant away the rights of their ward. From this perspective, the question of overlordship could not properly be raised until the succession had been decided, and there was a king of Scots with the authority to settle the matter. Edward, however, turned to the claimants, one of whom could logically be counted as 'he who shall be king', and required them all to recognize his overlordship, and to grant him seisin of the kingdom and its castles, so that he could deliver the kingdom after making judgement.

By this stage, eleven men had put forward a claim, including Edward himself, on the grounds of his descent from Matilda, daughter of Malcolm III (d.1093). Alongside Balliol and Bruce, and Count Florence, was John Hastings, an English baron descended from the youngest daughter of David, Earl of Huntingdon. John Comyn of Badenoch was descended from a daughter of Donald Ban, King of Scots (1094–7), but specified that he did not wish his claim to prejudice that of his brother-in-law, John Balliol. The other five were descended from bastard daughters of Alexander II or William; and while their claims omitted to mention any taint of bastardy, they had no chance of success, for illegitimate offspring could not inherit. In fact, four of the five held lands in England (as indeed did all but three of the final fourteen claimants), while Florence was in receipt of a pension from Edward. Indeed, Edward may have encouraged some of them to put their claims forward, for the more claimants the easier it was to justify his demand to give judgement rather than arbitration; and the greater the number of his clients among the claimants, the easier it was to impose his will over them as a whole.

Bruce, who appears to have considered his claim to be weaker than Balliol's, immediately accepted Edward's overlordship, along with all the other claimants save Balliol and Comyn. The latter, fearing that judgement would proceed without them, had little choice but to follow suit, and on 5 June Edward was granted seisin of the kingdom by the claimants. Once the claimants had conceded overlordship, Edward quietly abandoned his own claim, as he could hardly judge a case in which he himself was a party. The record of these events subsequently drawn up by the notary John of Caen after 1296 omitted all reference to his claim, ignored the protestations of the Scots, and presented his actions straightforwardly as those of the rightful overlord of the Scottish realm. Edward would have considered such rewriting of history fully justified, on the grounds that the overlordship of Scotland was a longstanding right of the kings of England, and the record of the proceedings needed to be adjusted to reflect that historical reality. In this, he was only following the example of the Church, which had frequent resorted to the forgery of charters to make up for deficiencies in documentary records.

Having achieved recognition of his overlordship, Edward began the hearings to decide the succession (known to later historians as the 'Great Cause') at Berwick in August 1291.[8] The case was to be heard before 104 auditors; and in an implicit recognition that they had been the only serious contenders all along, 40 were appointed by Balliol and 40 by Bruce, with the remaining 24 appointed by Edward. Nevertheless, the final judgement remained with Edward and his council. Leaving aside the complications introduced by the additional claimants, the succession hinged on whether the kingship should descend by primogeniture to Balliol, as the grandson of the eldest of David of Huntingdon's daughters, or by degree to Bruce, the son of the second daughter, as a nearer relative to David. Bruce also argued that the succession should pass to the senior male in each generation, therefore bypassing his cousin Dervorguilla, and hence her son John Balliol. Balliol's claim conformed to feudal law, while Bruce had a case under Roman law. Unfortunately, in the absence of any authoritative precedents, it was by no means clear what law should apply to the royal succession.

The proceedings began with a ten-month adjournment while Count Florence tried, and failed, to find proof to support his claim. In the meantime, Edward ruled as overlord. In fact, when the hearings were resumed in June 1292, such were the complexities of the case that the Scottish auditors were unable to offer much in the way of useful advice. After a month of hearings had settled nothing, Edward adjourned the case until October, so that he could call on a wider range of legal opinions, including experts from the universities of Oxford and Cambridge, and from Paris.

When the hearings resumed again in October, Edward's preferred option was to proceed by feudal law. On 3 November, Edward's councillors came to the unanimous conclusion that descent from the senior line trumped nearness of degree. On 6 November, this was accepted by the Scottish auditors, including those nominated by Bruce, and Bruce's claim was therefore disallowed. Demands from Bruce and Hastings that the kingdom should be divided between the co-heirs were then dismissed on the grounds that the kingdom of Scotland should be considered indivisible; and those claimants remaining were disqualified either because their claims were invalid, or because they had failed to pursue them. This left Balliol as the only contender, and so finally, on 17 November, judgement was given in his favour.

The judgement made sense in political terms, for Balliol had the support of the Comyns, the most powerful noble faction in Scotland, while from Edward's viewpoint, Balliol's largely English background must have recommended him. Yet there is nothing to suggest that such immediate political considerations determined the judgement. Edward was concerned only to establish the principle of his overlordship, and not with imposing a particular candidate for the kingship. Edward's rejection of Roman law met with little opposition, probably because most of Scotland's political establishment were more familiar and comfortable with the customs of feudal law which had shaped Scottish common law. After 1306, Bruce's grandson, King Robert I, would claim that Balliol had been imposed on the Scots by the king of England, against their will. Yet Bruce consistently acted as though he considered his claim to be weaker than Balliol's; and he accepted the judgement, if not with good grace, then at least without overt opposition. Instead, he resigned his claim to his son; his son, in turn, resigned the earldom of Carrick to his own son (the future King Robert), leaving him with no Scottish lands, so that he would not have to do homage to Balliol, and could therefore leave the family claim uncompromised.

John Balliol was duly inaugurated as king of Scots at Scone on 30 November 1292. And then he came across the border to Newcastle upon Tyne, where, on 26 December, he did homage to Edward I as his sovereign overlord, for the whole realm of Scotland.

ii. *English Conquest, 1292–1306*

On 7 December 1292, just three weeks after the end of the 'Great Cause', and three weeks before John's act of homage, Roger Bartholomew, a burgess of Berwick, appealed to Edward against judgements given against him in court by the guardians. Over the course of the thirteenth century, notions of sovereignty and overlordship had been increasingly closely defined and clarified by legal theorists, developing concepts derived from Roman law. It was now widely held that overlordship entailed the right of supervision of justice. So, as Edward saw it, the hearing of appeals from Scotland in the royal courts of England followed directly from the establishment of his overlordship, embodied in John's homage. To the Scots, however, this was an intrusion which undermined the sovereignty of the Scottish realm, and a clear breach of the promises made by Edward in the treaty of Birgham. In fact, there were not many appeals to Edward from Scotland, just eight over the next two years. The most important was that of Macduff, a scion of the comital house of Fife. Macduff had already appealed to Edward in 1292, while the latter was acting as ruler of Scotland during the Great Cause. John subsequently gave a new judgement against him, so Macduff appealed again in 1293. Edward now summoned John himself to appear before royal justices at Westminster, where he was convicted of contempt of court – a gross humiliation for a reigning king.

Equally unwarranted from the Scottish viewpoint were Edward's demands for military service. In 1294, war broke out between England and France over the issue of Gascony, held by Edward I, as Duke of Aquitaine, of Philippe IV of France. Edward summoned John and 26 Scottish nobles to serve against the French. In the event the expedition was cancelled, due to rebellion in Wales; but the war did provide the Scots with a potential ally. They were reluctant to risk defying Edward's increasing demands by themselves; but the prospect was much less daunting in conjunction with an ally as powerful as France. In December 1294, the Scots gained a significant diplomatic advantage when they obtained papal absolution from any oaths extorted by Edward by force. Shortly thereafter, negotiations began with the French – though which side instigated them is not clear.

Equally unclear is the extent of John's personal involvement in these decisions, for according to contemporary English accounts, by July 1295, a council had been appointed to advise him, comprising twelve prelates and magnates and dominated by the Comyns. These English accounts portray this as a *coup*, effectively sidelining John; one describes his situation as 'like a lamb among wolves'.[9] However, no Scottish account describes him as losing power at this stage, and it may be that the council was appointed in order to bolster John's authority in Scotland, as war with England became inevitable. The negotiations with the French led to the treaty of Paris, sealed in October, which committed the Scots to war with England. The 'Auld Alliance' with France would be a major factor in provoking and prolonging Anglo-Scottish conflict for the next 250-odd years.

Edward was already intent on confrontation. Although there is no evidence that he knew of the Franco-Scottish negotiations, he may well have suspected something. But his invasion of Scotland was presented as the conclusion of the legal process against John for his failure to provide justice to Macduff, requiring judgement to be imposed by force. By the time the treaty of Paris was sealed, Edward had already ordered the seizure of all lands and goods held by John in England, and those of any other Scots who remained in Scotland. And in December, he summoned his magnates to muster at Newcastle upon Tyne. The army which mustered was a striking demonstration of the power that Edward wielded across the British Isles, including men from across England, Wales, Ireland and Scotland itself.

For many who held lands on both sides of the border, the conflict had something of the complexion of a civil war, presenting them with the stark choice of which king to rebel against. It began with a skirmish in Northumberland, when an English force was sent to recover the border castle of Wark on Tweed. Its lord, Robert de Ros, a baron who held lands in England and Scotland, had sided with the Scots; according to English chronicles, his allegiance was determined by his love for a Scottish lady. Others chose their allegiance for more prosaic motives. Robert Bruce, son of the competitor in the Great Cause (who had died in 1295), and his son the earl of Carrick (the future king of Scots), remained in the English allegiance, having little inclination to risk the family's English lands in the cause of John Balliol's kingship. Also remaining in Edward's allegiance were Gilbert de Umfraville, Earl of Angus, and Patrick Dunbar, Earl of March. Both held extensive estates in Northumberland, and Umfraville was more English than Scottish in outlook, while Dunbar was a Bruce partisan. But others faced real conflicts of loyalty, such as Dunbar's wife Marjory, a daughter of Alexander Comyn, Earl of Buchan. Left in charge of Dunbar castle, she handed it over to Balliol's supporters; evidently, familial loyalties outweighed matrimonial ties in determining her allegiance.

At the end of March Edward advanced to Berwick, called on its inhabitants to submit, and when they refused, took the place by assault. According to contemporary customs of war, the inhabitants of any town captured under these circumstances were classed as rebels, and had no right to mercy. Nor did they get any. A terrible massacre followed, as Berwick was plundered. A Scottish force, led by the earls of Mar, Ross and Menteith, mounted a counter-raid into Northumberland, where they burned many villages. Returning to Scotland, they went to

Dunbar castle, and were admitted by the countess Marjory. An English force was dispatched to capture it, commanded by John, Earl Warenne, who was Balliol's son-in-law – another indication of the close familial ties which linked the aristocracy of England and Scotland. On 27 April, a Scottish force arrived to relieve the besieged castle; when Warenne began to manoeuvre his troops into battle formation, the Scots assumed he was retreating and launched a rushed attack, which was easily routed. Edward himself arrived on the following day, and the castle surrendered, landing the three earls in captivity.

After this defeat, Scottish resistance rapidly collapsed. A prime function of a medieval king was leadership in war, and John conspicuously failed to provide such leadership; unlike Edward, who was at the head of his army, John did not take to the field. Coupled with the ease of the English victory at Dunbar, this lack of leadership left his adherents with little will to resist. Edward was able to march north as far as Elgin virtually unopposed, taking Edinburgh and Stirling castles without difficulty, and accepting the fealty of many Scottish magnates and knights. Amongst those offering their submission was John himself. Initially, Edward appointed Warenne and Antony Bek, Bishop of Durham, to handle the negotiations. However, the terms they offered were deemed too generous by Edward, who demanded that John submit unconditionally. This he did, in a protracted process starting on 2 July, when he sealed a letter admitting that, 'by evil and false counsel, and our own folly', he had 'grievously offended and angered our lord Edward', and surrendering to him, 'the land of Scotland and all its people, and the homages of all of them'.[10] A few days later, he formally repudiated the treaty with France. Finally, on 8 July, at Montrose, he was brought before Edward and humiliated by having the lining stripped from his cloak, symbolising the stripping of the dignity of his kingship – an act which earned him the derisory nickname of 'Toom Tabard', or empty tabard.[11] He was then sent to the Tower of London. Scotland's royal insignia, including the Stone of Scone (used in the inauguration of kings of Scots), was sent to Westminster abbey, to be kept with the regalia of the vanquished Welsh principality of Gwynedd as trophies of war.

According to a later Scottish source, Robert Bruce the elder approached Edward after Dunbar, and asked him to grant him the kingdom. But he got short shrift, for Edward replied, 'have we nothing else to do but to win kingdoms for you?'.[12] This caustic rejoinder was all too typical of Edward's attitude to Scotland, revealed by another comment made when, on 3 September, he entrusted the custody of Scotland to Warenne:

'he does good business, who rids himself of shit'.[13] Much of Edward's contempt must have stemmed from the seeming ease with which Scotland had been conquered, a task which had proved much less difficult than the subjugation of Wales. Having initially justified his invasion as a legal process against a contumacious vassal, Edward now treated Scotland as a conquest of war, and every substantial landholder was required to swear fealty to him. Having effectively abolished the Scottish kingship, he set up his own administration, based (for the convenience of the English) at Berwick, rather than Edinburgh. Although Warenne was nominally in charge, he showed little enthusiasm for the task, and the effective head was the treasurer, the energetic and rapacious royal clerk Hugh Cressingham.

This was an administration staffed by Englishmen; Edward's new Scottish subjects were given no role in it, and thus had little reason to support it. Nor did they derive any great advantage from it; to the contrary, it rapidly became apparent that Scotland was to be exploited for England's benefit. In less than a year, Cressingham was able to extract over £5,000 for the English exchequer. This was not a large sum by English standards, but such exactions were unusual for Scotland, which was not wealthy. Wool levies added a further burden on top of this. The demands made by Edward's government south of the border were enough to provoke vehement protest in England in 1297. So it is small wonder that the imposition of a similarly exacting English administration should have aroused violent opposition in Scotland, a kingdom accustomed to a rather lower level of royal government.

This opposition erupted around the end of April 1297, when William Wallace killed the English sheriff of Lanarkshire, and raised the men of Clydesdale in revolt. In the north, Andrew Murray led a rising which started with an assault on Urquhart castle, by Loch Ness. Neither Murray nor Wallace were from the higher echelons of the nobility. Murray, the son of the lord of Petty near Inverness, was from the middling ranks; Wallace, probably the son of a Crown tenant in Ayrshire, was of rather lesser standing. It must have been clear that the English administration in Scotland now faced widespread rebellion, though thus far one which was not openly supported by any of Scotland's greater magnates, still cowed by their defeat in 1296. Yet that May, writs were issued from the chancery at Westminster, addressed to 57 Scottish nobles, ordering them to serve on Edward's planned expedition to Flanders, despite the reaction such demands had provoked in 1294. Some of the Scots captured at Dunbar had already agreed to serve in return for their freedom, but in

Scotland, these demands served only to further enflame the situation, provoking some of the nobility to rebellion. With the eclipse of Comyn leadership following the defeat of 1296, this was led by Robert Wishart, Bishop of Glasgow, and James Stewart, both Bruce partisans and former guardians. And they were joined by Robert Bruce, Earl of Carrick.

Having defeated the Scots so easily in 1296, Edward clearly did not anticipate that they would present any great threat just a year later. His attentions were now set firmly on the war with France; consequently, English efforts to subdue the rising were characterized by a mixture of complacency and indecision. The northern magnates Henry Percy and Robert Clifford led an army across the border. Considering the performance of the Scots at Dunbar, Wishart, Stewart and Bruce were understandably reluctant to risk battle, and so a settlement was negotiated at Irvine, on 7 July. Meanwhile, Cressingham had mustered some 10,000 men at Roxburgh. There ensued a squabble over whether a second expedition was still necessary, so it was decided to wait for Warenne to arrive from Yorkshire before doing anything; 'and thus matters have gone to sleep', complained Cressingham, in a decidedly irascible letter to his royal master.[14] Warenne, who was probably in poor health, finally arrived in September, by which time Percy had joined Edward in Flanders. Nevertheless, the earl led the remaining troops to Stirling, where a Scottish army commanded by Murray and Wallace waited on the other side of the Forth. Again negotiations were opened, but this time they failed to reach any conclusion, while Warenne remained in his tent. Eventually, Cressingham lost patience and rashly led his men across the narrow bridge over the river. Presented with an easy target, Murray and Wallace were willing to risk battle. They waited until the English vanguard had crossed, and then attacked and slaughtered them, while the rest of the army watched helpless from the other side of the bridge. Cressingham was killed, and reputedly flayed, some of his skin being used to make a sword-belt for Wallace.[15] In the aftermath of the battle, the English administration rapidly disintegrated; even the border town of Berwick fell, although the castle remained in English hands. The Scots followed up their success with an ill-disciplined but devastating invasion of the English Marches.[16]

Murray, wounded at the battle, died in November, and so leadership of the rebellion fell to Wallace. His status was made official shortly after, when he was knighted and appointed guardian. The office was held in the name of King John, who, in his absence, provided a figurehead for Scottish resistance, lending Wallace a vicarious authority which his own modest social standing could not provide. Paradoxically though, these Scottish successes brought some political benefit for Edward too. Opposition to his expedition to Flanders had aroused great political controversy in England; now, however, the bad news from Scotland rallied his opponents behind him. Furthermore, the Flanders campaign had ended in a truce with France, and Edward was therefore able to organize a major expedition against the Scots for the summer of 1298.

A huge force of some 28,000 men, including 11,000 Welshmen, was mustered at Roxburgh on 25 June, and the exchequer was moved from Westminster to York to pay them. An army of this size was enormously difficult to feed, and supplies were soon running short (a situation exacerbated by the scorched earth policy adopted by the Scots), leading to riots amongst the Welsh. Edward therefore needed to achieve results as soon as possible. As for Wallace, he was dependent on further military success to maintain his leadership of the Scots; perhaps overconfident after Stirling Bridge, he was therefore determined to fight. The two armies met at Falkirk on 22 July, where Wallace is reputed to have told his men, 'I have brought you to the dance, now hop if you can'.[17] However, Edward rapidly routed the small contingent of Scottish men-at-arms, and was able to attack the footsoldiers at leisure. After a hard-fought battle the Scots were defeated, with massive casualties.

This defeat served to undermine Wallace's authority, and he resigned the guardianship. However, victory did nothing to alleviate the supply problems of Edward's army, and consequently, he was able to take only limited advantage of the situation, re-establishing control in south-east Scotland and the borders. Both sides had now inflicted considerable defeats on each other, but neither could gain a decisive advantage, and so the conflict bogged down into a slow war of attrition.

Edward's constant demands for money and supplies soon revived opposition in England, and although on a lesser scale, it was enough to hamper his efforts. He was unable to launch another expedition until November 1299, but faced with a winter campaign, few of the men summoned turned out – and many who did promptly deserted. Consequently, Edward was unable to prevent the Scots from recapturing Stirling castle. A major royal campaign to Galloway in the summer of 1300 took Caerlaverock castle, and defeated a Scottish army in a skirmish across the river Cree. However, the Scots were able to escape across the moors, and Edward achieved little else, as his army slowly evaporated through desertion. In October, at the request of Philippe of France, he agreed to a truce to last until Whitsun (21 May 1301).

In 1301, after the truce had expired, Edward tried again, leading a two-pronged invasion with another army commanded by the Prince of Wales (the future Edward II). The expedition managed to capture Bothwell castle near Glasgow, and this time Edward remained in Scotland into the winter. However, financial difficulties once again led to widespread desertion, and in January 1302, he was obliged to grant the Scots another truce, under the treaty of Asnières, made with Philippe. In fact, negotiations had been underway since the previous August, and the winter campaign may have been intended to achieve as much as possible before the truce was imposed.

The English administration in southern Scotland was gradually asserting its authority, by dint of its continuing operation. However, by the same token, the Scots were able to maintain a government beyond the Forth. Edward's military campaigns had achieved comparatively little, because he was unable to inflict a decisive defeat on the Scots as they grew wary of engaging in battle; and he was unable to keep an army in the field long enough to achieve any more than piecemeal gains. Nor was he able to advance north of the Forth, leaving a substantial part of Scotland untouched by the war. There was little chance of forcing the submission of Scottish magnates while English armies tended to disintegrate after a few months. Essentially, whenever Edward invaded, the Scots could afford simply to wait until he was forced to go away again.

Meanwhile, the war was also being fought on the diplomatic front, and here the Scottish alliance with France gave them an advantage. In 1299, a peace treaty was sealed between England and France, under the terms of which Philippe secured Balliol's release into the custody of Pope Boniface VIII. The Scots also managed to procure a bull from Boniface, calling on Edward to cease his interventions in Scottish affairs. A propaganda war ensued at the curia, as both sides attempted to influence papal policy (see Chapter 11, Section i); and the Scots gained the upper hand. In the summer of 1301, Balliol was released by the pope, and installed by Philippe on his ancestral lands in France. He was now able to take a more active role in directing the Scottish government which had been operating in his name, so much so that he now appointed his own guardian, John de Soules.[18]

News of this had reached England by October, along with rumours that Philippe intended to help Balliol return to Scotland. In fact, these rumours alarmed some in the Scottish camp as much as the English; by February 1302, Robert Bruce, Earl of Carrick, had submitted to Edward. It was one thing for Bruce to resist the English in the name of Balliol's kingship; it was quite another to carry on that resistance when there appeared to be a real prospect of that kingship being restored. The Scottish leadership was increasingly dominated by the Comyns, who had gradually reasserted their customary authority; consequently, Bruce was being sidelined, and the terms of his submission to Edward suggest that he was concerned for the security of his lands within a Scotland controlled by his rivals. The terms included a studiedly ambiguous reference to Bruce's 'right', which may – or may not – have referred to the Bruce claim to the Scottish kingship.[19]

Now, however, the situation in Scotland was transformed by external factors, for in July 1302, the French suffered a massive defeat at the hands of Flemish rebels at the battle of Courtrai. Beset with his own problems, Philippe now wanted to improve relations with Edward, resulting in the treaty of Amiens, sealed in December 1302, which excluded Scotland. At the same time, relations between Philippe and Boniface were deteriorating, leaving the pope anxious to gain Edward's goodwill. The Scots were left isolated, and Edward was already planning an expedition for the following summer. Nevertheless, under the direction of John Comyn, now sole guardian, the Scots took to the offensive. They were able to capture a newly constructed fort at Selkirk, and in February 1303, inflicted a defeat on the English in a confused skirmish at Roslin, near Edinburgh.

The English army mustered at Roxburgh with some 7,500 foot soldiers and 580 men-at-arms, where it was joined by some contingents of Scots, including Bruce. Edward led them across the Forth early in June. Previous expeditions had been confined to the summer months, allowing the Scots to recover during the winter; crucially, this time Edward managed to maintain a substantial force with him over the winter, despite the usual chronic problems of supply and desertion. Allowed no respite, abandoned by Philippe and Boniface, and with no prospect of their king's return, increasing numbers of Scots came to the conclusion that there was nothing to be gained by prolonging their resistance, and early in 1304 Comyn negotiated a surrender. Edward had not, however, inflicted a decisive military defeat on the Scots, and given his continuing financial difficulties he had little choice but to offer lenient terms, allowing them to keep their lands. Stirling castle still held out, but after a three-month siege the garrison had little choice but to surrender – though Edward refused to let them leave until he had tried out his new siege engine, the 'Warwolf'. William Wallace, pointedly excluded from the peace terms, was eventually captured by Scotsmen. He was taken to London and ritually hanged, drawn and quartered as a traitor.[20]

In 1305, Edward decreed an ordinance 'for the good order of the land of Scotland'.[21] The Scottish kingship was effectively abolished, and Scotland relegated to the status of a 'land', to be governed by Edward's lieutenant, his nephew John of Brittany. Nevertheless, the settlement demonstrated that Edward had learned from past mistakes, and was prepared to compromise – to an extent. Although the highest ranking offices remained in the hands of Englishmen, many Scots were employed in positions of authority: 18 of the 22 sheriffs were Scots, while another 22 were appointed to John's council. The ordinance also went some way towards meeting Comyn's demands that Scottish law be maintained. A committee of Englishmen and Scots was to examine and reform the 'laws made by King David' (ruled 1124–53) and subsequent kings, with Edward himself having the final say on what should be rejected as 'displeasing to God'. However, the 'custom of the Scots and the Brets' (i.e., Gaelic customary law) was to be abolished. Essentially, Edward was prepared to tolerate such Scottish law as had developed under Anglo-French influence and which conformed to contemporary legal theory.

Edward clearly believed that he had subjugated Scotland once and for all. Thus, apparently, was completed the centuries-long process by which the kings of England (or more precisely, the English kings of Wessex) had gradually destroyed or subjugated all other kingships across the British Isles.[22] With the destruction of the Scottish kingship, Edward was the only remaining king in Britain. But this was to prove the high-water mark before the ebb-tide. Already, the English lordship in Ireland was faltering; and no king of England would rule throughout mainland Britain again until the accession of James VI of Scotland in 1603.

Chapter 2: Scottish Civil Wars, 1306–37

i. Good King Robert, 1306–28

On 10 February 1306, the civil war which had been smouldering in Scotland since the death of Alexander III finally ignited, when Robert Bruce killed John Comyn in the Greyfriars church at Dumfries. He subsequently re-ignited the Anglo-Scottish war as well, by having himself inaugurated as king of Scots at Scone, on 25 March. This bid for the kingship was motivated by political considerations as well as regal ambition. Robert had submitted to Edward in the winter of 1301/2, while the Comyns had continued to resist for another eighteen months, yet his early submission had gained him little. Edward's settlement of 1305 was intended to pacify Scotland by co-opting his Scottish opponents and trying to work with the grain of Scottish political society, an approach which meant leaving the Comyns' dominance comparatively intact.[1] But despite Edward's efforts, disaffection with English rule, and with the continuing influence of the Comyns, was widespread. Robert was able to garner significant support, from the earls of Atholl, Menteith and Lennox, and the bishops of St Andrews and Glasgow, and he rapidly captured a number of towns and castles.

These events brought about a dramatic upheaval in the patterns of Scottish resistance to the English. Robert now portrayed himself as the defender of Scotland's liberties against English tyranny. Conversely, the Comyns and their supporters, natural leaders of the 'community' of Scotland and the mainstay of resistance to Edward I until 1304, now cleaved firmly to the English allegiance. For these Scots, Robert was a divisive and factional figure, who had now proved himself a sacrilegious, perjured murderer and usurper. The prospect of his kingship was even less palatable than English rule; and they were certainly not prepared to overturn their newly sworn allegiance to Edward in his cause.

By this stage, Edward's health was failing, a factor which undoubtedly encouraged Robert in his *coup* (see Chapter 11, Section ii). Nevertheless, he reacted with a furious determination, persuading the pope to excommunicate Robert, and dispatching English forces north of the border yet again. Robert was defeated at Methven near Perth, and forced to flee westwards, only to be defeated again at Dail Righ, by followers of the MacDougall lords of Argyll, who supported the Comyns. The castles taken by Robert quickly fell, and many of his supporters were captured.

Edward's response was marked by unprecedented savagery, for he considered that he was putting down a rebellion, not fighting a war, and so the usual laws of war did not apply. Robert's supporters were treated as recidivist traitors, and most received a traitor's death, including the earl of Atholl – the first earl to be executed by a king of England since 1076. Robert's sister Mary, and Isabella, Countess of Buchan (who had assisted at his inauguration), were imprisoned in cages. These brutal punishments were influenced by developing theories of sovereignty which emphasized the authority and majesty of kings, and thus the iniquity of rebellion against them. Their novelty can be judged from the comments of an English chronicler, who noted with surprise that, 'among those who were hanged were not only simple country folk and laymen, but also knights and clerics'.[2]

There was nothing inevitable about Robert's eventual success. Indeed, after Methven, he must have seemed doomed to failure, leading many of his followers to submit. Robert only just escaped, and was forced to hide out, either in Ireland or the Western Isles. Yet he was able to stage a remarkable recovery. Early in 1307, he landed in Carrick with a small force of Irish and men of the Isles. His position remained perilous, and two of his brothers were captured, and gruesomely executed. But Robert himself managed to evade the forces pursuing him by 'lurking in the moors and marshes', as an English report put it.[3] In May, he beat an English force at Loudon Hill, a victory which though minor in itself, lent much-needed credibility to his cause.

Robert was greatly aided by the death of Edward, on 7 July 1307, as he struggled to lead yet another force into Scotland. The unfortunate Edward II inherited a parlous financial and political situation at home, which he rapidly made worse by his favouritism towards his unpopular Gascon intimate, Piers Gaveston. Facing demands for Gaveston's removal, and the reform of his government, he had other problems to worry about than Scotland, and campaigns planned for 1308 and 1309 came to nothing in the face of domestic opposition. Instead, Edward authorized the negotiation of a series of short truces. This enabled Robert to establish his kingship without effective opposition from the English. There was now widespread enthusiasm for his cause, though he also employed intimidation to enforce the recognition of his rule. Thus after defeating John Comyn, Earl of Buchan, Robert's forces systematically ravaged his earldom, to terrorize its inhabitants into obedience, and to warn others of the price of opposition. Edward's failure to protect his Scottish adherents left them with little choice but to submit. As for English garrisons in Scotland, they were generally isolated, undermanned, undersupplied and underpaid; when they were left unsupported as well, there was little difficulty in picking them off.

The English position in Scotland was now collapsing; but when Edward finally did mount an expedition in 1310, it had as much to do with the situation in England as his expressed desire to go to the aid of his Scottish subjects. A faction of powerful magnates led by Thomas, Earl of Lancaster, was trying to impose reform; Edward hoped that his absence from London would frustrate this, as well as keeping Gaveston safe from his English enemies. Opposition to Edward was such that many magnates refused to serve; and so when he eventually crossed the border in September, his army included only three English earls: Warenne, Gloucester (Robert's cousin) and Gaveston himself, recently created earl of Cornwall. Richard de Burgh, Earl of Ulster (Robert's father-in-law), recruited an additional army in Ireland; but bad weather prevented him from crossing the Irish Sea. Edward remained in Scotland for nearly a year, shoring up the defences of Lothian and wintering at Berwick, but was forced to return south by increasing political unrest in England, without having significantly impeded Robert's progress.[4]

In the wake of Edward's departure, the Scots began a series of destructive raids into England. The English border communities were forced to buy the raiders off, providing Robert with a source of ready cash to finance a series of prolonged sieges of English-held castles in Scotland, such as Perth and Dumfries, which both fell in 1312. Both were demolished, for Robert could not afford the costs of garrisoning them (Chapter 8). It quickly became apparent that the English could ill-afford such expenses either. Continuing turmoil in England left Edward unable to raise sufficient taxes to pay the remaining garrisons north of the border adequately; consequently they were reduced to banditry in order to feed themselves, thereby alienating the very people they were supposed to be protecting. In late 1313, those Scots still remaining in Edward's allegiance petitioned him, complaining bitterly that although they had negotiated a truce, their livestock was being plundered, 'partly by the enemy and partly by the garrisons of Berwick and Roxburgh castle'.[5] Their prospects were further diminished in October, when Robert decreed that all Scots who had not come to his peace within a year should forfeit their lands. However, Edward did manage to reach an accommodation with his English opponents, enabling him to announce a royal expedition to Scotland for the following summer.

Faced with a major English campaign, Robert set out to take the castles remaining in English hands, so that Edward could not use them as bases. Roxburgh was taken by surprise in February 1314, and Edinburgh stormed soon after. This left Stirling isolated, and Edward Bruce, Robert's brother, was put in charge of besieging it; following the conventions of siege warfare (see Chapter 8), he accepted an offer from its captain to surrender if he had not been relieved by Midsummer (24 June), when Edward's expedition was due.[6] The Scots were therefore obliged either to abandon the siege or to prevent the English from reaching Stirling.

Edward was able to muster a very sizeable army, for although the earls of Lancaster and Warwick declined to take part, many of his magnates did turn out, along with several thousand Welshmen, and possibly a contingent from Ireland. Nevertheless, delays prevented the army from crossing the border until 18 June. Meanwhile, Robert had summoned the host which mustered south of Stirling.

Edward's army approached on 23 June, only for the vanguard to be beaten back in two fierce skirmishes – defeats which left the English demoralized. Encouraged by this success, and by the advice of Sir Alexander de Seton, a Scot who defected from Edward's camp overnight, Robert determined to stand and fight, rather than withdraw across the Forth, as he had intended. At daybreak on Midsummer Day, Robert's army formed up on foot in *schiltroms* and advanced. Caught out by the speed of the advance, the English were pushed back against the Bannock Burn (the stream after which the battle is named), where hundreds were drowned, and the army rapidly disintegrated (see Chapter 8).[7] Edward was led from the field, and escaped by sea. Many of his subjects were not so fortunate; the thousands of English dead included the earl of Gloucester, while many other nobles were captured and ransomed.

The spectacular victory was widely regarded as a God-given confirmation and validation of Robert's kingship; even hostile English chroniclers now began to refer to him as king of Scotland. The battle was also a victory in the civil war he had been waging with the Comyns. Amongst those who died fighting for the English was John Comyn, the son and heir of the man killed by Robert in 1306. Other Scots who had previously served assiduously in the English allegiance now submitted to Robert, including Patrick, Earl of March, who thereby forfeited his estates in Northumberland. Some Scots, however, remained obdurate, such as David Strathbogie, Earl of Atholl, who made an ill-judged return to the English allegiance on the eve of the battle. At a parliament in November, Robert's 1313 decree of forfeiture was put into effect. This led to the final dismantling of the cross-border landholdings which had linked the nobility of England and Scotland so closely for two centuries, completing the process begun by Edward I in 1295.

Bannockburn has been seen as the crowning triumph of Robert's career, but in many ways it served merely to confirm existing realities. English lordship in Scotland had already effectively collapsed, and even without the battle, it is hardly likely that Edward's expedition could have done much to restore it. In terms of Scotland's wider relations with England, the victory settled nothing; Edward was no more inclined to recognize Robert's kingship after Bannockburn than he had been before it.

Within a month of the battle, the Scots raided the English border counties again. The next few years saw a series of intermittent but vastly destructive and increasingly wide-ranging incursions, intended to put pressure on Edward to come to a peace agreement. Accordingly, raids were interspersed with peace negotiations – or more usually, talks about peace negotiations. In July 1315, the Scots made a serious attempt to take Carlisle, attacking the walls with siege engines, but after ten days the defenders, led by the Westmorland knight Sir Andrew Harclay, beat them off with heavy losses. After this, there were no major raids on England for a year, while the Scots turned their attention to Ireland.

In May 1315, Edward Bruce invaded the English lordship of Ireland, announcing his intention of installing himself as king.[8] He soon over-ran Ulster, although Carrickfergus, the earldom's main castle, was captured only after a seventeen-month siege (during which the garrison was reputedly reduced to eating eight Scottish prisoners). But while the cash-strapped Anglo-Irish administration was little more able to mount an effective defence than its counterpart in northern England, Edward Bruce was equally unable to build on his initial success. A series of Scottish raids wreaked immense destruction, but were hampered by widespread famine and poor weather. Even the arrival of Robert with another army in January 1317 failed to revive the venture. The army starved, and Robert returned to Scotland after just four months, having achieved nothing. Edward Bruce remained hemmed into Ulster until the summer of 1318, when an improved harvest allowed him to resume the offensive. But the Anglo-Irish were able to raise a large army against him, and in October he was killed and his forces annihilated at Faughart, the only significant battlefield victory won by any of Edward II's subjects against the Scots during his reign.

From a strategic viewpoint, an attack on the English lordship of Ireland made sense; John MacDougall, an exiled Comyn adherent, had used Ireland as a base for attacks on the Western Isles, while the lordship had provided the English war effort in Scotland with a constant stream of men and supplies. Robert doubtless hoped that these could be used to support the Scottish war effort in England instead. But the expedition was also motivated by the dynastic aim of extending the Bruce family hegemony, and by the close historical and cultural links between the Gaelic Irish and the Scots. As well as being the son-in-law of Richard de Burgh, the Anglo-Irish earl of Ulster, Robert had close ties to the Gaelic Irish, which had helped to save his neck in 1306–7; and the Bruces hoped to bring them into an anti-English alliance. In this, however, they were overly optimistic. Gaelic Irish lords did not see the Scottish invasion as their chance to throw out the English; rather it provided an opportunity to use Scottish support to further their personal interests, usually at the cost of other Gaelic Irish lords. Consequently, the Scots were drawn into a complex world of longstanding rivalries and feuds, where gaining the allegiance of one Gaelic kin-group inevitably drove a rival kin-group into the arms of the Anglo-Irish.

In the end, the Irish expedition served mainly to highlight the limitations of Scotland's military resources; not only did it end in disaster, but it demonstrated the inability of the Scots to wage war successfully on more than one front. It was only a lull in the fighting in Ireland during the summer of 1316 which allowed the Scots to mount another incursion into England. Conversely, Robert's absence in Ireland in 1317 enabled the earl of Arundel to lead a raid into Scotland, though it achieved little beyond persuading Robert to return.

Meanwhile, the English, forced on to the defensive since Bannockburn, sought the respite of a truce. A mission to the newly elected Pope John XXII resulted in the dispatch of two cardinals to negotiate peace, to which end he promulgated a two-year truce. But the cardinals' efforts were in vain; Robert refused to accept their letters, as they were not addressed to him as king of Scots. Ignoring the papal truce, the Scots recaptured Berwick on the night of 1 April 1318; it was betrayed to them by Peter Spalding, an English man-at-arms in the town's garrison. This flagrant breach of papal authority earned Robert another excommunication.

Having driven the English from their last outpost north of the border, Robert now aimed at forcing Edward to recognize his kingship. To this end, he ordered another raid into England, which reached as far south as Skipton in Yorkshire. Since Bannockburn, the English war effort had been undermined by continuing political dissension, but in the autumn of 1318, Edward managed to patch up a settlement with Thomas of Lancaster. This paved the way for another expedition to Scotland, planned for the following summer.

The English eventually crossed the border in September 1319, laying siege to Berwick. Robert was anxious to break the siege, but unwilling to risk a battle. Instead, he sent the earl of Moray across the border, bypassing the besiegers and raiding deep into Yorkshire. The archbishop of York cobbled together a scratch force, but it was easily routed by the battle-hardened Scots, at Myton – a battle derisively denominated the 'Chapter of Myton', due to the number of clergymen killed or captured there. This aroused consternation among the many northerners in the English army at Berwick, who understandably cared more for protecting their country than pressing home the siege. After acrimonious arguments amongst Edward's commanders, the siege was lifted so that they could intercept Moray's invasion force. This they signally failed to do, and the army dispersed. Foremost in calling for the abandonment of the siege was Thomas of Lancaster; and it was widely rumoured that he was in league with the Scots.

With the failure of the siege of Berwick, the Anglo-Scottish wars were now effectively at stalemate. The English, riven by dissent and faction, had proved incapable of defending the Marches; but equally, the Scots were unable to use their undoubted military advantage to impose a political settlement. In the long term, the raids on England did achieve a belated measure of political success; Edward's failure to defend his realm was one of the factors which led to his deposition in 1327. In the shorter term, he remained unmoved by the north's plight, and steadfastly refused to countenance any recognition of Robert's kingship. Although parts of Northumberland had been effectively overrun, the Scots proved unable to capture major border strongholds such as Carlisle or Norham castle; and English administration continued to function in the Marches.

And while Edward remained more concerned about his English opponents than the Scots, continued raiding could achieve nothing beyond plunder and the extortion of money – although many Scots regarded these as worthwhile ends in themselves.

Meanwhile, Robert was facing difficulties in Scotland, where his authority had been weakened by the loss of his brother Edward. By 1319, all his brothers had been killed by the English, and he had no surviving children, leaving his three-year-old grandson, Robert Stewart, as his only male heir. There were also signs of unrest from disaffected former Balliol supporters, which would come to a head in the Soules conspiracy of 1320, aimed at the overthrow of his kingship. Robert therefore agreed to English proposals for a two-year truce, from Christmas 1319.

Edward, too, had problems; by 1321, the political situation in England had deteriorated to the point of widespread rebellion. As with the Comyns after 1306, the exigencies of civil war overcame national enmities, and Thomas of Lancaster opened negotiations with the Scots. But for many English marchers, rebellion against Edward served only to distract him from the task of war with Scotland. Indeed, as soon as the truce ended, the Scots took advantage of the unrest to start raiding again – possibly in collusion with Lancaster. Such considerations undoubtedly determined the continued loyalty of prominent marchers such as Andrew Harclay, who led the army which finally defeated Lancaster at Boroughbridge in March 1322.

Flushed with victory over the English rebels, Edward now felt ready to deal with the Scots. In August, having raised an army of some 20,000 men, perhaps the largest of his reign, he invaded Lothian. The Scots simply retreated northwards, taking all the region's livestock with them. The enormous size of the English army proved a liability, for it was too large to feed. With his men starving, Edward was forced to turn back, having achieved nothing. Worse, once the army had dispersed, Robert led another incursion into England, routed a sizeable English force near Byland abbey in Yorkshire, and almost managed to capture Edward himself.

The abject failure of this expedition, and its disastrous aftermath, threw into stark relief Edward's inability to wage successful war against the Scots. With his English opponents utterly defeated, he had been able to bring the entire military might of the English state to bear against his Scottish enemies; yet still he had failed. It was now increasingly apparent that some sort of peace agreement was the only realistic option for the English. Accordingly, in an act of astonishing lese-majesty, Harclay took matters into his own hands and negotiated a treaty with Robert on his own authority, which stipulated that Scotland and England should remain as separate kingdoms, and recognized Robert as king of an independent realm. In return, Robert promised to pay 40,000 marks (£26,666 13s. 4d.) if Edward would consent to the treaty, while provision was made for enforcing the terms on anyone unwilling to accept it, a veiled threat to Edward if he refused to comply.

Edward was indeed unwilling to accept this abrogation of his authority. Harclay was arrested, summarily tried as a traitor, and messily executed for his pains.[9] Nevertheless, having put to death his chief supporter in the Marches, and one of the few captains who had had any success in fighting the Scots, Edward had little alternative but to follow his example, and to come to terms with Robert. The defeat of Lancaster had, however, left Edward in a much stronger position (notwithstanding the failure of the 1322 expedition), and Robert evidently realized that there was little chance of imposing any peace agreement on him by force. Negotiations were opened just three months after Harclay's execution, leading to the sealing of a thirteen-year truce in May 1323, leaving the issue of Robert's kingship unresolved.

Negotiations for a final peace were pursued in a desultory fashion, without result. There was, however, movement on the diplomatic front. Robert had obtained little support from the French beyond recognition of his kingship and fulsome expressions of goodwill. This changed in 1324, with the outbreak of war between France and England over Gascony. Although the war was short-lived, the French once more regarded the Scots as a useful ally against England. The treaty of Corbeil was duly sealed in April 1326, reviving the Franco-Scottish alliance on similar terms to the treaty of 1295.

Robert's health was now failing, and he was more anxious than ever to reach a permanent settlement with England, to secure the unhindered succession of his young son, David (born in 1324). Although Edward remained obdurate, the shifting of English politics provided Robert with his opportunity. In January 1327, Edward was deposed in a *coup* led by his queen, Isabella, and her intimate, Sir Roger Mortimer. In his place, they installed Edward's son and heir, the fourteen-year-old Edward III, who remained under their tutelage.

Robert took immediate advantage; Norham castle was attacked – unsuccessfully – on the very day of the new king's coronation. This presented Mortimer and Isabella with an awkward dilemma; one of the charges they had laid against Edward II was that he had lost Scotland, yet their regime rested on slender foundations, and they were reluctant to risk war. Accordingly, they confirmed the existing truce, and peace negotiations were held at York. However, these had broken down by mid-June, when the Scots raided Cumberland. Edward III was dispatched north at the head of a large army. He spent three weeks chasing the invaders around the rain-soaked woods and valleys of Weardale, in the bishopric of Durham, only for the Scots to slip away in the middle of the night, leaving the young Edward weeping tears of frustration. Robert kept up the pressure, leading a devastating invasion of Northumberland. In an escalation of their previous tactics, the Scots besieged the castles of Norham, Alnwick and Warkworth, while Robert gave out charters granting Northumbrian lands to his followers, thus presenting the alarming prospect of an occupation of the county.[10]

The threat worked. Isabella and Mortimer could sustain neither the financial nor the political costs of such a conspicuously unsuccessful war, and so had no alternative but to come to terms. By the treaty of Edinburgh, negotiated in March 1328, Edward recognized 'the eminent prince Lord Robert, by the grace of God illustrious king of Scots',[11] and renounced any claim to overlordship; Robert's son and heir David (aged 4) was to marry Edward's sister, Joan (aged 7); and the English would help to obtain the annulment of Robert's excommunication. This they duly did, and Scotland's status as a fully sovereign realm was further confirmed when the pope subsequently granted that Scottish kings should be inaugurated with the rites of coronation and anointment. The Franco-Scottish alliance was exempted from the terms of the treaty, leaving the Scots free to attack England in the event of an Anglo-French war. The Scots agreed to pay £20,000, perhaps to compensate Edward for the loss of his rights. Otherwise, the treaty offered the English nothing to show for 32 years of war.

For much of the population of England, particularly in the north, the cessation of the war can only have been an unalloyed blessing. However, the political classes took a rather different view, and a number of English chroniclers would denounce the treaty as the 'shameful', or 'cowardice' peace. This view was evidently shared by the London mob which prevented the Stone of Scone from being returned to Scotland, as the terms of the treaty demanded. Edward made clear his opinion of the proceedings by refusing to attend his sister's wedding to David. For Robert, the treaty offered everything he had been fighting for since 1306. In the event, however, the peace endured for less than five years. From then on, England and Scotland would remain formally at war until 1502.

ii. *Edward Balliol and the Disinherited, 1332–7*

In the negotiations for the treaty of Edinburgh, one issue above all proved particularly contentious – that of cross-border landholding. Before 1296, many Englishmen and Scotsmen had held land in both realms (see Introduction, Section ii). But with the outbreak of war, cross-border landholders were forced to choose between allegiances which had suddenly become incompatible, leading to the forfeiture of lands in the realm they rejected. The situation was further complicated by the grants of lands in Scotland made by Edward I to English magnates, to encourage them to serve there.

Initially, Robert I was strongly opposed to any restoration of forfeited lands, particularly as he had granted many of them to his own supporters. However, Mortimer and Isabella were obliged to pursue the issue because they could ill-afford to alienate powerful magnates such as Henry Percy and Henry Beaumont, who had claims to lands in Scotland. Consequently, they insisted on some degree of restoration. Percy was able to recover his family's Scottish estates (even though these had been acquired only since 1299), largely because he was one of the main English negotiators. Similarly, James Douglas, the leader of the Scottish delegation, recovered his lands in Northumberland, as did a minor Scottish landowner, Henry Prendergast. A number of religious houses were also able to recover their cross-border holdings. Thereafter, the process stalled, probably because Beaumont had fallen out of favour with Mortimer.[12]

There were many other magnates, both English and Scots in the English allegiance, whose claims had not been addressed (dubbed the 'Disinherited' by a contemporary English chronicler).[13] They included David Strathbogie, whose father had forfeited the earldom of Atholl, after going over to the English (Section i, above). John, Alexander and Geoffrey Mowbray were sons of Roger Mowbray, a Scottish baron who had forfeited his lands for his involvement in the Soules conspiracy (Section i). The Northumbrian Umfravilles remained steadfastly English in their allegiance, and consequently forfeited the Scottish earldom of Angus in 1314. Beaumont had married a Comyn heiress, and Richard Talbot, a baron of the Welsh Marches, had married another; both claimed forfeited Comyn lands. But of all the Disinherited, the biggest loser was Edward Balliol, son of King John. Edward had spent much of his youth in England, vainly trying to recover the family's English estates, forfeited to Edward I in 1295. By the time of the treaty of Edinburgh, he was in his late forties, and had retired to the remaining family lands in France.

In 1329, the death of Robert I and succession of the five-year-old David II presented an opportunity for the Disinherited to recover their lands by force. The initiative for the expedition seems to have originated with Beaumont, who persuaded Balliol to head it, in the hope of drawing on lingering pro-Balliol sentiment in Scotland. This also lent legitimacy to the adventure, for Balliol could claim to be fighting to recover his sovereign rights, and the expedition could thus be presented as a just war. By this time, Mortimer had been executed, and Edward III had seized control of his own government. Officially, he disowned the expedition, for any support would have constituted a breach of the treaty of Edinburgh. The magnates who joined Balliol did so in a private capacity, and served at their own expense. In fact, Edward gave them his tacit backing, and may have received Balliol's homage for Scotland, although he appears to have had no great expectations of the expedition.

The Scottish guardian, Thomas Randolph, Earl of Moray, died on 10 July, just as the expedition was preparing to sail, a coincidence which led to rumours of poisoning. A parliament was summoned at Perth, where, on 2 August, Donald, Earl of Mar, was chosen to succeed him as guardian, but only after heated debate. Mar, a nephew of Robert I, was the obvious candidate, as the nearest legitimate adult relative of King David (Robert Stewart was a nearer relative, but was only sixteen years old). But Mar had been brought up at the court of Edward II, only returning to Scotland after Edward's deposition; and he was widely suspected – by the English as well as the Scots – of sympathizing with the Disinherited. These doubts about his loyalty were to have disastrous consequences.

The Disinherited sailed for Scotland with around 1,500 or 2,000 men. They landed on 6 August, at Kinghorn on the Firth of Forth, where Alexander III had come to grief 46 years before. Mar had mustered a huge army at Perth, and met the invaders at nearby Dupplin Moor on 11 August, where the Disinherited formed up their small force across a narrow valley. Meanwhile, a furious squabble broke out amongst the Scottish commanders, when Mar was accused of being in league with the enemy by Robert Bruce, the bastard son of King Robert. Refusing to accept Mar's precedence, Bruce led his men in a headlong and disorganized assault. He was quickly followed by Mar with his division, determined to prove his loyalty to David's cause; and with too many men trying to advance down the valley, the Scottish army effectively defeated itself, rapidly disintegrating into a fatally constricted mob. Thousands died in the crush, including Bruce, Mar, and three other earls.

With many of the dead unmarked by the blow of any weapon, this overwhelming victory by a vastly outnumbered army was widely seen as the judgement of God. Just as trial by battle at Bannockburn had vindicated Robert I's seizure of the kingship, so victory against the odds at Dupplin Moor justified Balliol's claim, and many Scottish nobles now submitted to him. On 24 September, Balliol was made king of Scots at Scone. For Edward III and his council, these events offered an unexpected opportunity to recast Anglo-Scottish relations in England's favour – although they were not yet sure how to go about it. In part, they were driven by apprehension of the threat posed by the recently renewed French alliance with Scotland, for England was once again in dispute with France over Gascony. But Edward personally detested the treaty of Edinburgh, imposed on him by Mortimer against his will, and he was also determined to expunge the shame of the abject failure of the Weardale campaign in 1327 (Section i, above).

There were three main options open to Edward: he could support Balliol against David, in return for his acceptance of English overlordship; he could do without Balliol and try to impose direct English rule (as his grandfather, Edward I, had done); or he could support David, his sister's betrothed (as David's government requested under the terms of the treaty of Edinburgh), and take the opportunity to extort concessions. Balliol himself still faced considerable opposition in Scotland, and was all too aware that he needed Edward's support; in order to secure it, he issued letters recording his homage and fealty to Edward and his heirs, 'as sovereign lords of the said realm of Scotland and the Isles'.[14] He also promised to grant Edward £2,000 worth of lands on the Scottish Marches, including Berwick. He sent envoys with these terms to the parliament which met at York in December.

Edward III now claimed that he was not bound by the Edinburgh peace treaty. His council justified this on two grounds: firstly, that the treaty had included a provision that the Scots were allowed to retain their alliance with France, and as the French were now the king's 'open enemies', then so were the Scots (a somewhat sophistic reading of the terms); and secondly, because the renunciation of English overlordship had applied only to the overlordship conceded by John Balliol; as Edward Balliol was now offering a new fealty, therefore, 'from a new cause, a new war'.[15] It was also pointed out that Edward III had been a minor in 1328 when the treaty was sealed, with the clear implication that he was therefore not bound by it.

Meanwhile, it had become clear that although David's supporters had been badly bloodied at Dupplin Moor, they were far from defeated. A week before Christmas, Balliol's household was caught in a surprise attack at Annan, near the border. John Mowbray, one of his main Scottish supporters, was killed, and Balliol himself was forced to flee ignominiously to Carlisle, reputedly in his nightshirt. With David's party resurgent, and therefore unlikely to offer any concessions, Edward finally opted for war in support of Balliol, despite a marked lack of enthusiasm for his plans in parliament.

Balliol and the Disinherited regrouped their forces, now with the financial assistance of the English exchequer, and, in March 1333, set out to besiege Berwick. David's supporters, wary of risking battle after their catastrophic defeat at Dupplin Moor, responded by raiding Cumberland, to try to draw the attackers away from their siege. This gave Edward III the excuse he needed; and citing this raid as a breach of the treaty of Edinburgh, he led an army to join Balliol.

At the end of June, after nearly four months of siege, the defenders of Berwick agreed to surrender if they were not relieved. The Scots again tried to draw off the besieging army by invading England, as they had successfully done in 1319; but although the smoke from burning Northumbrian villages was clearly visible to the English army across the Tweed, Edward was not to be distracted. The Scots were now placed in the same position as Edward II before Bannockburn; if they were to break the siege, they had no choice but to attack the besiegers. They duly crossed back over the Tweed, and advanced towards Berwick on 19 July. Edward drew up his army on foot on nearby Halidon Hill, in a strong defensive position; the Scots, forced to attack uphill, were slaughtered in their thousands. Among the dead lay five earls, and the guardian, Sir Archibald Douglas.[16]

Immediately after the battle, Edward exacted the first instalment of the price of his support, taking Berwickshire under English control. He complacently regarded his victory as decisive; a writ issued on 4 August, just two weeks after the battle, referred to 'the late war against the Scots', as though it was already over and won.[17] Edward had returned to England, leaving to Balliol and his supporters the task of consolidating their rule in Scotland. In this, they were initially almost completely successful, and the Disinherited were able to take possession of the lands they claimed without serious opposition. David's remaining adherents were reduced to holding out in a few isolated fortresses, with the young David sheltering at Dumbarton castle, on the Clyde. However, no effort seems to have been made to reduce these remaining outposts. The opportunity to gain custody of David was passed over, leaving the way open for his supporters to stage a recovery.

Balliol's position was in fact weaker than it appeared, for the re-instatement of the Disinherited had left many of David's adherents dispossessed, creating a new class of disinherited who were hardly likely to be reconciled to Balliol's kingship. Similarly, the rewarding of his English supporters with offices in Scotland aroused considerable resentment amongst Scots. And his authority was further undermined by the cost of Edward III's support. Although he prevaricated for as long as possible, he was obliged to make an exceedingly generous interpretation of the terms he had offered in 1332. And so in June 1334 at Newcastle, he performed homage to Edward, and ceded the sheriffdoms of Roxburgh, Peebles, Selkirk, Dumfries and Edinburgh (in addition to Berwick, which was already in English hands). This amounted to the dismemberment of the realm, granting away a large part of Scotland south of the Forth, perhaps the wealthiest region of the kingdom, to English control – though it did not entail a northwards shift of the border (Chapter 9, Section i).

The renewed outbreak of Anglo-Scottish hostilities had presented Philippe VI of France with something of a dilemma. Under the treaty of Corbeil, sealed by his predecessor, Charles IV, in 1326, he was obliged to support the Scots; yet he was intent on leading a crusade to the Holy Land, and such a venture could hardly be risked unless he was on good terms with Edward III. Indeed he hoped that Edward might accompany him. Therefore, despite the unresolved dispute over Gascony, his initial response to the Disinherited's invasion was limited to a letter of mild reproof (an approach made easier by the care which Edward had taken to avoid associating himself with it). However, John Randolph, Earl of Moray, went to France to remind Philippe of his obligations, and when the English besieged Berwick in 1333, he felt honour-bound to come to David's aid. He sent money and a fleet of ten ships laden with supplies, although in the event, storms prevented them from getting any further than Flanders. Critically, however, he also agreed to provide a haven for David, who took ship to France in May 1334. The ten-year-old king was established at Château Gaillard on the Seine, with a generous pension, enabling him to function as the figurehead of a court in exile.

Encouraged by Philippe's support, David's adherents, led by Moray, Robert Stewart and Douglas of Liddesdale, mounted a counter-attack.

They rapidly established themselves in the west, and were able to undermine attempts to establish an English administration in the counties ceded by Balliol. And unfortunately for the defence of what remained of Balliol's realm, a bitter squabble broke out between him and his main English supporters over the inheritance of John Mowbray, killed at Annan in 1332. David's supporters were able to defeat them piecemeal: Richard Talbot was ambushed and captured, and Beaumont was besieged at Dundarg. At the same time, Atholl was cornered and forced at sword-point to pledge his allegiance to David; and Balliol once again fled to England. This left Patrick, Earl of March, as the sole Scottish magnate remaining in the English allegiance.

These events finally persuaded Edward of the necessity of substantial military support for Balliol, and he summoned an army to muster at Newcastle in October. The prospect of serving in Scotland in winter did not meet with great enthusiasm, and the subsequent campaign was plagued by poor recruitment and desertion, and achieved little. Edward was unable to relieve Dundarg, which was forced to surrender, while March now went over to David's party, a mark of the ineffectiveness of Edward's efforts. He did, however, rebuild Roxburgh castle (demolished by Robert I after its capture in 1314), which provided a secure base for future operations.

In the summer of 1335, Edward finally brought to bear the full resources available to the English Crown. A summer campaign proved much easier to recruit for, and he was able to lead a two-pronged invasion of Scotland with Balliol, wreaking immense devastation, and forcing the submission of many Scottish magnates. Among these were Atholl and Stewart who negotiated terms which included, alongside personal concessions, the wider recognition that 'the laws of Scotland ... in the lands of the king of Scotland should be used according to the ancient usages and customs of Scotland'; and that 'the offices of Scotland should be ministered by men of the same nation' – a telling indication of the issues which continued to concern Scotsmen about English overlordship.[18] They were followed by John MacDonald, Lord of the Isles, who submitted to Balliol in September, and entered into Edward III's allegiance. David's remaining followers were under severe pressure, and agreed to a truce, to be followed by negotiations for a permanent settlement.

It seems that the truce applied only to Edward III's men, leaving Balliol free to send Atholl to subdue the lands north of the Forth, a task which he set about with enthusiastic brutality. After a campaign of burning and ravaging, he besieged Kildrummy castle, held by the wife of Andrew

Murray, the guardian. Murray gathered an army and attacked Atholl, killing him and dispersing his army at Culblean, on 30 November.[19] This was undoubtedly a major blow for Balliol, putting an end to his attempts to subdue the north. And after the disasters at Dupplin Moor and Halidon Hill, success on the battlefield was a much-needed boost to the morale of David's adherents. Nevertheless, it was not a decisive victory, for Edward III's expedition had greatly strengthened Balliol's authority in the south.

The negotiations continued, and it was agreed that David should succeed Balliol as his heir, and rule Scotland on the same terms after the latter's death. But when the terms were taken to David in France, they were rejected by his advisers. Such a settlement would have left Scotland subordinate to England; and it would also have left some of the most prominent of David's supporters dispossessed of their lands, including Moray (who was not party to the negotiations as he had been captured by the English), and Douglas of Liddesdale.

In the event, the course of the Anglo-Scottish conflict was in large part determined by events on the Continent. Relations between England and France had steadily deteriorated as the dispute over Scotland prevented any settlement over Gascony. The pope realized that this was an insurmountable obstacle to Philippe VI's proposed crusade, and in March 1336, he cancelled it. Philippe had already assembled a fleet to take him to the Holy Land; he now planned to use it to send an expedition to Scotland instead, to restore David. Edward responded by leading a small force on a *chevauchée* into north-eastern Scotland, where he relieved Lochindorb castle, defended by Catherine Beaumont, the widow of the earl of Atholl. Having chivalrously rescued this damsel in distress, he thoroughly ravaged the coastal plain, and burned Aberdeen to the ground, so as to hinder any French landing, and prevent them from feeding themselves if they did land.[20]

Edward's expedition met with little resistance, and he was able to march across the region unimpeded. It was, however, merely a pre-emptive strike, presaging a shift towards a defensive strategy, marked by the rebuilding of castles and town walls at key points such as Edinburgh, Stirling, Roxburgh and Perth, which Balliol adopted as his capital. As a strategy, this could only have worked with the commitment of large numbers of English troops on a permanent basis, including a standing field army to protect garrisons by quickly breaking Scottish sieges. Edward could not however make such a large-scale commitment to Balliol's cause, because of his deteriorating relations with France.

In effect, English apprehension about the alliance of 1326 proved to be self-fulfilling: the potential threat it posed was one of the considerations which led Edward to attack Scotland in 1333; yet this attack eventually served to ensure the threat became a reality. In November 1336, a Franco-Scottish fleet attacked the Channel Isles, and by the following January, Edward was set on war with France. For the next hundred years, Scotland would take second place to France in the English Crown's priorities.

Chapter 3: The Hundred Years War: War on Two Fronts, 1337–1453

i. Edward III and David II, 1337–71

Looking back from the beginning of the fifteenth century, the Scottish chronicler Andrew Wyntoun commented that Edward III's decision to go to war with France was 'a good chance for Scotland'.[1] England was now fighting on two fronts. In September 1337, it was decided to send another expedition to Scotland, in the absence of Edward, who was planning to lead an army to France. The Scottish expedition would be led by Richard, Earl of Arundel, and Edward's favourite, William Montague, newly ennobled as the earl of Salisbury. Their objective was Dunbar castle, on the coast of Lothian. It had been rebuilt at Edward III's expense in 1333, while its owner, Patrick, Earl of March, had been in the English allegiance; but he had then gone over to David. The castle was boldly defended by Patrick's resourceful countess, Agnes (daughter of Thomas Randolph, the former guardian), and Salisbury conspicuously failed to capture it despite maintaining the siege for more than four months. In July, Edward III led his expedition to the Continent, taking Salisbury with him. The army he had led to Scotland, at great expense, had nothing to show for its efforts except for a truce, to last until 30 September 1339. Small wonder that one contemporary English chronicler commented, 'the Scots were cheerful and happy, the English were unhappy and dolorous'.[2]

In the event, the truce lasted only until May 1339. Facing an English army in Flanders, Philippe stepped up his support for David, and William Douglas of Liddesdale returned from visiting David's court in exile with a force of French knights – the first direct military assistance for the Scots since the sealing of the Franco-Scottish treaty of 1295.

With their help, David's supporters besieged Perth, which fell in August. Over the next two years, the position of the Anglo-Balliol regime gradually deteriorated, while Edward III was busy bringing England to the verge of bankruptcy through his prodigious expenditure on the French war. With Balliol and the English on the defensive, starved of troops and resources, David's adherents waged a war of attrition, besieging English-held castles, and wearing down Balliol's remaining Scottish supporters by a campaign of devastation. The success of this strategy was marked by the capture of Edinburgh, in April 1341. David was now seventeen, and his supporters felt secure enough to bring him back from France. He crossed to Scotland in early June, after seven years of exile. His return was marked by a major raid into Northumberland, which he accompanied.

Having run out of money, Edward III had been forced to return to England in 1340; and he finally reacted to events in Scotland by ordering an expedition, appointing Henry Grosmont, Earl of Derby, as its leader. In the event, it was Edward himself who led the expedition north in November 1341, at the head of an army some 2,500 strong. He remained in Scotland until after Christmas, his army ravaging and burning in the customary fashion; but the Scots, as usual, simply retreated. Nevertheless, this show of force was enough to convince them to agree to a truce, until May 1342. The negotiations were enlivened by splendid tournaments at Roxburgh and Berwick in which Derby distinguished himself, a reminder of a shared chivalric culture which might, on occasion, transcend national hostilities (Chapter 10). Derby remained in the borders to continue negotiations. However, he was unable even to ensure the maintenance of the truce, for on 30 March, Roxburgh fell to a surprise attack. Ten days later, David received the surrender of Stirling. This left Lochmaben, Jedburgh and Berwick as the only remaining English strongholds in Scotland.

In the five years since the beginning of the French wars, the English had lost virtually all the gains they had made since the re-installation of Edward Balliol as king of Scots in 1333. The garrisons the English maintained across the border had not been adequate to defend these lands by themselves, and expeditionary armies were sent too infrequently, and stayed for too short a time, to make a significant difference. Northern England now once more seemed vulnerable to Scottish raiding, and in expectation of this, a standing force of 1,200 men was contracted in May 1342 to remain in the field for as long as necessary for the defence of the Marches. Had such a scheme been implemented in Scotland in 1337 for the defence of the English lands there, then they might have remained in English hands for longer. On the other hand, the Crown's finances could hardly have stood the prohibitive expense of maintaining such an army indefinitely. Quite simply, Edward III could not afford to raise forces adequate to the task of waging war against France and Scotland at the same time.

However (fortunately for the state of English finances), the Scots made little concerted effort to follow up their successes after 1342. For the next four years, David's policy towards England – insofar as he had one – was driven not by any overarching strategic aim, but rather by the vicissitudes of internal Scottish politics, and his need to establish his personal authority in his own kingdom. This set him at odds with many of his magnates who had become used to operating in his absence, untrammelled by royal power. Foremost among these was Robert Stewart, David's nephew (though some eight years his senior), who – until David should sire an heir – stood next in line to the kingship.

More immediately, the fall of Roxburgh brought about a major crisis when David appointed its captor, Alexander Ramsey, as sheriff of Roxburghshire. Taking this as an unwarranted interference in his sphere of influence, Douglas of Liddesdale seized Ramsey and had him starved to death. In the aftermath, the Scottish borders were embroiled in a major feud, which effectively curtailed aggression against England. Indeed, in 1343, Douglas flirted with entering the English allegiance. Well might a contemporary Scottish chronicler comment that following Ramsey's murder, 'all campaigns undertaken for the benefit of the kingdom straight away took an unfortunate turn ... because ... an almost eternal quarrel and unending strife arose in the kingdom'.[3]

Meanwhile, Edward III's attention returned to France, and in the summer of 1345, he sent expeditions to Gascony and Brittany. David undoubtedly felt an obligation to aid his French allies, who had provided him with a refuge in exile. But perhaps more importantly, he still needed to reinforce his authority as king. For the son of Robert Bruce, the obvious way to do so was through leadership in war with England. Over the course of the next year, three cross-border raids left large areas of Cumberland and Westmorland devastated; but events on the Continent then inspired David to escalate this belligerent policy. On 26 August 1346, the French suffered a terrible defeat at Crécy at the hands of Edward III, who went on to besiege Calais. Philippe now invoked the Franco-Scottish alliance, imploring David to invade England, in the hope that this might distract Edward.

The English were well-informed of David's intentions, not least because they had sent out spies. David, however, remained singularly ill-informed about the state of the English defences. Many chronicles, both Scottish and English, report that he laboured under the unfortunate conviction that all of England's fighting men were in France, leaving only 'priests, friars and clerks, craftsmen and tradesmen',[4] a belief in which he had been encouraged by Philippe. The opportunity of attacking England while it was apparently defenceless was not to be passed up, and so he summoned a large army from across his realm, boasting that they would march to London. Nevertheless, while an invasion of England was undoubtedly popular, it did not serve to unite his magnates behind him. The earl of Ross, for instance, used the muster as an opportunity to murder a local rival, before going back home.

Despite these difficulties, the Scots crossed the border at the beginning of October. However, the invasion lacked any clear strategic aim. Five days were spent besieging the minor border fort of Liddel Peel, chiefly in the interests of Douglas of Liddesdale. After this, the Scots meandered slowly round the Marches, ravaging and extorting blackmail. Scottish armies under Robert I had moved rapidly, allowing the English little chance of gathering defensive forces to repel them. By contrast, the leisurely progress of David's invasion allowed the English plenty of time to muster an army, recruited from across the northern counties.

The Scots were taken aback when they ran into this army at Neville's Cross, near Durham, on 17 October. Unable to avoid battle, they had no choice but to attack, despite unfavourable terrain. The ensuing battle was hard fought, but after onslaughts by the Scottish vanguard and the main division had failed to break the English line, Robert Stewart (David's heir) and Patrick, Earl of March, the commanders of the rearguard, led their division from the field, leaving David to be captured.[5] From a tactical viewpoint, the discretion of Stewart and March was probably the better part of valour, given the disasters which had befallen the Scots at Dupplin Moor and Halidon Hill. But equally, they may have been unwilling to risk themselves in the cause of a king whose interference they resented. Either way, Stewart's tactical withdrawal did nothing to endear him to his king, and this enmity was to influence the course of Anglo-Scottish relations for the rest of David's reign.

Many Scottish nobles joined their king in captivity. The earls of Menteith and Fife were sentenced to death as traitors, because the former had been sworn as a member of Edward's own council, while the latter had done homage to Balliol; and though Fife was reprieved because he was related to Edward, Menteith was duly executed. This still left the problem of what to do with David. He had never sworn fealty to the English Crown, and so unlike Menteith, he could hardly be put to a traitor's death – a fate which would surely have befallen his father Robert, if he had ever had the misfortune to fall into the clutches of Edward I or Edward II. More positively, his capture gave Edward the possibility of a negotiated settlement; and at the very least, he could fetch – quite literally – a king's ransom. However, any such negotiations would amount to a *de facto* recognition of his kingship.

In the interim, Edward Balliol (the king currently recognized by the English) was appointed to lead an expedition. An army of some 1,000 men crossed the border in May 1347, and succeeded in re-establishing English hegemony across most of Berwickshire, Roxburghshire and Dumfriesshire. Balliol was established at Hestan, a small island on the Galloway coast, where a second English army served with him in October, though it achieved little beyond extorting the sum of £9,000 from the Scots for a truce. Over the next decade, the Scots would gradually erode the English position, and recapture much of the land occupied in the aftermath of Neville's Cross.

With David in captivity, Robert Stewart had secured the post of guardian, and he proved in no great hurry to negotiate the release of his king. After all, Balliol had been defeated in David's absence before, and there were few grounds for supposing that he would do any better this time round. Furthermore, Stewart was busy using the authority of the guardianship to extend his family interests. Thus it was not until April 1348 that a Scottish embassy came to London. The terms initially demanded for David's release included his homage; military support for the English in France; the restoration of the Disinherited; and the succession of Edward III, or one of his sons, as king of Scotland, should David die without heirs. This would have reduced Scotland to a state of abject subjugation, and disinherited Stewart. Unsurprisingly, the Scottish envoys went home having agreed to nothing beyond an extension of the truce.

Here matters effectively rested (in part due to the disruption caused by the Black Death in 1348–9), until a new round of negotiations commenced in 1350. The background to these talks is revealed by a memorandum to the English negotiators. Balliol was now in his late sixties and had no heir; he lacked any support in Scotland outside Galloway, and Edward III had come to regard him as an obstruction to any settlement. It was also anticipated that David would have difficulty persuading his subjects to accept the proposed terms.[6] These provided for a ransom of £40,000; the restoration of the Disinherited; possible Scottish military service against the French; and the succession of a younger son of Edward III (possibly John of Gaunt). For David, the latter proposal had much to recommend it, and it may have been his own suggestion. The succession of an English prince would occur only if he did not produce an heir himself, and he was still young enough to expect to do so. Given the animosity between him and Stewart, the prospect of Stewart's disinheritance could hardly have displeased him, while he seems to have admired Edward as an exemplar of chivalric values. Crucially, the demand for homage had been dropped, while the succession of a younger son offered a guarantee of the continuation of Scotland as a separate kingdom (barring dynastic accident).

The terms were taken to Scotland by Douglas of Liddesdale, where they were discussed at a parliament held in May 1351, summoned by David from captivity. In November, David himself was allowed to go north of the border to try to gain agreement for improved terms, including the remittance of any ransom, and the return of all lands occupied by the English. Still aggrieved by the 'shameful peace' of 1328, Edward could not quite bring himself to agree to a permanent peace, but offered the next best thing, a truce of 1,000 years. If put into effect, these terms would have led to a return to something like the conditions before 1286, with a sovereign Scotland and a partially revived Anglo-Scottish nobility united by cross-border landholdings.

However, the concerns about David's ability to persuade his subjects proved to be well-founded. Clearly, Stewart had nothing to gain from any settlement which displaced him as heir. Other Scottish magnates stood to lose from the restoration of the Disinherited. But opposition to the proposals was more widespread; after more than 50 years of hostility, an English heir to the throne was simply not acceptable for too many of the Scottish political establishment.

Faced with a king who seemed bent on removing him from the succession, Stewart turned to France. He received assurances from Jean II (who succeeded Philippe in 1350), who offered to pay for 1,000 men-at-arms and archers if the English invaded Scotland, or, more remarkably, if David himself were to invade. Evidently, Stewart feared that David might try to impose a settlement on his recalcitrant subjects by force, with English support. In fact, Edward had no desire to invade Scotland, for after a long period of fruitless negotiations, the war with France was hotting up again, and the last thing he needed was the distraction of war against the Scots. Instead, in the absence of any viable alternative, he settled for a straightforward ransom. An agreement was drawn up in July 1354 by which David would be released for 90,000 marks (£60,000), to be paid over nine years. But the settlement was undermined by the reluctance of Stewart and his allies to implement it, encouraged as they were by the diplomatic efforts of the French, who were determined that the Scots should indeed provide a distraction. To this end, Eugene, Sire de Garencières, was sent to Scotland in March 1355, with 50 men-at-arms and their retinues and – more significantly – 40,000 *écus* (£8,000 by the reckoning of Andrew of Wyntoun) to pay to suitably bellicose Scottish magnates.

The English got wind of this, but the threat appeared to have been averted when the English March wardens managed to negotiate a truce with their opposite number, William, Lord Douglas. Presumably on the strength of this, Edward took a number of northern magnates across to France in October, including the keeper of Berwick. However, other Scots were happy to take Garencières' money, including the earls of Angus and March; and in November, they seized Berwick, in the absence of its keeper.

In the short term, the capture of Berwick did have the effect that the French had hoped, as it immediately brought Edward III back to England. But the diversion proved short-lived. He rapidly mustered a large army which recaptured Berwick, and then advanced to Roxburgh. Here, on 20 January 1356, Edward Balliol surrendered his right to the kingdom of Scotland to Edward III, in belated recognition that his claims were no longer relevant. The English expedition was curtailed by a storm which scattered its supply fleet; but before going home, the army took the trouble to ravage Lothian thoroughly – a devastation that was remembered in Scotland as the 'Burnt Candlemas'. Commenting on Garencières' expedition, a contemporary Scottish chronicler reckoned that 'from this agreement and greed of gold, there followed ... the destruction of Lothian', adding wryly that his fellow countrymen 'often for a penny lose a shilling'.[7]

The French intervention had done nothing for the Scots; and nor had any great benefit accrued to the French, for English campaigning in France was not noticeably impeded by events on the Scottish borders. Yet neither did the wasting of Lothian do much to bring David's release closer. Negotiations continued, but again events in France were to set the pace. In September 1356, Jean II fought an English army at Poitiers. In his company was William, Lord Douglas, who reputedly advised the French to fight on foot; they took his advice, but were decisively defeated anyway. Douglas narrowly escaped capture, but Jean joined David II in English captivity.

This marked a high point for Edward who now held prisoner the kings of both France and Scotland. The Scots could no longer look to the French for aid, which had anyway availed them little, and Edward now threatened to exclude them from any Anglo-French truce. They had little choice but to come to terms. The treaty of Berwick, October 1357, allowed for David's release in return for a ransom of 100,000 marks (£66,666), to be paid in ten annual instalments, with a ten-year truce. In effect, this amounted to the recognition of David's kingship, and he was explicitly referred to as 'the noble prince, Sir David, King of Scotland'; otherwise, it addressed none of the underlying causes of Anglo-Scottish conflict since 1296.[8]

In 1360, one of the immediate driving forces towards Anglo-Scottish war was removed with the sealing of the treaty of Brétigny, which brought peace between England and France. Peace negotiations were resumed between England and Scotland when the Scots proved unable – or unwilling – to make continuing ransom payments. At a conference at Westminster in 1363, attended by David in person, Edward proposed that he himself should succeed to the Scottish kingship; in return, he offered to restore what remained of the English lands in Scotland, to buy out the claims of the Disinherited, and to cancel the ransom. David, still childless, seems to have been prepared to accept one of Edward's younger sons, probably John of Gaunt, as his heir; or at least, he was prepared to negotiate on that basis. His subjects, however, proved rather less amenable, and the proposals were comprehensively rejected at a Scottish parliament in 1364. After further desultory peace talks had led nowhere, both sides settled for a new ransom agreement, in 1369. This provided for a fourteen-year truce, along with an increased ransom of £100,000, which was, however, to be paid in smaller instalments of just £4,000.

In 1333, Edward III had thrown over the treaty of Edinburgh and gone to war with the Scots. Three decades later, all he had to show for it was a gradually shrinking English dominion over Berwick, Roxburgh, Jedburgh and Lochmaben and their environs. He had failed in his attempt to install Edward Balliol, or to enforce English overlordship, or an English succession to the Scottish kingship. French aid to the Scots had been a major factor in deciding Edward on war with France; but the outbreak of the French war led Edward to abandon any serious attempt to impose overlordship on Scotland by force. For their part, despite catastrophic defeats at Dupplin Moor, Halidon Hill and Neville's Cross, and the captivity of their king, the Scots had managed to maintain their sovereignty intact. Anti-English sentiment was now so strongly rooted that Robert Stewart was able to maintain his influence by presenting himself as the protector of Scottish independence against David's attempts to impose an English heir. But despite the failure of peace negotiations (which left England and Scotland still legally at war), and the continued level of mistrust, the 1360s saw a definite thaw in relations between the two countries. The outbreak of comparative peace offered a welcome opportunity for peaceful contacts, and many merchants, traders, pilgrims and scholars took advantage of the truce to cross the borders (see Chapter 10). However, the thaw was not to outlast the 1360s.

ii. England at Bay, 1369–1406

In 1369, war broke out again between England and France; and in February 1371, David II suddenly died, to be succeeded by the pro-French Robert Stewart (as Robert II). Together, these two factors served to undermine the Anglo-Scottish *détente*.[9] The new direction of Scottish policy was marked by a new alliance with France, the treaty of Vincennes, sealed in June. This required both realms to make war on England if either was attacked, but with the important proviso that the Scots would not be required to break the existing truce – a clause which effectively made their treaty obligations voluntary. The French had negotiated for a more active alliance, offering to pay off David's ransom (a debt which remained binding, despite his death), and to send an army to Scotland to launch a joint invasion of England; but Robert was not, at this point, ready for open war.

Nevertheless, the renewal of the French war left the English at a disadvantage. Even before David's death, there had been a marked upsurge in violent incidents on the Marches, despite the truce. This period in Anglo-Scottish relations has been characterized as one of private feuding between over-mighty border magnates, acting in their own interests, and beyond the control of their respective governments. Certainly, this was the view recorded by Jean Froissart, a chronicler from Hainault in Flanders, who visited both England and Scotland. He presented Anglo-Scottish warfare at this time as a series of chivalric encounters, devoid of any wider political context, which a weak Robert II could do nothing to prevent. Indeed, Robert himself deliberately fostered this version of events; faced with English complaints about breaches of the truce, he regularly protested his innocence, replying that although he wanted peace, he was unable to restrain his own nobles.

Robert, however, may well have connived at his magnates' actions, maintaining a duplicitous front to placate the English, in order to recover the occupied lands without bringing down the truce.[10] The Scots were anxious to avoid open war; the last time they had provoked the English to the point of retaliation, by taking Berwick in 1355, they had brought upon themselves an immensely destructive *chevauchée* (see Section i, above). The English, busy losing their war with France, were even more desperate to avoid open war with Scotland. Thus it suited both sides to maintain at least the semblance of truce. To this end, the English were prepared to respond to Scottish breaches of the truce by negotiation, so long as such breaches were not too egregious. What ensued was a sporadic, low-intensity war, kept from escalation by March days (Chapter 9, Section ii). The Scots gradually chipped away the cross-border English lordships by intermittent, small-scale raiding, while English reprisals were generally confined to piracy at sea (at least some of which was licensed by the Crown).

There were occasional outbreaks of more serious fighting. In 1373–4, William Douglas, now Earl of Douglas, mounted an aggressive campaign against the lordship of Jedburgh, held by Henry, Lord Percy, to which Douglas had a claim. As both were March wardens, the conflict could hardly be settled through the usual mechanisms of March law, so special commissions were appointed from outside the borders to try to broker a settlement. Generally, though, Scottish aggression was carefully and cautiously calibrated, and there was a falling-off of Scottish attacks during the two-year Anglo-French truce of 1375. However, this truce expired in midsummer 1377, three days after the death of Edward III and succession of his ten-year-old grandson, Richard II. With England under a minority government and once again preoccupied by war with France, there was a marked escalation of Scottish attacks, and Robert felt confident enough of English weakness to stop further payments towards David's ransom. Nevertheless, the Scots were careful not to violate the truce too flagrantly. When Berwick castle was captured by Scottish bandits in 1378, the earl of March, warden of the Scottish East March, apparently volunteered to help Henry Percy (now earl of Northumberland) to take it back. This kind offer was, however, declined and Northumberland recovered it through his own efforts.

The English council's reaction to the deteriorating situation was to appoint the king's uncle John of Gaunt, Duke of Lancaster, as lieutenant of the Marches, in February 1379.[11] As the greatest magnate in England he had the standing to negotiate with the Scots at the highest level; and in particular with John, Earl of Carrick, Robert II's eldest son, who took a leading role in the Scottish Marches (Carrick was himself appointed as Robert's lieutenant of the Marches soon afterwards, to match Gaunt). The council also hoped that Gaunt's power and status, coupled with the authority of his office, would be sufficient to deter English Marchers from breaching the truce. Indeed, he had a particular incentive to maintain a lasting truce, for he had a claim to the kingship of Castile, which could not be pursued while there was a threat of war with Scotland.

Despite Gaunt's assiduous efforts in punishing English breaches of the truce, the threat of war continued to increase. The summer of 1380 saw the Scots crossing the border, and burning Penrith during its annual fair. They also ambushed and captured Ralph, Baron Greystoke, on his way to take command of Roxburgh castle. These raids were finally enough to provoke an English response. When Gaunt arrived at a March day with Carrick in October, he brought an army of 3,500 men. They proceeded to burn Dumfries (as well as plundering the unfortunate inhabitants of Northumberland), a show of force sufficient to secure a new truce, and to deter any further large-scale Scottish incursions for the next three years. Evidently, Gaunt was able to establish a good relationship with his Scottish counterparts, for in the following June, he fled to Scotland when England was convulsed by the Great Revolt of 1381. He was received with honour, and lodged at Holyrood abbey in Edinburgh. He did not, however, take up a Scottish offer of troops to put down the rebels.

Since 1369, the Scots had managed to recover much of the remaining English-occupied land north of the border, but none of the major castles of Berwick, Roxburgh, Lochmaben or Jedburgh; nor had they secured any English concessions on the issue of overlordship. By 1383, the continuing failure of the English war effort against France had persuaded the Scots that they could again risk open war with England. Therefore, in June, a Scottish embassy to France agreed terms committing the Scots to war, for which the French were to provide 1,000 men-at-arms, 40,000 gold francs, and arms and armour, the following May. Even before the treaty had been ratified by King Robert, a Scottish force launched the first major cross-border raid for three years, sacking Wark castle in Northumberland.

Although negotiations followed, the Scots were now set on war, and declined to renew the truce, due to expire the following year. The French, on the other hand, now agreed to peace talks, and a nine-month Anglo-French truce was sealed on 26 January 1384. Provision was made to include the Scots, but by the time news of this reached Scotland, it was too late. Striking as soon as the Anglo-Scottish truce expired, on 2 February, the Scots had already captured Lochmaben, the last remaining English outpost in Annandale. They now faced war with England without French support, an outcome their entire strategy since 1369 had been intended to avoid. The English, however, were beset by mounting financial and political problems arising from the unsuccessful conduct of the French wars, and although they now pursued a more aggressive policy towards Scotland, they proved unable to exploit her isolation effectively. Gaunt led another army across the border; but although he inflicted considerable devastation, he failed to deter further Scottish raiding. In December, Berwick was captured again; this time, the earl of Northumberland resorted to the expedient of buying it back for 2,000 marks (£1,333).

The Anglo-French truce was not renewed, and the plans for co-ordinated Franco-Scottish action were finally put into effect in May 1385, when the admiral of France, Jean de Vienne, landed in Scotland with an army of 1,500 men. At the same time, a vast French invasion force assembled in Flanders. England now faced the dire prospect of simultaneous invasion from France and Scotland. In the event, the continental invasion force was diverted to put down a Flemish rising; but the Franco-Scottish army in the Marches had already crossed the border, sacking Wark castle once again.

This was the first time a French army had invaded England since 1216, in the reign of King John (although the south coast had been subject to French raids since 1337), and the English response had to match the gravity of the situation. It had been planned that Richard II should lead his first expedition to France; this was now directed to Scotland instead. Some 14,000 men were raised, the largest English army of Richard's reign. They marched as far as Edinburgh which they burned, before a lack of supplies forced a return to England. Also put to the flames were Dryburgh, Melrose and Newbattle abbeys (see Chapter 10), though Holyrood was spared at Gaunt's insistence, from gratitude for its hospitality during the Great Revolt.

Once the English had withdrawn, the Franco-Scottish army attacked Carlisle; having failed to take it, they planned an attack on Roxburgh.

However, the expedition broke up in acrimony when Vienne demanded that, if captured, Roxburgh should be held in the name of Charles VI. Soon after, the French returned home in disgust. Despite the near panic they aroused in England, they achieved little beyond falling out with their Scottish hosts, and leaving a trail of unpaid bills.

Richard's expedition has been seen as a failure, or as an unnecessary diversion from the French war.[12] However, the potential threat from the Franco-Scottish army was real enough – the English could not have known that it would be largely nullified by squabbling between the allies. Although Richard did not manage to bring his enemies to battle, his army wrought considerable destruction in southern Scotland; and it was sufficiently large to have a deterrent effect, bringing the Scots to accept another truce. With annual renewals, this lasted three years, and was tolerably well observed.

This was just as well for the English, for the country was riven by political dissension, culminating in a brief outbreak of civil war, and the imposition on Richard of a council dominated by his opponents. The new regime embarked on an aggressive policy towards France, dispatching a naval expedition in the summer of 1388; meanwhile, the English Marches had been weakened by the death of one of the main Marcher magnates, John, Lord Neville. The issues of English overlordship and occupation of lands in Scotland had not, of course, been resolved by Richard's expedition, and the Scots took advantage of the political conflict in England to attack again, launching simultaneous and devastating invasions of both Marches.

Henry 'Hotspur' Percy, son of the earl of Northumberland, and the most energetic of the English March wardens, force-marched his army and caught one of the Scottish armies at Otterburn. He attacked at once in the twilight, and the resulting battle, confused but hard-fought, ended with his capture. The battle has been considered a disaster for the English.[13] However, it was a pyrrhic victory for the Scots, for amongst the casualties was James, Earl of Douglas, and disputes and feuding over his inheritance would seriously disrupt southern Scotland for years. In the long run, the battle at Otterburn may have been almost as damaging for the Scots as for the English.

More raiding and counter-raiding followed; and Richard announced another expedition to Scotland. Negotiations with the French were close to agreement on a long-term truce; the English now pressed for the Scots to be excluded, so that they could fight them without interference. However, the French refused to abandon their allies, and when the terms were finally settled in June 1389, the truce encompassed all three realms. This met with a degree of opposition in Scotland, but realistically the Scots had little option; they could not risk war against England without French support while southern Scotland remained embroiled in feuding over the Douglas inheritance.[14]

Scottish strategy between 1369 and 1389 had been carefully calculated to take advantage of England's war with France, and in the latter stages, depended on close and co-ordinated planning with the French. For these 20 years, the Scots had undoubtedly retained the initiative and the military advantage, recapturing most of the English-held lands north of the border, and inflicting extensive devastation on the English border counties. Yet the Scots had failed to achieve all their war aims, for the English had not renounced their claims to overlordship, and Berwick, Roxburgh and Jedburgh still remained in their hands. Nor had English defences collapsed as they had after Bannockburn. Scottish raiding had been confined to the border counties, while the Scottish borders had suffered a series of destructive English invasions and raids, and English privateers had inflicted heavy losses on Scottish shipping. In particular, military alliance with France did not bring the advantages the Scots had hoped for. The failure of the French to launch their invasion across the Channel in 1385 had left the Scots exposed to invasion from England, while the French expedition to Scotland had ended in rancorous disagreement.

In 1390, Robert II died, to be succeeded by his son John, Earl of Carrick, who took the name Robert III – 'John' being tainted by association with John Balliol. The truce was maintained (despite occasional breaches such as the Scottish night-time assault on Jedburgh castle in 1395), and in many respects, as in the 1360s during the Anglo-French peace, Anglo-Scottish relations became more cordial. Trade increased as piracy declined; Scottish clerics were granted leave to study at Oxford; and Scottish knights came to London to joust in 1390 (see Chapter 10). Peace talks were held in 1394, but with the French truce holding well, the English felt no need to make concessions. Richard demanded that Robert should do him homage, and restore the Scottish lands granted to England by Balliol in 1334, although he was prepared to settle for only the restoration of the lands the English had still held in 1369. In return, he offered to drop demands for payment of the remainder of David's ransom. Such terms were completely unacceptable, and the talks petered out; although the Scots were included in the 28-year Anglo-French truce of 1396, a series of shorter truces were negotiated separately between England and Scotland.

Again, the improvement in Anglo-Scottish relations did not last. In July 1399, John of Gaunt's son, Henry Bolingbroke, led a successful *coup* against Richard II, being crowned as Henry IV in October. He hoped to avoid any destabilizing foreign entanglements while he established his regime, and even before his coronation, he wrote to Robert III requesting a renewal of the existing truce, which expired at the end of September. Robert prevaricated, replying that any extension would have to be confirmed by a Scottish parliament. Nevertheless, for some Scots, the temptation to take advantage of English political disunity once again proved irresistible; Wark castle was ransacked and burned while its owner was at parliament, assisting in the deposition of the unfortunate Richard. Further incidents followed, despite Henry's continuing efforts to renew the truce; nor were relations improved by Robert's refusal to recognize him as king. He therefore began preparations for an expedition to Scotland, partly in response to the Scottish raids, but also as a means of uniting the English political community behind him in a common military endeavour.

Meanwhile, the Scots were suffering political difficulties of their own. Robert's son and prospective heir, David, Duke of Rothesay, seized control of the government, denouncing his father as unfit to rule. But Rothesay's actions aroused resentment. In particular, George Dunbar, Earl of March, was incensed because Rothesay had married and then repudiated his daughter, preferring the earl of Douglas's daughter instead. This was a gross insult in itself; but in an age when marriages were a mark of political allegiance, it signalled that Dunbar had lost influence. He reacted by going over to the English allegiance, where he was employed in a prominent military role in the Marches. It may have been the adherence of such a major Scottish magnate which now prompted Henry to once again put forward claims to the overlordship of Scotland; and like Edward I before him, he looked to historical precedent to back his claim.

In August 1400, Henry led an army some 13,000-strong across the border.[15] In contrast to previous expeditions, the men were restrained from the usual course of burning and ravaging, partly to avoid damaging Dunbar's lands, and partly because Henry wished to present himself as a good lord to the Scots. He even described himself as 'half a Scot, having the blood of the Comyns in my veins'.[16] While this more pacific approach earned him the praise of Scottish chroniclers, it failed to produce any tangible result, beyond a vague promise from the Scots to consider his claims. And like so many previous expeditions, it was written off by English chroniclers as a failure. It failed even to serve as a deterrent. There followed a round of raiding and counter-raiding, interspersed with negotiations. However, as neither side was prepared to offer any meaningful concessions, these rapidly descended to petty point-scoring. When the English put forward the claim to overlordship, the Scottish negotiators countered by suggesting that Henry IV's right to the realm of England should be put to arbitration.[17]

Around this time, a man claiming to be Richard II turned up at Islay, in the Western Isles, and was brought to the Scottish court. Derisively labelled the 'Mammet' by the English, who identified him as one Thomas Warde of Trumpington, Cambridgeshire, he was maintained by the Scots at considerable expense until his death in 1419, when he was given a prestigious burial. Nevertheless, it is evident that they did not take his claim seriously, making no attempt to use him in diplomatic relations with England. Rather, they seem to have valued him as a source of annoyance and embarrassment to Henry IV's regime, for he was the focus of a number of seditious rumours and would-be conspiracies in England, which – with some encouragement from Scotland – persisted into the reign of Henry V.[18]

The Scots' espousal of the Mammet's cause did nothing to improve Anglo-Scottish relations; but it was a change of regime in Scotland which led to the outbreak of war. At the end of 1401, Robert III's brother, Robert, Duke of Albany, mounted a *coup* against Rothesay, who was imprisoned and starved to death (leaving the king's younger son James as the prospective heir to the throne). Albany ruled as the king's nominal lieutenant, but to shore up his position, he needed the support of Archibald, Earl of Douglas, the most powerful Scottish magnate outside the Scottish royal family. Douglas favoured war with England; and so Albany duly obliged. It was probably Douglas's influence which was behind the embassy sent to Paris at the end of 1401 to seek French military aid (notwithstanding that the Franco-Scottish venture of 1385 had ended in mutual recrimination). The following spring, a party of thirty French knights arrived in Scotland, while a Franco-Scottish fleet ranged across the Channel, capturing at least 25 English ships. In response, the English mounted a naval expedition which seems to have been equally successful against Scottish shipping.

Scottish raiding by land met even sharper resistance; in June 1402, a Scottish raiding force was defeated by Dunbar in a skirmish at Nesbit in Berwickshire. In retaliation, a much larger Scottish army crossed into Northumberland in September, led by Douglas, and Albany's son,

Murdoch. Hotspur set off in hot pursuit, accompanied by Dunbar, and they caught the invaders at Humbleton Hill, in the foothills of the Cheviots, on 14 September. The Scots took up a strong defensive position on the hilltop, but were driven off it by murderous English archery, and thousands were slaughtered in the subsequent rout. Amongst the many prominent prisoners were Douglas and Murdoch, as well as the earls of Moray, Angus and Orkney.

The battle changed the dynamics of Anglo-Scottish relations; having suffered such a catastrophic defeat, leaving so many leading magnates dead or in captivity, the Scots were in no position to carry on the war. But fortunately for them, neither were the English. A revolt had broken out in Wales during Henry's Scottish expedition of 1400, led by Owain Glyn Dŵr (a veteran of the Scottish wars, who had served in the English garrison of Berwick). By the end of 1402, much of Wales was in rebel hands, and English resources were therefore increasingly directed towards the suppression of this revolt. At the same time, Hotspur was engaged in an increasingly acrimonious dispute with the Crown over a number of issues, including unpaid fees for his service as March warden, and the custody of the prisoners he had captured at Humbleton (principally the earl of Douglas).

Nevertheless, despite these difficulties, in March 1403, Henry IV (as putative overlord of Scotland) granted all of Douglas's lands to the earl of Northumberland, on the understanding that the earl should invade Scotland to take them. In fact, Henry was probably constrained by the need to accommodate Dunbar, who was anxious to recover his Scottish estates. If Dunbar was to be kept in the English allegiance, his demands could hardly be ignored, and so Henry had little choice but to authorize a military campaign; and this could hardly be contemplated without the co-operation of the earl of Northumberland. And so, Dunbar joined Northumberland and his son in an expedition across the border. Here, they ran into stubborn resistance at Cocklaws tower, in Roxburghshire. Faced with the prospect of a siege, Hotspur entered into an agreement with its defenders that they would surrender unless they had been relieved by 1 August.

By 1 August, however, Hotspur was dead, having been killed in rebellion against Henry, at Shrewsbury. Fighting alongside him was his prisoner, the unfortunate Douglas, who lost one of his testicles in the battle. Arrested for complicity with his son's rebellion, Northumberland was stripped of his Crown offices, but managed to avoid forfeiture. Nevertheless, some of his Northumbrian castles continued to hold out against the king, and in these circumstances, any further English aggression against the Scots was out of the question. The Scots were thus saved from the consequences of the English victory at Humbleton Hill by rebellion in England. Northumberland was finally forfeited in 1405, following a rising in Yorkshire. He now followed the example of the earl of March, by allying himself with his national enemies. He handed over Berwick, the town he had defended against the Scots for most of the last three decades, to a Scottish force led by the earl of Orkney. Reacting quickly, Henry IV marched northwards with an artillery train. Still cowed by the disaster at Humbleton Hill, the Scots made no attempt to stop him. Orkney and Northumberland fled, and Berwick returned to English hands.

Four years of more-or-less constant warfare between 1399 and 1403 had settled nothing. By this stage, the Scots had been incapacitated by military defeat, the English by rebellion: neither side was in a position to carry on fighting. And then, in 1406, events in Scotland conspired to put the king of Scots into English hands.

iii. Stalemate, 1406–53

The death of James, Earl of Douglas, at Otterburn in 1388 had led to an outbreak of prolonged feuding in the Scottish borders. The capture of Archibald, Earl of Douglas, at Humbleton Hill in 1402 led to another bout of feuding, but this time the consequences would affect Anglo-Scottish relations for decades. As Archibald was not dead, he could not be succeeded, but his absence left a vacuum of power. Into this vacuum stepped the earl of Orkney, a supporter of Robert III, bringing him into conflict with Archibald's younger brother, James Douglas. In 1406, this conflict erupted into civil war. Orkney had custody of Robert's eleven-year-old son and heir James; and when, defeated in battle, he fled for France, he took James with him. Unfortunately, their ship was captured by English pirates, who delivered the hapless pair into the custody of a delighted Henry IV. On hearing the news that his only surviving son was now an English captive, King Robert promptly expired.

The duke of Albany managed to make a relatively smooth transition from Robert III's lieutenant to governor of the realm during the enforced absence of James, who was recognized as Robert's heir, but not as king. A statute was passed in the Scottish parliament obligating Albany to work for James's release, but having secured his own authority in Scotland, he was in no great hurry to do anything to undermine it; his efforts on James's account were therefore somewhat perfunctory. Nor was the renewal of the Franco-Scottish alliance, in 1407, calculated to improve relations with England.[19]

As for Henry IV, with the military organization of the Marches impaired by the removal of the Percies, and still facing rebellion in Wales, he could not contemplate an actively aggressive policy towards Scotland. He was also afflicted by a debilitating illness which would periodically undermine his health for the rest of his reign. Nevertheless, he – or his council – was reluctant to concede too much, particularly while the pseudo-Richard II was being maintained at the Scottish court. Consequently, negotiations resulted only in a series of short-term and ill-kept truces – so ill-kept that at times England and Scotland verged on open war, as in May 1409, when Jedburgh was stormed by the Scots. With no prospect of recovering his lands through English invasion, the earl of March now returned to the Scottish allegiance.

By 1412, however, there were signs that relations were starting to improve. Henry's health recovered sufficiently for him to assert a greater degree of control over his own government, and he was able to impose his own policy of using James to obtain a favourable settlement with Scotland. At seventeen, James himself was now old enough to begin to take a personal role in negotiations; and he was increasingly able to wield a degree of influence in his realm – albeit remotely. Meanwhile, Albany was increasingly anxious to secure the release of his son and heir Murdoch (captured at Humbleton Hill). And then there was the situation in France. With Charles VI incapacitated by recurring bouts of madness, French politics were dominated by two rival factions, the Burgundians and the Armagnacs; and their rivalry was escalating to the point of civil war. This presented opportunities for the English to exploit French weakness, which in turn required relative peace on the Anglo-Scottish borders. It also left the Scots with little prospect of support from their French allies in the event of Anglo-Scottish war.

Together, these developments cleared the way for serious negotiations for the release of both James and Murdoch. A six-year truce was sealed, and talks had almost reached the point of settlement when they were halted by Henry IV's death, in March 1413. Even during his lifetime, his son and prospective heir, Henry, Prince of Wales, had advocated a hard line against the Scots. As King Henry V, he now ordered that James and Murdoch be closely confined in the Tower. The Scots responded by refusing to renew the truce (which they held to have lapsed on Henry IV's death).

Henry was intent on war with France, and having effectively ruled out peace with Scotland, he needed to make alternative arrangements for the security of northern England. The English Marches had been in a parlous state since the forfeiture of the earl of Northumberland in 1405, for the wardens who succeeded him lacked his experience, and were unwilling or unable to apply the same resources to the task. Henry therefore decided to restore the Percy family to their traditional role of defence against the Scots. The family heir, Hotspur's son (another Henry Percy), was still in exile in Scotland. Henry now arranged with Albany to exchange Murdoch for Percy. Unfortunately, Murdoch was kidnapped on his way to the border. This may have been connected with the Southampton plot against Henry, or the plotting of religious dissidents known as Lollards. But whatever the cause, and although Murdoch was rescued after a week, the deal collapsed, and open war broke out. The Scots put Penrith to the flames; and the English burned Dumfries in revenge, while another Scottish raiding party was defeated at Yeavering in Northumberland.

In spite of these hostilities, negotiations were soon resumed. Albany remained determined to secure his son's freedom, and the exchange duly took place in February 1416. Negotiations were also resumed for James's release; but they soon stalled, for Henry now raised the issue of overlordship, while James's own efforts to reach an agreement aroused fears in Scotland that he would concede too much. By this stage, in the wake of their catastrophic defeat at Agincourt in 1415, the French were desperate for aid from their Scottish allies. With Murdoch safely home, Albany felt free to respond. In 1417, now well into his seventies, he led an attack on Berwick, while Archibald, Earl of Douglas, attacked Roxburgh; but they were easily beaten off, and their venture was denounced even in Scotland as the 'foul [i.e., foolish] raid'.[20] A bout of retaliatory raiding by the English followed in its wake.

This tit-for-tat border fighting did little to hinder Henry's war effort in Normandy. Far more significant was the recruitment of Scottish soldiers to fight in France, in response to an embassy sent in 1418.[21] Although the Franco-Scottish treaty did not oblige the Scots to send men to France, Albany saw another opportunity to undermine the negotiations for James's release. He therefore called a council where it was agreed to send an army led by Albany's second son, the earl of Buchan. A force of perhaps 6,000 men sailed in October 1419, with their wages paid by the French.

The removal of so many Scottish warriors to France did at least have the benefit of bringing comparative peace to the Anglo-Scottish Marches. But given the priority Henry placed on the French war, this can hardly be counted a triumph for his Scottish policy, for they were crucial to the resistance of Henry's invasion. He reacted by wheeling out the captive James. In May 1420, he was brought across to Normandy to the siege of Melun, defended by a Scottish garrison; when they eventually surrendered, Henry had them hanged as traitors to their king. Nevertheless, James's presence in Normandy in Henry's company signally failed to deter his compatriots from serving against the English. Instead, *la grande armée Ecossaise* proved its worth, beating the English at Baugé, in Anjou, on 21 March 1421, where Henry's brother and heir presumptive, the duke of Clarence, was killed – the worst battlefield defeat inflicted on the English in France since the start of the Hundred Years War. Faced with this unexpected setback, Henry again turned to James; he knighted him (pointedly on St George's Day), and gave him joint command of the siege of Dreux. After Dreux had been taken, the army marched south in pursuit of a Scottish force led by Buchan. In September, the two forces almost met. Had they done so, James might have faced thousands of his future subjects across a battlefield – but in the event, Buchan withdrew, unwilling to risk battle.

By this time, Henry had fallen ill with dysentery, and in August 1422, he died. His policy towards Scotland was marked by an aggressive assertion of English rights, which served merely to antagonize the Scots. He was unable to prevent the recruitment of large armies in Scotland whose service helped to save the French from defeat. Equally, his attempts to use the captive James against his future subjects proved ineffective; and in the long term, this may have created enough mistrust to undermine James's later efforts to impose a peace settlement with England in Scotland.[22]

Henry was succeeded by his nine-month-old son Henry VI, during whose minority England was ruled by a council.[23] Under the terms of the treaty of Troyes, 1420, the young Henry was also the heir of Charles VI of France, who died two months later. The council's immediate concern was to complete the conquest of his French inheritance, for Charles's son, the Dauphin, also claimed his father's throne. To this end, it was necessary to stem the flow of Scottish soldiers to France. In a change of policy, it was decided that this could best be brought about through peace with Scotland, to be obtained by James's release, and his marriage to an English lady, which – it was hoped – would maintain his links with England. The English royal family suffered from a dearth of eligible princesses, and so the choice fell upon Joan Beaufort, daughter of the earl of Somerset and granddaughter of John of Gaunt. Moreover, the Beaufort line had been excluded from the succession to the English Crown by Act of Parliament, making her all the more suitable from the English viewpoint. She was also the niece of Henry Beaufort, bishop of Winchester, a leading figure on the council.

In negotiating with the Scots, the council was constrained by the fact that Henry VI was a minor. Contemporary legal doctrine held that a minor's estate should be maintained undiminished until he came of age; and this applied especially to a king. English negotiators were therefore reluctant to offer any permanent concessions regarding Roxburgh or Berwick, or the claim to overlordship. Although they had hoped for a more permanent settlement, the best they could achieve in these circumstances was a seven-year truce, sealed in March 1424, with a ransom of £40,000, euphemistically described as reimbursement for James's expenses in England. To guarantee payment, a number of Scottish nobles were handed over as hostages.

The Scots also agreed that no new forces would be sent to France. The value of this concession was, however, somewhat undermined by the departure, in February, of a major expedition under Archibald, Earl of Douglas, who carefully arranged to sail before the truce came into effect (doubtless encouraged by the magnificent offer of the duchy of Touraine, a prize which demonstrates how desperate the French were to secure his services). In the event, the English managed to deal with this issue by more direct methods, annihilating Douglas's army at Verneuil in Normandy in August 1424, along with its commander and several leading Scottish magnates. The ransom proved more difficult to extract, and no more than 9,500 marks (£6,333 6s. 8d.) was ever paid. The hostages proved worthless, for James simply left them to rot in English prisons.

Meanwhile, James was being courted by the Dauphin, desperate for more Scottish aid against the English. A high-ranking embassy arrived in Scotland in 1428, offering, in return for the service of 6,000 Scots, a marriage between James's daughter, Margaret, and the Dauphin's son and heir, Louis. This marriage was potentially enormously prestigious, far more so than James's own match to an English noblewoman who was only a first cousin once removed to the king. A treaty was duly agreed, and was ratified by the Dauphin in October. Nevertheless, despite the additional incentive of the offer of the French county of Saintonge (on the Atlantic coast, bordering Gascony), James proved in no hurry to fulfil its terms. The English were anxious to keep the Scottish reinforcements out of France, and Joan's uncle, Henry Beaufort, was dispatched to Scotland to remind James of his ties and obligations to England. He found him amenable, indeed so much so that James proposed a marriage between another of his daughters and Henry VI. Nevertheless, although negotiations dragged on for the next eighteen months, the English were able to obtain nothing more than a renewal of the truce for another five years.[24]

By this stage, the war in France had started to turn against England, with Joan of Arc's dramatic breaking of the siege of Orléans in 1429. Consequently, peace with Scotland was more necessary than ever; it was a mark of increasing desperation that by 1433, Henry's council was prepared to offer the return of Berwick and Roxburgh, his continuing minority notwithstanding. James summoned a general council to discuss these terms, but they were rejected. This may have been a deliberate ploy, playing off England and France against each other to extract greater concessions, and to delay any final commitment to either. Certainly, the English regarded James as a wily and skilful opponent; one of the English envoys in 1430 characterized him as 'a fell, a farseeing man and having great experience'.[25]

Yet James's machinations may have stemmed not from policy, but rather from political stalemate in Scotland. Like David II before him, James was unable to persuade his subjects to accept English peace terms, even terms as favourable as these. England was too well-established as the Auld Enemy; and too many Scottish nobles had gained wealth and advancement, and – just as important – honour and renown, through service to the French (such as the cadet branch of the Stewart family, established as the seigneurs d'Aubigny in central France). They saw no reason to throw over a valued ally, and were quite prepared to countenance war with England – a war which the English would have to fight on two fronts.[26]

With any settlement with England effectively ruled out, James had nothing to gain from further putting off the implementation of his treaty with France. Indeed, his bargaining power was declining as the situation of the Dauphin, now crowned Charles VII of France, improved; already, the offer of Saintonge had been withdrawn, and so the arrangements for the marriage of James's daughter were hastily completed, while the agreement was still on the table. The French no longer needed Scottish troops in any great numbers, and instead reverted to their time-honoured strategy of encouraging the Scots to attack the north of England, in the hope of diverting English resources away from France. Tension on the Anglo-Scottish borders had already been heightened, for in January 1435, the English had received into their allegiance George Dunbar, Earl of March, who followed the family tradition of defection, after his forfeiture for feuding with William Douglas, Earl of Angus.

Seeking to take advantage of Scottish disunity, an English force was sent across the border to support Dunbar's son, who was staging a rebellion, but they were ambushed and defeated at Piperden. Having failed to improve the security of the Marches by force, the English once again resorted to negotiation, hoping to secure a renewal of the truce. However, the French were still pressing the Scots to attack. Having previously fought with Henry V against the French, James now finally went to war against Henry VI in their support; and in August 1436, shortly after the expiry of the truce, he besieged Roxburgh. It appeared to be a propitious moment, for the English were distracted by the collapse of their alliance with the Burgundian faction in France, and their subsequent attack on Calais. James had raised a large army and acquired an artillery train, and he was confident of capturing Roxburgh. In a fit of hubris, he appointed a new herald in anticipation of his victory; but a large English relief expedition forced James to flee ignominiously, abandoning his expensive new guns. The abject failure of the siege badly damaged his authority in Scotland, and was one of the factors which led to his murder by a faction of his own nobles in February 1437.

The killing of James proved a boon for the English, for it led to a prolonged period of political instability in Scotland, during the minority of his successor, the six-year-old James II. The Scots were thus in no position to contemplate war with England, and a nine-year truce was negotiated in 1438, and extended for another seven years in 1442. As in 1360 and 1389, this outbreak of peace was certainly welcome to some Scots, including a number of merchants, clerics and pilgrims to Canterbury who obtained licence to come to England (Chapter 10).

In the event, the truce held only until 1448. The immediate causes of renewed conflict are obscure; in general terms, however, it stemmed in large part from developments in Scottish politics, and French patronage of the Scottish royal family. Factional infighting subsided as James's minority neared its end, and consequently, an aggressive policy towards England became a practical possibility again. The death of James's English mother, Joan Beaufort, in 1445, had removed a pro-English influence; and Scotland was being drawn closer to France by a series of marriages which Charles VII arranged for James's sisters, culminating with the marriage of James himself to Mary of Guelders, the niece of Philip, Duke of Burgundy, in 1449. The sealing of an Anglo-French truce in 1444, marked by Henry VI's marriage to Margaret of Anjou, Charles's niece, meant that closer ties between Scotland and France did not initially present any threat to England. However, squabbling rapidly broke out over the implementation of the terms of the truce, and as tension grew between England and France, so did tension between England and France's ally, Scotland.

While the truce with France still held, however shakily, the English were able to take an aggressive stance against the Scots. A bout of cross-border raiding followed in the summer of 1448, leading to the burning of Dumfries and Dunbar in Scotland, and Alnwick and Warkworth in England. In the autumn, Henry VI led an army north, but he only got as far as Durham, where he stayed for three days before returning to Westminster; typically, he described the expedition as a pilgrimage to St Cuthbert (whose remains lay at Durham), on which he had been 'right merry'.[27] The Scots simply waited until he had gone away, and then burned the suburbs of Carlisle. A retaliatory English raid met with disaster, in a battle on the banks of the river Sark on 23 October, which ended with Sir Henry Percy and many of his men as Scottish prisoners. Another expedition led by Richard Neville, Earl of Salisbury, warden of the West March, was little more successful. With relations with France rapidly deteriorating towards war, the English government returned to a more conciliatory approach. The Scots were suffering financial and political problems of their own, and so the truce was renewed.

For the first half of the fifteenth century, Scotland was largely subordinated to France in English policy. Diplomatic relations with Scotland veered inconsistently between assertiveness and conciliation, driven largely by the situation in France. Military resources were applied haphazardly, usually in reaction to an immediate threat, and after Henry IV's expedition to recapture Berwick in 1405, no English king would cross the border until Henry VI fled to Scotland in 1461. Despite this, the English were generally reluctant to make the concessions that might have gained a lasting peace, and their insistence on maintaining the claim to overlordship was a standing impediment to any settlement. In fact, as the negotiations of 1433 demonstrated, support in Scotland for the French alliance was so strong that there was little chance of any peace terms with England being accepted anyway. Nevertheless, the shadow of the disastrous defeat at Humbleton Hill hung heavy, and the Scots remained wary of taking on the English on the battlefield. Only in 1448 were they able to gain a real military advantage. As a consequence, the Anglo-Scottish Marches saw decades of ill-kept truce, punctuated by short bursts of open war, which produced no great change in relations between the two realms. This would change with the end of the French wars and the descent of England into civil war.

Chapter 4: The Wars of the Roses, 1453–1502

i. English Civil Wars, 1453–80

The English defeat at the battle of Castilion in 1453 crowned a series of disastrous reverses in France. The 'vasty fields' of Henry V's conquest were now reduced to a foothold in Calais, while defences on the Scottish border were suffering the effects of long-term under-funding. The struggle between Richard, Duke of York, and the Lancastrian Edmund Beaufort, Duke of Somerset, for domination of Henry VI's government escalated into civil war, as York took to the battlefield to assert his claim to the succession. And then Henry succumbed to a mental illness so severe that York was appointed Protector of England.

Meanwhile, in Scotland, James II was preoccupied with cutting the comb of one of his own powerful nobles: William, Earl of Douglas. In 1452, James stabbed the earl to death in a fit of rage, and a full-scale revolt ensued, led by William's brother and heir. The king was forced to conciliate this new earl of Douglas, and the two reached apparent accord. But in fact, James was more determined than ever to subdue the family.[1]

For neither side, then, was a return to war desirable, and in May 1453, the truce agreed in 1450 was extended to 1457. Even while at truce, however, each realm frequently provided support and refuge for the other's rebels, particularly those of rank and power. While such men remained in their native land, their activities weakened and distracted their government. In exile, too, they were valuable guests: commanding affinities whose services their hosts might call upon, or as diplomatic bargaining pieces. Such a relationship existed between the English government and the very Douglases who were such a thorn in James's side. In July 1451, while the Scottish ambassador was confirming the truce, Douglas secretly sent his brother to Henry VI, where he was 'mickle made of'.[2] In June 1452, at the height of his rebellion, Douglas offered his personal homage to Henry, and even as he made peace with James that August, he requested an English safe-conduct as a back-up. Conversely, it was natural that the Lancastrian duke of Exeter and Thomas Percy, Lord Egremont, should appeal to James, Somerset's nephew, for assistance in their revolt against York's protectorate in 1454, and Scottish violations of the truce that month may have been intended to provide a helpful distraction.[3]

In March 1455, James launched his final assault against the Douglases, culminating in the siege of their stronghold of Abercorn. The earl's wife and mother were received at Carlisle, while the garrison of Roxburgh supported his resistance in the Scottish Middle March. When Abercorn fell, Douglas fled to England, and in summer 1455 bestowed Threave, his final remaining stronghold, upon Henry VI – shortly before it fell to James. The Douglases were forfeited for 'treasonous bonds and confederations ... made ... with the English',[4] and York, now in his second protectorate, granted the earl a pension of £500.

James's routing of the Douglases left the way clear for action against their English hosts. In June, he launched a raid on Berwick. He also wrote to Charles VII of France, proposing a joint venture to recapture Calais and Berwick (which he presented as an act of support for Henry VI against York, depicting the latter's resumption of the protectorate as an act of rebellion). The Yorkists were widely perceived to be strongly anti-French, and to favour the resumption of war in France; nevertheless, James's proposal found little favour with Charles, for whom the value of Auld Alliance was significantly reduced with the English expulsion from most of France. French interests could now best be served by preserving the *status quo*; hence in early 1456 Charles proposed a three-way peace between England, Scotland and France, instead.

Although York's protectorate had come to an end in February, the council which ruled in Henry's name was still dominated by his chief supporters, Richard Neville, Earl of Warwick, and his brother John; and Douglas's pension continued to be paid. James sent an embassy to England in May, but shortly thereafter announced his renunciation of the truce, on the grounds of its continual violation by the English. He then threatened Henry VI with another invasion, and wrote to Charles requesting military aid, now claiming – in a complete *volte face* – to be acting in support of York's 'clear right to the crown ... of the kingdom of England'.[5] He made a similar approach to York himself, who was now acting as lieutenant of the North.

York's response put paid to any hopes of harnessing the Yorkist cause to Scottish ends. On the same day in which the council addressed James as a rebellious vassal of the English king, York rebuked him for his breach of the 'faith and troth, that of his duty he should owe and keep' to Henry, and challenged him to battle.[6] York could not afford to invite a hostile power into England, particularly as his principal supporters were the Nevilles, who had made a career of fighting the Scots. Invoking the overlordship claim made his position as a loyal English subject very clear.

Undeterred, that summer James launched raids into Northumberland, and there were rumours he was preparing to lay siege to Berwick. The keepers of Roxburgh and Berwick wreaked retaliatory havoc in southeast Scotland, while in February 1457 James made an abortive raid on Berwick. But the enthusiasm of his subjects for such inconclusive and expensive campaigning soon waned, and in June 1457, a year's truce was agreed. The English government was now controlled by the Lancastrians – Somerset and his allies, plus Henry's wife, Margaret of Anjou, whose son stood to be disinherited if York's claim succeeded – and it was keen to come to terms in order to neutralize possible Scottish support for the Yorkists. Douglas's annuity was reduced to £200 that November, and a marriage alliance between Somerset's sons and James's sisters was proposed. In 1459, Margaret, now in full control of the English government, entered into secret negotiations to secure Scottish help against the Yorkists.

But James was not interested in aiding an insecure English regime against its enemies; rather he sought to take advantage of the situation to pursue his own ends. While his ambassadors negotiated with Margaret (the French king's niece), James's half-brother, James Stewart, was listening to the counter-bids of Philip, Duke of Burgundy, who was allied to the Francophobe York (on the grounds that Burgundy's independence was best preserved by France's containment).[7] And in 1460, James began secret negotiations with York himself, who now sought the Scottish support he had previously spurned.

In July, however, events in England took a dramatic turn. Yorkist forces triumphed at the battle of Northampton, and Henry VI was captured. Margaret and her supporters remained at large and the full-scale civil war which ensued provided James with the perfect opening for an invasion of England. By the end of the month, he was besieging Roxburgh.

But on 3 August, disaster struck – James was 'unhappily ... slain with a gun, the which broke in the firing'.[8] It was his eight-year-old son and successor, James, to whom the Roxburgh garrison surrendered on 8 August, and who presided over the capture of Wark castle the same day.

Important dynastic events were also taking place further south. In October 1460, York made the symbolic gesture of placing his hand on the throne before the English parliament. The Act of Accord which followed duly recognized him as Henry VI's successor, setting aside Henry's son, and convincing Margaret that she must look abroad for support. In January 1461, she met Mary of Guelders, James II's widow, and regent of Scotland, at Dumfries. Mary was the great-niece of Philip of Burgundy, who pressed her to embrace the Yorkist cause, while Charles VII of France urged her to support the Lancastrian.

In fact, Mary and the regency council were more interested in Scotland's cause, continuing James's policy of dealing with whichever side offered the best terms. At this point in the conflict, the Lancastrians had considerable strength in the north, while the Yorkists were struggling. York's death at the battle of Wakefield probably proved decisive for Mary. She provided a Scottish contingent to reinforce Margaret's army, which then marched south. In April, York's son, Edward, seized the English crown and routed the Lancastrians at Towton, accompanied by a small contingent paid for by Philip. Mary gave refuge to Margaret, her son Prince Edward, and the deposed Henry VI. But the price of Scottish support reflected the urgency of Lancastrian need. Berwick, held by the English since 1333, and still in Lancastrian hands, was given over to the Scots that April. Margaret also promised Carlisle, but a combined Scottish and Lancastrian force in June failed to capture it from its Yorkist captain John Neville, now Lord Montagu.

To the newly crowned Edward IV, the king and queen he had deposed were now his rebels. Mary's aiding and abetting of them, and her invasion of his realm, were now repaid in kind. Edward demanded the restoration of Douglas, and in February 1462, entered into a private agreement (the 'treaty' of Westminster-Ardtornish) with Douglas and John MacDonald, Earl of Ross and Lord of the Isles. MacDonald promised to swear allegiance, support the Douglas restoration, and to aid a projected English invasion to establish Edward's overlordship, with Scotland to be divided up between the two earls as his vassals.

However, having handed over Berwick, Mary's guests had made all the returns for her hospitality of which they were capable. She now saw them principally as bargaining counters, to squeeze the best possible peace terms out of Edward, and so, shortly after occupying Berwick, she sent ambassadors to England. With Lancastrian loyalties persisting in Northumberland, Edward preferred not to risk war if he could cut off Scottish support for Henry and Margaret through negotiation, and a year's truce was concluded in November. In April 1462, Margaret's departure to France probably provided further impetus towards peace, and at the end of that month Mary and James III met with Warwick at Dumfries, and again in Carlisle in July.

But Mary's was not the only foreign policy in Scotland. Her influence over government was contested by James Kennedy, Bishop of St Andrews, who had returned from France in 1461 at the exhortation of Charles VII, to 'support and aid King Henry, his cousin'.[9] He duly mounted a traditionalist Auld Alliance platform, opposing negotiations with Edward IV, advocating aid to the Lancastrians as English rebels, and accusing Mary of acting according to Burgundian, rather than Scottish interests. Edward's support for Douglas helped to sway opinion towards Kennedy's anti-English policies among the earl's opponents and those who had profited from his downfall. Over the next year, as Kennedy gained ground, Mary's negotiations with Edward were undermined, and Scotland's policy towards England would become steadily more hostile.

On her return to Scotland in October 1462, Margaret initially received little support, despite the letters she carried from the new king of France, Louis XI, urging the Scots to this course. The army with which she invaded England that month was largely composed of Lancastrians, and the retainers of her cousin Pierre de Brézé, seneschal of Normandy (acting in a purely private capacity – Louis' solicitude for Margaret did not extend to military aid).[10] She succeeded in capturing Alnwick, Dunstanburgh and Bamburgh castles, but her army was chased back into Scotland by the English, who promptly re-took the latter two. Desperate for Scottish aid, Henry VI offered the earl of Angus, one of Kennedy's chief allies, an English dukedom (and, it was rumoured, promised the see of Canterbury to Kennedy himself). In early January 1463, de Brézé and Angus mounted an expedition to relieve the Lancastrian garrison at Alnwick, but after a brief stand-off, they retreated back to Scotland taking the garrison with them, and the castle was surrendered.

It was clear that unless Edward could cut off Scottish support for the Lancastrians, he would struggle to gain permanent control of the border region. In March, the exiled Douglas led a successful counter-raid on the Scottish West March and Galloway, but stronger measures were required. Mary's pro-Yorkist policies had clearly been eclipsed, as

Kennedy held a council of war with the Lancastrians, plotting an attack on Norham. That June, the English parliament granted Edward an aid of £37,000 to lead an army against the Lancastrians and their Scottish allies. The Scottish attack on Norham, however, proved a fiasco. The castle was relieved by Warwick and Montagu (wardens of the East and West Marches respectively), who chased the besiegers into the Scottish East March, which they then proceeded to devastate. Leaving Henry in Scotland, Margaret and her son sailed for the Continent, in the hope of finding stronger allies.

In the event, Edward's projected military offensive failed to materialize. Instead, in October 1463, he sealed a year's truce with Louis, who promised to abandon the Lancastrians, abjure the Auld Alliance, and even to aid an English conquest of Scotland. Bishop Kennedy's hopes of a Franco-Scottish alliance had evaporated, and he had little choice but to abandon his Anglophobe position. In December, he sealed a nine-month truce with England, during which period each side was to refrain from supporting the other's rebels; and while Douglas's allegiance to Edward was recognized, Kennedy was not to harbour the Lancastrians once their existing safe-conducts had expired. In April 1464, Kennedy's last-ditch attempt to entice Louis away from his agreement with the English having failed, the truce was extended for fifteen years. Edward granted Kennedy a pension of £366 (cheap at the price, if it secured Scotland's abandonment of the Lancastrian cause). Henry duly left his Scottish hosts, and, following Lancastrian defeats at Hedgeley Moor and Hexham in 1464, was finally captured in July 1465.

Anglo-Scottish *détente* prospered in the short term, owing to mutual distraction by domestic problems. After Kennedy's death in May 1465, succeeding Scottish administrations lacked a broad base of support, while in England, the political *status quo* was upset by Edward's controversial marriage to Elizabeth Woodville. That December, the truce was extended for 55 years, suggesting that the issues which had motivated war in the past were no longer so pressing. In 1470, Scotland proved a mere interested spectator of Henry's brief return to the English throne.[11]

France, however, did support Henry's readeption, and when Edward regained his crown the following year, his foreign policy focussed on revenge. He made an alliance with Louis' enemy Charles the Bold, Duke of Burgundy, and offered a full peace to Scotland. James III, now ruling in his own right, considered that he was not bound by the truce made in his name in 1465, and would only confirm a two-year truce, in March 1473. Scotland had ties with both Burgundy and France, but initially James was keen to favour Scotland's traditional ally. In May, it was reported that the Scots would 'adhere to their ancient league and confederation', in return for a pension of 60,000 crowns a year, 'so that they may be able to oppose the king of England in favour of his majesty [Louis XI]'.[12] Relations between England and Scotland were strained by the plundering of the Scottish ship *Salvator*, shipwrecked off Bamburgh, and by the cross-border depredations of the reivers of Liddesdale, Tynedale and Redesdale (see Chapter 9, Section i).[13] Rumours of forthcoming English raids prompted James to summon the host. Anticipating that the Scots would soon be at war with England anyway, Louis offered James a mere 10,000 crowns: a one-off payment to be made only if he prevented an invasion of France by successfully diverting Edward's army.

Such miserliness was ill-judged. Less than two weeks after the war scare, James sent an embassy to England to negotiate the settlement of Scottish grievances, but also to discuss a marriage alliance. In October 1474, a truce was sealed, to last until 1519. James's heir, James, Duke of Rothesay (born 1473), was betrothed to the five-year-old Princess Cecilia, Edward's eldest daughter. Edward thereby secured his northern border, while Cecilia's dowry of 20,000 marks (£13,333 6s. 8d.) gave James an additional income independent of the frugal Scottish parliament. Both sides appeared to be committed to the alliance. Edward proved keen to settle Scottish grievances, and made payments of the dowry on schedule, while in May 1477, James proposed further matrimonial links: his sister Margaret to be married to Edward's brother, the duke of Clarence; and his brother, Alexander, Duke of Albany, to Edward's niece, Mary of Burgundy (Charles the Bold's heiress). These came to nothing; Albany refused to co-operate after James forced him to divorce his existing wife, and Clarence would shortly be executed for treason. Nothing daunted, James proposed instead that Margaret should marry the queen's brother, Anthony Woodville, Earl Rivers, and by August 1479, preparations for their wedding were being made in both countries.

ii. *'Rigorous and Cruel War' to Perpetual Peace, 1480–1502*

Lasting peace between the two realms now seemed a serious prospect. The issues of Roxburgh and Berwick had apparently been settled; the Auld Alliance had crumbled, and Edward had agreed a seven-year truce with France in 1475, thus removing Anglo-French war as a potential source of Anglo-Scottish conflict. Yet war broke out again between England and Scotland as soon as 1480. What led to a renewal of the conflict which had seemed so far from the desires of both kings?[14]

The main factor was simply that James's was not the only policy operating in Scotland with regard to England. Prolonged truce was detrimental to the lordship of Scottish border magnates, whose patronage was expressed partly through the spoils of cross-border raiding (Chapter 9, Section i). One such magnate was James's own brother, Albany. Anti-English sentiment remained common in Scotland, exemplified by Blind Hary's *The Wallace* (a polemical history in verse, violently hostile to Anglo-Scottish peace), and the ambitious Albany now jumped on this bandwagon. His absence from the 1479 parliament, which voted the taxes to fund the English marriage, marked him out as the focus of resistance to it. As warden of the West March, he had opportunities to disrupt the peace by rather more direct methods. That spring, a March day ended in the kidnapping of Sir Henry Percy, deputy warden of the English East and Middle Marches, and the murder of Robert Lisle 'in the presence and by the authority of the wardens lieutenant of Scotland'.[15]

James's response demonstrates the importance he attached to his English alliance, and how closely it was identified with his personal authority. In April, he took the field against his brother, who fled to France, and was indicted for treason in October; the charges included abuse of his office of warden, and violation of the truce. However, wider opposition to James's Anglophile policy was revealed when his parliament refused to find Albany guilty; and by resistance to the collection of taxes to provide for Margaret's marriage. Two safe-conducts for her journey to England lapsed as James was unable to fund it.

This seeming laggardliness, combined with Albany's aggression, must have looked suspicious to Edward. Anglo-Scottish relations were also increasingly influenced by wider European conflicts: Louis XI's assault on Flanders had been decisively defeated by the Emperor Maximilian, and he now needed the Scottish ally he had so recently slighted. Seeing in Albany a tool to manipulate James, Louis received him warmly, arranging a prestigious marriage for him. Under the cloak of effecting a brotherly reconciliation, Louis secretly urged James to invade England. Though Franco-Scottish diplomacy was not incompatible with the terms of the Anglo-Scottish treaty, these talks seem to have aroused Edward's suspicions that James was about to embrace the Auld Alliance once again.

In January 1480, Edward delivered a stinging rebuke. Remonstrating about the March day incident, he also resurrected grievances which had lain dormant for over ten years. The earl of Douglas had been wrongfully disinherited; James was wrongfully occupying Berwick and Roxburgh; and – crucially – had failed to do homage to the English king 'as he owes to do and as his progenitors have done'. Edward demanded that Cecilia's promised husband, the six-year-old Rothesay, should be given into English custody, and that Berwick should be handed over. If these conditions were not met by 1 May, Edward would make 'rigorous and cruel war' on Scotland.[16]

Such insupportable terms suggest that in fact Edward had already determined on war. In early spring 1480, advance payments were made to English march wardens, who were ordered to prepare for Scottish attacks. When the May deadline expired without the delivery of either Rothesay or Berwick, Edward appointed his brother, Richard, Duke of Gloucester, lieutenant-general in the north, charging him with the invasion of Scotland. Hostilities were delayed, however, partly because Edward was preoccupied with negotiating an Anglo-Burgundian alliance against France, which was not sealed until August. In the event, the opening move in the war was made by Archibald Douglas, fifth Earl of Angus, who launched a raid into Northumberland in September. Louis was reported to have encouraged this attack, to distract Edward from pursuing his alliance with Maximilian; and James was said to have requested French gunners and artillery.

In fact, Angus's raid was a private enterprise by a Scottish border magnate motivated by the same considerations as Albany. The English counter-raid, however, ordered as it was by Gloucester, Edward's lieutenant-general, must be regarded as the expression of royal policy. Around April 1481, James made a last-ditch attempt at reconciliation, offering redress for all Scottish breaches of the truce. But Edward refused to receive the Scottish ambassadors, and the following month referred to his 'primeval right [of overlordship] left dormant for a while for the sake of foreign affairs', and his intention to lead an army against Scotland in the summer.[17] The same month, he commissioned a naval force to keep the western seas, with power to take Scottish ships. Edward also sought to exploit internal opposition to James. However, Scottish domestic politics had shifted in the 20 years since 1461, and Edward's envoy to John McDonald, Lord of the Isles, was rebuffed, and later captured. Only three Scots responded to his blanket offers of lands and other enticements in return for military service.

In June 1481, Edward began his campaign proper with an innovative use of naval power: John, Lord Howard, sailed a squadron of ships into the Firth of Forth, attacking Scottish vessels moored at Leith and Kinghorn, and landing several hundred soldiers to burn the town of Blackness. The land-based invasion which followed proved something of an anti-climax; the campaign was restricted to a raid on Dumfries, and an unsuccessful siege of Berwick, possibly owing to resistance to war-taxation (although the strategic combination of traditional cross-border invasion with naval-based attacks on the heart of Scotland would be further developed in the sixteenth century: Chapter 6, Sections i and ii). James mustered a host, but it disbanded, allegedly at the insistence of papal envoys, but more probably owing to reluctance to risk fighting the English for Berwick, and James's own inability to meet the costs of his army (see Chapter 8). His urgent appeals to Louis for aid against the English received little response – hardly surprising, as Louis was by now negotiating with Edward for the renewal of the Anglo-French treaty, which was sealed in October.

In March 1482, the Scottish parliament made plans to deal with 'the reiver Edward, calling himself king of England' (a pointed reference to Edward's seizure of the throne in riposte to his demand for homage), who intended to 'invade and destroy and ... make conquest of this realm'.[18] Unusually, the Estates agreed to pay for 600 soldiers to be stationed in garrisons in the Marches (Chapter 8); the defence of Berwick, however, would be funded by the king, another indication that James's preoccupation with the fortress was not shared by his subjects.[19] The parliament also sent ambassadors to Louis, appealing to his 'brother and confederate' to 'help and supply his highness and his realm now at war waged by their common enemy England',[20] apparently unaware of the renewal of the Anglo-French truce.

England was also preparing for war, and in February, Gloucester was paid 10,000 marks (£6,666) for the defence of the West March. In June, Edward recognized Albany, James's forfeited brother, as King Alexander of Scotland. By the treaty of Fotheringay, Edward promised to help him obtain the Scottish throne in return for his homage. King Alexander was then to renounce the Franco-Scottish alliance, and hand over not only Berwick, but Liddesdale, Eskdale, Ewesdale, Annandale and Lochmaben castle. And, if Albany could extricate himself from his French marriage, Edward would give him the hand of his daughter Cecilia.

Both parties were being somewhat disingenuous. Albany was unlikely to be accepted as king by the Scots, for he would first have to dispose not only of James III, but also his three sons. The most he could hope for was to sideline James and impose a new regime; but no Scottish government would either recognize Edward's claim to overlordship, or hand over any part of Scotland. For his part, Edward may have adopted Albany's cause in order to emphasize his claim to overlordship, rather than in any real hope of putting him on the throne. On the other hand, if Albany did succeed in gaining any authority over Scottish government, then he might at least provide a pro-English influence. On 12 June, Gloucester was appointed to command an army of 20,000 men, at least 1,800 of whom were professional soldiers: Burgundian, German and Swiss mercenaries (an innovation which heralded the future composition of English armies fighting in Scotland). He was on the march within a week; however, Edward had made provision for only one month's wages, far too short a period for the task supposedly envisaged.

The Scottish host was encamped at Lauder, and a clash seemed imminent. But some of James's nobles were convinced that this would result in a major military disaster for Scotland, and others wished to be rid of him. On 22 July they acted. James was arrested by the leaders of his army, and imprisoned in Edinburgh castle. The Scottish army disbanded. Meanwhile, the English had received the surrender of the town (though not the castle) of Berwick. On 2 August, Gloucester marched into Edinburgh, meeting no resistance. However, with only a week's pay remaining, there was no possibility of his army's mounting a siege of Edinburgh castle and Gloucester was obliged to come to terms with James's councillors. It was agreed that Albany would be restored to his lands, and pardoned his offences, including his aspiration to the Scottish throne. On 4 August, the provost and community of Edinburgh promised that, if the marriage between Prince James and Cecilia was not ratified, the instalments Edward had made on her dowry would be repaid. Gloucester left the city, and disbanded his army, retaining 1,700 men with whom he completed the capture of Berwick, which had probably been the principal objective of the expedition all along. Edward IV wrote to the pope, gloating over the achievement of 'our loving brother, whose success is so proven, that he alone would serve to chastise the whole kingdom of Scotland'.[21] Berwick had changed hands for the last time.

Albany now headed the government acting in his brother's name, but when James regained control, he fled to Dunbar, and in February 1483, again pledged allegiance to Edward. Edward again agreed to support Albany's bid for the throne. In return, Albany agreed to support the king of England against all his adversaries, 'and namely against the occupiers of the Crown of France' – for Louis had abandoned his English alliance after sealing a treaty with Burgundy in late 1482.[22] Albany also agreed to restore the earl of Douglas; surrender any claim to Berwick; and marry one of Edward's daughters without a dowry. In January, Gloucester had been granted hereditary possession of the wardenship of the West March; all royal lands in Cumberland; and, significantly, an appanage of the Scottish lands promised by Albany the previous year, with licence to conquer them – giving him a vested interest in pursuing the war in the longer term.[23] Edward had effectively put the prosecution of the Anglo-Scottish conflict into his brother's hands.

Once again, however, Albany came to terms with his brother and abandoned his English allies. In March 1483, James granted him full remission of his treasons, and allowed him to keep his office of March warden. In return, Albany was to denounce a rumour that his brother was attempting to poison him; guarantee not to come within six miles of him; renounce his allegiance to Edward; and to promise to work towards what was still James's principal aim: an English peace, and a renewal of the on-again off-again marriage of Cecilia and Prince James.

Three weeks later, Edward was dead. Gloucester hurried south, first to head a short-lived minority government on behalf of his nephew, and then to usurp the throne, as Richard III. In the meantime, Albany failed to show up at the Scottish parliament to fulfil the terms of his agreement; instead he admitted an English garrison to Dunbar, and then fled to England. However, these events made little difference to James's policy. He wrote to Richard in August, blaming the late wars on the machinations of 'evil disposed persons',[24] and offering to send an embassy to negotiate the resumption of peace. Unimpressed, Richard determined to continue his brother's aggressive policy, and in February 1484 announced his intention of leading an army against the Scots.

Richard also took an aggressive stance against France, where Louis XI had died and been succeeded by the minor Charles VIII. The French government therefore favoured a resumption of the Auld Alliance. By November 1483, James was discussing a joint invasion to put Henry Tudor, Earl of Richmond, on the English throne, and in February 1484, the Scottish parliament began to make war plans. In March, James confirmed the renewal of the Auld Alliance, and the French ambassador returned home with a contingent of Scots. The same month, Richard described to the pope 'this most serious war which we are waging with the very cruel and fierce people of the Scots'.[25] It seemed that the default positions of the Hundred Years War had been resumed.

By the summer, however, over-commitment to foreign adventures had forced Richard to draw in his horns. He cancelled the projected Scottish campaign, requested negotiations for a truce, and declined to support Albany and Douglas's invasion of Scotland in late July. They were defeated, Douglas was captured and Albany fled back to England. Truce negotiations began that September at Nottingham, James's secretary optimistically hoping that 'with the Kings of England and Scotland joined in mutual love, affection, friendship and affinity, their subjects should enjoy the blessings and pleasures of peace and tranquillity'.[26] The two principal obstacles to this peace and tranquillity proved to be Berwick and Dunbar, and only a three-year truce could be agreed. The fortresses were to remain in English hands, but, as the treaty was careful to note, James did not surrender his claim to them. Provision was made that after six months he should be allowed to besiege Dunbar without breaking the truce, provided he first informed Richard of his intentions. The truce was accompanied by a new marriage alliance for Rothesay, this time with Richard's niece, Anne de la Pole. With no prospect of support from England, Albany fled to France.

There is no reason to suppose that James was not serious about the alliance, which was consistent with his policy of peace with England, and in May 1485, the Scottish parliament appointed an embassy to arrange the details of the marriage. When Henry Tudor defeated Richard at Bosworth that August, his army did include a Scottish contingent. However, it was probably composed of the men who had left with the French ambassador before the meeting at Nottingham; nor did this constitute a breach of the treaty, for the men were not serving their king, but as mercenaries for Charles VIII. Nevertheless, James probably welcomed the removal of Richard, whose long-term commitment to Anglo-Scottish peace was doubtful, given his earlier hawkish policy – certainly, one of the Scottish captains at Bosworth was subsequently rewarded by James for his service. The death of Albany, the would-be English puppet-king, a few months later, must also have come as a relief.

As king 'by the grace of Charles VIII', with an even narrower base of support than his predecessor, Henry VII had much to do to establish his rule over his new kingdom, a task which would take a decade to complete. James took advantage of the political disarray in England to pursue the two goals closest to his heart – the recovery of Berwick and

Dunbar. Less than a month after Bosworth, commissions of array were sent to the northern counties to prepare for a Scottish invasion, and in October 1485, a similar commission specifically named Berwick as the Scottish objective. In the event, it was Dunbar which was besieged and taken, uncontested by Henry.

Possession of Dunbar was a position from which James was prepared to negotiate, and by the end of July 1486, a new three-year truce had been sealed. Its terms included proposals for another marriage alliance, between James's second son, and Catherine, Henry's sister-in-law and the daughter of Edward IV. That autumn, a further meeting heralded an early and more permanent settlement. Marriages were proposed between James (now a widower) and the 50-year-old Elizabeth Woodville (Henry's mother-in-law); and Rothesay and an unspecified daughter of Edward IV, 'for the increasing of more love and amity between the said princes, and for the sure observation of the truce'.[27] However, the truce was extended by a mere three months. As ever, the stumbling block was Berwick, the deliverance, or destruction, of which James continued to demand as the price of a permanent peace. More negotiations over the proposed matrimonial alliances and 'the appeasing of the said matter of Berwick' were scheduled for May 1488, the two kings to meet personally in July.[28]

Yet again, however, an Anglo-Scottish treaty was to be torpedoed by domestic events. In February, civil war erupted in Scotland, with the fourteen-year-old Rothesay at the head of the faction which opposed his father. Both sides looked to England for support – the first time that both sides in a Scottish factional conflict had appealed to the English since 1332 (see Chapter 2, Section ii). That spring, several of the rebel leaders obtained safe-conducts from Henry (although these were never used). James sent his favourite, John Ramsay, to appeal to Henry, who, however, declined the invitation to invade Scotland on James's behalf. Rothesay's party freely employed anti-English propaganda against his father (conveniently overlooking their own solicitation of Henry). James was presented as a vindictive father, influenced by wicked Anglophile counsellors, who had poisoned his wife and now threatened his heir through 'the inbringing of Englishmen to the perpetual subjection of the realm'.[29]

In June, the two factions clashed at Sauchieburn, where James III 'happened to be killed'.[30] The recently agreed Anglo-Scottish peace died with him. Henry was faced with a new regime, whose credibility depended on blackening the reputation of the late king of Scots, a process which involved whipping up anti-English feeling (James was crowned on 24 June, the anniversary of Bannockburn). The new minority government was dominated by Patrick Hepburn, Earl of Bothwell, and Alexander, Lord Home, whose spheres of influence centred on the south-east border region. As was frequently the case with border magnates, war with England suited their own interests (see Chapter 9, Section i), and so they advocated closer ties with France. Within a week of Sauchieburn, safe-conducts were granted to Ricardian rebels, and James would later receive embassies from Margaret of Burgundy, Richard's sister, and Henry's implacable enemy. Equally, Henry had received supporters of James III who had fled to England, including Ramsay. In July, Henry strengthened the garrisons of Berwick, Norham and Newcastle; and the same month, Bothwell went to France, to discuss a renewal of the Auld Alliance. However, lacking widespread support, the new regime could not afford war with England, and in September another three-year truce was agreed.

Once again, however, Scottish foreign policy became caught up in a power-struggle at the court. Archibald Douglas, Earl of Angus, whom Bothwell had displaced as warden of all three Marches in July 1489, now embraced an opposing Anglophile policy. In November 1491, Angus entered into a private – and potentially treasonable – agreement with Henry's commissioners, aimed at inducing James to make a firm peace. Failing this, Angus would attack opponents of the peace, namely Bothwell and Home, and their supporters. As a last resort, Angus agreed that he would give up Hermitage castle in Liddesdale, in return for English lands. However, he was unable to mount an effective challenge, and in December agreed to give up Liddesdale to James, in exchange for lands in Ayrshire, reducing his power on the borders. Liddesdale was promptly granted to Bothwell, and in March 1492, James ratified a renewal of the Auld Alliance, while the truce with England was extended for a mere eight months. The same month, James received letters from Perkin Warbeck, a pretender to Henry's throne, claiming to be Edward IV's younger son, Richard, Duke of York (one of the 'Princes in the Tower').

However, Bothwell's preference for the Auld Alliance came up against the same stumbling block which had caused James III to abandon this approach: French indifference. In November 1492, Charles VIII sealed the treaty of Étaples with Henry. Even before this, however, Scottish policy had been veering towards rapprochement with England, as Angus made a political comeback, and other pro-English ministers such as

William Elphinstone, Bishop of Aberdeen, rose to prominence. In the same month, an eighteen-month extension of the Anglo-Scottish truce was agreed. Henry was still pursuing his quest for security, and in Perkin Warbeck, he faced the most serious threat to his rule to date. He was thus anxious to secure a more permanent arrangement, and so ensure that Warbeck found no support in Scotland. In June 1493, Henry secured an extension of the truce to 1501, and, at his own insistence, the terms included a payment of 1,000 marks (£666 13s. 4d.) in compensation for damages caused by English pirates. He also offered a peace, to be strengthened by a marriage alliance. Now 20 years old, James saw a suitable bride as an important part of his foreign policy. However, Henry offered only his cousin, Catherine: hardly a splendid match for a king whose predecessors had married European princesses.

In 1494, James IV attained his majority; and Henry feared that he would pursue a more warlike policy. In March 1495, he informed Charles VIII that he expected a Scottish invasion before the year was up, and requested that Albany's son be sent to England – clearly hoping to field an equivalent pretender to the Scottish throne, should James decide to support Warbeck. The same month, commissions of array were issued in the English border counties, and arrangements made to convey artillery to Berwick. Henry's fears proved justified. In June, James met with Hugh O'Donnell, a powerful northern Irish magnate, committed opponent of Henry, and a longstanding supporter of Warbeck. The same month, he approached Maximilian (Warbeck's patron *du jour*), proposing a league against Henry, and offering to support the pretender in an invasion of England (hoping thereby to recover Berwick, as the Venetian ambassadors to Maximilian's court reported).[31] The deal was to be sealed with James's marriage to Maximilian's daughter Margaret.

As an alternative, James proposed himself as the husband of a Spanish infanta. However, Ferdinand and Isabella of Spain were interested in Scotland only inasmuch as it posed a threat to their 'Holy League' against France. They hoped to persuade Henry to abandon his French alliance and join the league; but he was unlikely to risk committing himself to war with France if he feared a Scottish invasion. When James used the threat of just such an invasion to press his suit, Ferdinand and Isabella instructed their ambassadors to Scotland to offer false hope that it would be favoured, in order to manoeuvre him into sealing a long Anglo-Scottish truce. Unfortunately, the ambassadors' instructions arrived in Scotland before they did; and James read them. He moved swiftly, receiving Warbeck as 'Prince Richard of England', in November, and marrying him to a distant kinswoman. According to the contemporary chronicler Polydore Vergil, writing in England, few of James's council believed Warbeck's claim, but some:

> only too pleased to be given this fresh opportunity of fighting the English ... urged that it would be greatly to the advantage of the country if ... under the guise of giving him assistance, they might wage war on the English.[32]

Having raised the stakes, James wrote to Ferdinand and Isabella, again urging an alliance; and around Easter 1496, sent his ambassadors back to Spain, to press once more for a marriage with one of their daughters, dangling the promise of the expulsion of Warbeck, and a perpetual peace with England. Anglo-Scottish relations, of such importance to James III, were, for his son, a mere bargaining counter on the gameboard of European diplomacy.

Ferdinand and Isabella's attitude towards Scotland, however, had not changed. All they wanted from James was that he should abandon Warbeck. The marriage offer was not seriously entertained, but they hoped that James might be 'put ... off some time longer with vain hopes' from making war on England, or allying with Spain's enemy, France.[33] However, James was not to be so easily manipulated. He had begun to prepare for an invasion of England even before receiving an answer from Spain. Around Whit Sunday, 1496, he summoned the host to Lauder; that summer a tax was agreed to fund the forthcoming campaign, and in September, he and Warbeck agreed on terms – once again, James's principal concern was the re-acquisition of Berwick.

James's support for Warbeck had wider implications for Henry's dynastic plans. He was himself in the midst of negotiations for a Spanish marriage: that of his son and heir, Arthur, to the Infanta Catherine of Aragon. However, Ferdinand and Isabella would not proceed with this alliance while the security of Henry's throne was in doubt. In July 1496, Henry joined the Holy League, with the proviso that he would not make war on France until his relationship with Scotland was satisfactorily arranged. Henry was certainly doing his best to achieve this. That March, he again offered James a marriage alliance, and this time proposed a properly prestigious bride: his daughter Margaret. James was unmoved by this improved offer, perhaps because he did not believe it to be sincere (Henry was simultaneously contemplating a match with the heir apparent of Denmark). James may also have relished the chance to lead an invasion of England, in order to win his spurs, and to enhance his popularity with those of his subjects who regarded any campaign as an opportunity for plunder.

Henry adopted the usual gambit of suborning his enemy's dissident subjects: principally James Stewart, Earl of Buchan, and James III's erstwhile favourite, John Ramsay, who had never truly been reconciled to James IV's regime. These two conspired in an abortive scheme to assassinate Warbeck before the Scottish campaign began. In September, Ramsay wrote to Henry, providing details of when and where James planned to muster the host, the date of the planned invasion, and the terms of the deal reached by James and Warbeck.

James's army crossed the Tweed on 14 September.[34] The force principally concerned itself with plundering and laying waste to the Tweed and Till valleys. No Englishmen flocked to Warbeck's banner, and within 24 hours, he retreated back to Scotland. James and his army remained, continuing their campaign of destruction and looting. A siege of Heaton castle was abandoned on the 26th, following news of the approach of the English army, and the Scots withdrew across the border. The campaign was a disaster for Warbeck; but James and his subjects, enriched by their spoils, took a different view. The Spanish ambassador opined that James had developed a taste for war, as profitable both to himself and his country; he had also displayed his martial prowess both to his countrymen and to Henry. And there was always next year.

In October and November, the English parliament made a grant of £120,000, to meet the threat of further invasion by the Scots. James now abandoned his support for Warbeck's claim and dismissed his supporters, although he retained him for the time being as a potentially useful diplomatic pawn. James began his own preparations for the next round of hostilities, rebuilding Dunbar castle, and siting fifteen guns at Coldingham, to train on any English army advancing from Berwick. He launched a raid in February 1497, and mustered the entire host in April. A Spanish delegation, still hopeful of conjuring up an Anglo-Scottish peace, achieved little; and negotiations in May foundered on English demands that Warbeck be handed over.

For Henry, however, the impetus to seek a peace was intensified by domestic disturbances. In May, he had to divert troops bound for the border to Cornwall and Devonshire, to suppress a revolt sparked by the imposition of the war tax. In June, James took advantage of the situation to launch a series of raids on Northumberland, and an English riposte against the Scottish East March was repulsed. He brushed aside Henry's attempts to negotiate a truce in early July, in favour of another campaign offering further opportunities for glory and plunder. James was clearly not yet ready to abandon the role of war leader, but he may also have been looking to improve the terms of a future peace. At any rate, he clearly wanted to keep his options open for a future agreement, for he abandoned any remaining pretence of support for Warbeck and dispatched him and his wife to Ireland. Warbeck's pension was a significant drain, and as his inglorious part in the previous year's invasion made clear, he could not offer James any prospect of help from dissident English Yorkists.

James mustered the host on 20 July, and in early August laid siege to Norham castle. However, the siege of a well-defended fortress was a different proposition from a smash-and-grab raid, and James could not keep his host in the field indefinitely (see Chapter 8). On 10 August, he withdrew, and an English army crossed the border and laid siege to Ayton castle. Summoning the remnants of the host, James set off to Ayton, but was unable to prevent its fall. After negotiations with the English command, James called off hostilities on the grounds that the English army was being disbanded.

Both sides had reached an impasse. Henry was still dealing with the western risings, while James had reached the limits of what he could expect from the Scottish host (Chapter 8), and of his financial resources. Having established his credentials as a force to be reckoned with, he was now ready to negotiate. In September, a seven-year truce was duly agreed, extended in October to last for one year after the death of either Henry or James. This was ratified in February 1498, with Ferdinand and Isabella agreeing to act as arbitrators of any future disputes. In January 1502, a full treaty of peace between England and Scotland was finally concluded, sealed by a marriage alliance between James and Margaret. This was the first full peace (as opposed to truce) between the two countries since 1333, when the settlement of 1328 had broken down. The state of war which had existed between the two realms for some 170 years was thus brought to an end.

Chapter 5: *Auld Alliance, New Europe, 1503–37*

i. *The End of the Perpetual Peace, 1503–13*

In 1503, the marriage of James IV of Scotland to Margaret Tudor, daughter of Henry VII of England, sealed a 'Perpetual Peace' between the two countries.[1] The arrangement was not universally popular among their subjects. Some of Henry VII's councillors opposed the marriage, fearing that Margaret's descendants – future kings of Scotland – might come to inherit the English throne (Henry reassured them with the prediction that, in such a case, England, as the larger country, would not be absorbed by Scotland, but rather *vice versa*).[2] According to the Spanish ambassador to Scotland, the majority of James's subjects had been opposed to peace with the Auld Enemy from the start.[3]

Both kings were aware of the strains which could be placed on international relations by cross-border disputes between their respective subjects. Accordingly, the treaty of Ayton contained provisions for dealing with breaches of the peace, supplementing the existing laws of the Marches (Chapter 9, Section ii). One such incident was the killing of Sir Robert Kerr, Scottish warden of the Middle Marches, by the Englishmen John Lilburn, the Bastard John Heron, and one Starhead, at one of the very March days designed to deal with such disputes. In 1508, James complained that, despite repeated requests, Henry had made insufficient redress for this. In fact Henry's response suggests his determination to preserve the painstakingly crafted peace: Lilburn had already been handed over to the Scots; Heron, the ringleader, had gone to ground, but his brother was acting as hostage for him; and Starhead was beyond

English, Scottish or March justice, having been murdered at the orders of Kerr's son.[4]

A greater threat to the continuation of the peace was the Auld Alliance between Scotland and France against England. It potentially threatened both the Anglo-Scottish peace, and the Anglo-French peace of 1492, and Henry's attitude to his son-in-law was heavily coloured by this. Shortly before the marriage, Henry requested that James repudiate the Alliance, but James promised only to consult him before renewing it.[5] Franco-Scottish relations remained cordial – indeed James's navy benefited significantly from French money, men and materials, in return for the promise of its use (Chapter 8). But when Louis XII requested Scottish troops to serve against the Spanish in 1507, James prevaricated, for with an English peace secured, there was little profit in committing himself to French interests.

However, these diplomatic exchanges awoke Henry's fears, leading him to adopt a policy which threatened to provoke the very action he was seeking to avert. In 1508, landing in England on his return from France, James's envoy, James Hamilton, Earl of Arran, was detained on the pretext that he had no safe-conduct. Thomas Wolsey, the ambassador Henry dispatched to James, reported that the renewal of the Alliance was imminent, and that there was strong pro-French feeling at his court. This was to some extent staged, however, and James subsequently promised to refrain from renewing the Alliance, providing, he stipulated pointedly, Henry treated him well. Arran was duly released, and the incident does not appear to have altered James's French policy. In June 1508, he dispatched Gavin Dunbar, Archdeacon of St Andrews, to Louis, bearing expressions of goodwill and assurances of his intention to maintain and strengthen the Auld Alliance – but no commitment to its formal renewal. Unfortunately, neither had James's promises lulled Henry's suspicions. When, upon his return, Dunbar was shipwrecked off the east coast of England, he, too was taken to Henry, although he was speedily released.

Thus, by 1509, when Henry VIII confirmed the Perpetual Peace on his succession to the throne, its fault-lines had already become apparent. While Henry VII lived, the treaty was not subjected to the test of hostilities between Scotland's Auld Ally and her new one, but, as soon became apparent, his son was determined on war with France. However, the face of Europe had changed. Of England's fifteenth-century allies against France, the duchy of Brittany had been absorbed by the French Crown, while the duchy of Burgundy had become part of the ever-expanding territories of the Hapsburgs. International relations in sixteenth-century Europe were dominated by the Italian wars: the contest between the French royal house of Valois, and the Hapsburg heirs to Spain and the Empire, for the duchy of Milan and kingdom of Naples. Anglo-Scottish relations would now become part of the complex and shifting web of alliances engendered by this conflict.[6]

In 1511, Henry VIII joined the Emperor Maximilian and Ferdinand of Aragon in the papal Holy League against Louis. That December, in a letter to the pope, James asserted that Henry's failure to offer redress for breaches of the peace had forced him to conclude that their treaty was dissolved. Henry's response came with ominous swiftness. He refused to hand over Margaret's inheritances from their brother, Arthur, and grandmother, Margaret Beaufort, and in January 1512, the English parliament declared the Scottish king to be the 'very homager and obediencer of right to your Highness'[7]: Henry was reviving the claim to English overlordship. James riposted with a claim of his own – as heir, in the right of his wife, to the as-yet-childless Henry. James had already asserted this claim, through his use of iconography since his marriage to Margaret Tudor, and more directly in writing to Henry VII in 1508.[8] From now on, the Stewart claim to the English throne would be a recurring factor in Anglo-Scottish relations.

By the end of February, James had opened negotiations for a renewal of the Auld Alliance, while seeking to persuade Louis to recognize his claim. Henry now attempted to use James's claim for his own ends, warning that James's hopes for the succession would not be furthered by a French alliance, for Louis had recognized the claim of the Yorkist Richard de la Pole. James remained unmoved. Terms were eventually agreed in May 1513: James undertook to invade England, and to send the Scottish fleet to France; Louis to equip and victual it, and to pay James a large pension. In June, James entered into another alliance, with Hugh O'Donnell of Tyrconnell in Ulster, probably intended to enlist his help for a Scottish attack on Carrickfergus, the chief English stronghold in that province.

Henry's army sailed to France at the end of June. By the end of July, the Scottish fleet, captained by Arran, had been dispatched to France, via Ireland. James summoned the host, and invaded Northumberland in late August. The capture of Norham castle was swiftly followed by that of the smaller fortresses of Etal and Ford. But the English army raised to defend the north, led by the veteran earl of Surrey, was close at hand. In contrast to the usual tactics adopted by Scottish invaders, James deliberately kept his army in England to meet the oncoming force. At the battle of Flodden, the Scottish army engaged an English army in the field for the first time since the skirmish at the river Sark in 1448 – and suffered a massive defeat (see Chapter 8). James died on the battlefield, alongside thousands of his subjects, including the archbishop of St Andrews, nine earls, and fourteen lords. He left a year-old son to succeed him.[9]

ii. England versus France: Minority Regimes in Scotland, 1513–24

The next fifteen years saw Scottish politics dominated by the contest between pro-English and pro-French factions to control the minority government of James V. Initially, the two main players were Margaret, the infant king's mother (and Henry VIII's sister); and John Stuart, Earl of Albany, his paternal uncle, who had been in the French king's service since the age of twelve. Margaret was named regent in her husband's will (as long as she remained a widow), but Scottish custom dictated that, as the king's nearest adult male relative, Albany should govern on his behalf. The council's decision to accept Margaret's appointment did not, however, prevent Henry from following up his victory at Flodden with a series of raids, designed to keep up the pressure on the Scots to abandon the French alliance.

The majority of the Scottish nobility also favoured the continuation of war. In October, orders were issued for wappenshaws throughout the country, and the council requested Albany to come to Scotland, to act as James's lieutenant-general in forthcoming campaigns. It also requested French aid to continue a war which had, it argued, been fought in the service of France. In November, Louis agreed both to renew the Auld Alliance, and to send Albany. Shortly afterwards, however, he made terms with Henry's allies, Ferdinand and the Emperor, leaving Henry with little choice but to reach his own agreement with the French king. As France's ally, Scotland was comprehended in the Anglo-French peace treaty of August 1514, sealed by Louis' marriage to Henry's younger sister, Mary. Albany's journey to Scotland – to which Louis' new brother-in-law would have taken strong exception – was now cancelled.

Events, however, dictated a swift turnabout. Margaret married the pro-English Archibald Douglas, Earl of Angus, one of the few Scottish nobles to oppose war with England in 1513. Their attempts to set up a rival centre of government to the council alienated other Scottish lords, who were unwilling to allow the powerful Douglas family to acquire such influence. The pair sent a letter in James V's name to Alexander, Lord Home, warden of all three Scottish Marches, commanding him to cease hostilities and meet with the English wardens to discuss a truce. However, a party led by Arran, Home, and the chancellor, Archbishop James Beaton of Glasgow, formally deprived Margaret of her regency and offered Albany the governorship of the realm. Although the new French king, François I, wished to maintain peace with England, the opportunity to install a pro-French administration in Scotland (thus preventing the pro-English party from regaining the upper hand) was too good to miss. Albany landed in Scotland in May 1515. That July, he was acknowledged by parliament as governor, and received the oaths of allegiance of the attendant Scottish lords.

Having failed to choke off the Auld Alliance, Henry now strove to undermine Albany's regime. However, any efforts in this direction would have to be covert, for Henry, too, wished to maintain the Anglo-French peace. He found allies in Angus and Home, who swiftly abandoned the allegiance they had so recently sworn to Albany. As Margaret's husband, Angus hoped to take power with English support, while Home was disaffected because Albany's lands had been restored partly at his expense. The pair were involved in an abortive plan to abduct James V and bring him to England. In early August, Home promised Thomas, Lord Dacre, warden of the English Marches, to hold Home castle for Margaret and Angus, and to make no agreements with Albany without Henry's consent. In the meantime, Dacre covertly aided Home's raids on Albany's lands.

As Henry would later remark, Albany '[was] and always has been at the French king's commandment'.[10] Consequently, the governor was hampered in his dealings with English-sponsored rebels by François' instructions to preserve the Anglo-Scottish peace. When Albany raised an army to capture Home's castles in the East March, Dacre protested, purporting to fear that he intended to attack Berwick. In response, Albany disbanded his force before Home himself could be taken. Nevertheless, Margaret and Angus were forced to flee to England that

September, and Home was eventually captured in October. The following spring, Albany accepted Angus's and Home's renewed oaths of allegiance and they returned to Scotland, though Margaret remained at her brother's court.

True to his master's instructions, Albany also made overtures for a renewed truce with England. Henry used this opportunity to try to undermine the council's support for Albany with a spot of black propaganda. He alleged that, as James's next heir, Albany coveted the Scottish throne, and that while he remained governor – or indeed in Scotland at all – his nephew's life was in danger. The council robustly dismissed these smears, defending Albany's right to the governorship. The truce was extended to the end of November, but Henry continued to pursue his goal covertly. When Albany executed Home for conspiracy with the English, his brothers, George and David, Prior of Coldingham, fled across the border, and were harboured by Dacre.

Anglo-Scottish relations continued to be shaped by developments on the Continent. Any hopes Henry may have had for a further campaign in France were dashed by the Hapsburg–Valois peace agreements of summer 1516, which deprived him of potential allies. In the autumn, in the light of the continuing Anglo-French amity, Albany sought a full peace with England. At the same time, he was attempting to secure French support for Scotland in the event of renewed English aggression, to be confirmed through a marriage between James and a daughter of the house of Valois. But France had only one use for Scotland – as an attack dog to set on England when French interests required it. Closer Franco-Scottish ties would inevitably raise Henry VIII's hackles, and, at present, François had no intention of provoking England. He politely prevaricated over the proposed marriage, and promised aid only so far as his honour and his peace agreement with England permitted.

Albany's hopes for a peace with England were also to be disappointed, for Henry would only agree to an extension of the truce until November 1517. The truce was ill-kept, and the English Crown continued to support the cross-border depredations of the Home brothers, denying all knowledge when the Scots demanded they be handed over. Nevertheless, it suited neither side to resume hostilities. The Scots did not want to risk action without François' support, while, for Henry, peace with France made the removal of Albany's regime less pressing. Indeed, in June 1517,

Albany himself returned to France, in order to press his pleas for a firmer commitment to Scotland in person. That October, the Anglo-Scottish truce was renewed for a further two years. Meanwhile, Albany's efforts had borne fruit in the Franco-Scottish treaty of Rouen, sealed the previous month. The degree of François' commitment, however, was still limited. He pledged 1,200 troops, and 100,000 crowns, but only in the case of an English invasion of Scotland. As a bride he offered James a putative third daughter (as yet, just a twinkle in François' eye – but, he regretted, the existing two were committed elsewhere). Worst of all, French ratification of the treaty was continually delayed.

In March 1518, England received more Scottish rebels, including David Home of Wedderburn, who had killed Antoine, Sire de la Bastie, the Frenchman appointed by Albany to head the council in his absence. A fairly accurate summation of Henry's policy was offered by the French ambassador in Scotland: the English supported Scottish rebels in order to keep James's government divided, weak, and unable to mount an attack on England, while English raids passed freely into Scotland. Arran (who had gained control of the council after the death of de la Bastie) complained to François that Henry had ignored the terms of the truce by refusing either to deliver the rebels, or to turn them out of England. Meanwhile, however, Thomas Wolsey, now a cardinal and Henry's chief minister, was presenting his master to the world in a new role: that of peacemaker and unifier of Western Christendom. In October, Henry and François were the first signatories of the treaty of London, a non-aggression pact in the face of the rising threat of the Muslim Ottoman Empire, subsequently ratified by the papacy, Spain and the Empire. Peacemaker Henry's objectives in Scotland remained the same, however. An early draft of the treaty had specified that Albany was not to be admitted to Scotland, and that Margaret was to be restored to the regency. While this clause did not make the final treaty, François' attitude remained the same: so long as he wished to keep the peace with England, he would not allow Albany to return to Scotland.

When this came to be understood in Scotland, open factionalism erupted between Arran, and Angus and Margaret (who had finally returned to Scotland after Albany's departure, and with his blessing). Neither party, however, wanted war with England. Arran feared Henry would invade Scotland in support of Angus, while Angus feared war would precipitate the return of Albany – a far more formidable opponent. In December 1519, the council accepted a further year's truce, with the proviso that Albany's governorship was not thereby prejudiced. This was followed by a series of short-term extensions, while the council attempted to speed Albany's return, informing François of Henry's attempts to prevent this by fostering civil strife, undermining affection for the governor and for France, and compelling a peace which would gain him control of Scotland.[11] They warned François that if he did not send Albany back by midsummer, France would indeed lose Scotland, for in that case they would 'treat with England surely and without any default'.[12] For his part, Henry was waiting to see how relations between François and the Emperor Charles V panned out; he had no intention of getting involved in a war with Scotland.

When the Hapsburg–Valois peace broke down, Henry abandoned his peacemaker guise, resumed the mantle of war leader (a role more in keeping with his own preferences), and threw in his lot with the Emperor. In summer 1521, a new treaty stipulated that, if a Franco-Imperial peace was not agreed by November, the English would join the conflict on the Imperial side by May 1523. As no such peace was agreed, François no longer had any reason to pacify England, and Albany was dispatched to Scotland. If England was preparing to enter into conflict with France again, then the Auld Alliance regained its customary value. Henry adopted the standard gambit of an English government wishing to move against Scotland without the expense of raising an army – he stepped up his support for Scottish rebels. Wolsey instructed Dacre to tell Angus and the Homes to make ready against their 'mortal enemy' (Albany), and to stir up dissension against him in Scotland; a payment of 500 or 1,000 marks (£333 or £666), it was considered, would do much to effect this.[13]

François was by no means resigned to Henry's alliance with the Emperor. In December, he offered a truce in Italy to Charles, provided that England agreed to a truce with Scotland; following this he would force Albany to leave Scotland. This proposal foundered on the English insistence that Albany's departure must come first, and in June 1522, François finally ratified the treaty of Rouen. Thus the stage was set for a conflict which neither England nor the majority of the Scottish nobility really wanted. Indeed, the Scots sought a truce as early as the end of June. Dacre reiterated the English position: no truce unless Albany left Scotland. He also recommended the Scots to consider that 'for lack of issue of my said sovereign, your sovereign is heir apparent to this realm'[14] (conveniently ignoring the existence of Henry's six-year-old daughter, Mary). The Stewart claim to the English throne, which had so infuriated Henry when asserted by James IV, was now deployed as a carrot to persuade the Scots into conformity with English wishes. It would not be the last appearance of this particular carrot.

Albany's task now was to persuade Scotland into war against England in the French interest. The lack of enthusiasm with which this proposal met forced him to deliver an ultimatum: either follow him in attacking England, or he would abandon Scotland for good. Accordingly, a tax was voted to fund the war and it was agreed to summon the host for 1 August. From the Scottish viewpoint, there was no good reason to invade England at this time. English backing for the rebels had lost its teeth: Angus had surrendered to Albany, and been packed off in exile to France in February, and even the Home brothers were on the point of being reconciled. Albany was also hampered by his master's niggardliness. François refused to stump up French men and money, on the grounds that the attack was not covered by the treaty of Rouen. The day after the muster, Albany perforce yielded to growing pressure to abandon war with England, promising that if no aid arrived from France, he would agree a two-month truce, and open negotiations for a full peace.

In the meantime, the Scottish army headed west to menace Carlisle (a fortress rendered vulnerable by 20 years of chronic neglect), but on reaching the border they baulked at crossing it. At the same time, lack of money and provisions had grounded the English army at York. On 10 September, therefore, Dacre requested a truce; true to his promise, Albany acquiesced. At the end of October, he returned once again to France, to attempt, once again, to extract from François the men, money and arms necessary for a successful Scottish invasion of England. In his absence, the truce was continuously extended until March 1523.

In December 1522, Henry suggested a sixteen-year peace, to be sealed by James's marriage to Mary (at this stage his only legitimate child) and the ceding of Berwick. In return, the Scots were to abandon Albany and give no further aid to France, effectively renouncing the treaty of Rouen. Henry's offer highlights the importance he attached to neutralizing Scotland, in order to proceed unhindered in his continental adventures. The Scots' rejection of it demonstrates the importance they attached to Albany's governorship – now regarded as the sole bulwark against the factionalism which would otherwise tear Scotland apart. Peace talks having failed, English preparations for war began in February 1523. If the Scots could not be persuaded to abandon Albany and the French alliance, they must be forced to. Parliament voted a war tax of £20,000, and in March, the earl of Surrey was appointed lieutenant-general in the north, and cross-border raiding began. The Scots began to mobilize in early April, and an urgent message was dispatched to France to speed Albany's return.

Surrey hoped to lure the Scots into a war of attrition, in which they would exhaust their troops and provisions chasing raiding parties. Between April and September, he and Dacre led a series of devastating raids in the Scottish borders. The Scottish defence strategy proved ineffective; their response to the fast-moving English attacks was slow and unwieldy. François was finally galvanized into action, bribing key players on the Scottish political scene (Arran and Margaret each reportedly received 1,000 crowns), and providing the much-requested military aid. That June, 500 French soldiers crossed to Scotland, and in September, when Albany at last returned, he brought with him a force of 5,000 infantry and 100 *Landsknechte*.

Albany did not, however, strike immediately, for François still hoped Henry might be persuaded to abandon his agreement with the Emperor. Accordingly, Albany proposed a truce, conditional on the inclusion of France. With an English army poised to invade France, Henry – unsurprisingly – refused. The Scottish host was summoned for 19 October, but the turnout was poor; the weather was bad, and there was growing resentment that French soldiers received wages while Scotsmen served without pay. The army crossed the border and laid siege to Wark on 1 November but, three days later, news of an approaching English army caused Albany to retreat back over the border, where he disbanded his army. Meanwhile, Surrey contacted the Scottish council, once again offering peace in return for the exclusion of Albany. Once again, this was decisively refused. The French soldiers were sent home, but the Scots confirmed the treaty of Rouen in November. No Anglo-Scottish truce could be agreed because the aims of the parties were diametrically opposed and apparently non-negotiable. Henry refused to consider any agreement which involved recognition of Albany's position; Scotland would not abandon Albany; and Albany stuck to it that any truce between England and Scotland must also comprehend France. But for Henry, the whole point of peace with Scotland was to free him to fight France.

In February 1524, the Scots launched another cross-border offensive, met by a series of English counter-raids in April, intended to expose Albany's government as unable to protect James's subjects. Faced with an apparent impasse, Albany won reluctant permission from François to leave Scotland. He set sail for France in May, warned by the Scottish lords that he would forfeit the governorship if his absence exceeded three months. He would never return.

iii. France Eclipsed: 1524–37

As soon as Albany left for France, Margaret staged a *coup*, neatly ousting him from the governorship by having the twelve-year-old James declared of age. Her timing was opportune. Many Scots were now wondering whether Albany was worth the price of war with England. As Henry's sister, Margaret was well placed to negotiate an end to English raiding and secure a longer-term peace. At the end of July 1524, a majority of the lords entered into a bond with James to support his administration and to reject Albany's authority. James's new status (and that of his mother) was confirmed in parliament, and from this point, the king no longer acted 'with the consent of the lords of council, in absence of the governor', but 'with the consent of his mother and the lords of the council.'[15]

With his sister back in power, Henry might reasonably hope for a more pro-English government. While English raids maintained the pressure to abandon Albany for good, English money rewarded Margaret's supporters, and a 200-strong English guard preserved her possession of her son. In August, Scottish ambassadors were sent to England for peace talks: the terms proposed were the marriage of James and Mary; recognition of James as Henry's heir; and the bestowal of English lands befitting this position. Should he be displaced by the birth of a son to Henry, he was to be compensated by the ceding of Berwick. In September, a three-month truce was agreed, and in November, the Scottish parliament formally expressed its approval of a peace with England. November also saw the return of Angus, who, after escaping from France, had stopped off in England to pledge allegiance to Henry (saving his allegiance to James), and commit himself to working against the French alliance, under Wolsey's advice. Any remaining hope of Albany's return was dashed in December, when François announced that he would be unable to spare him until at least summer 1525. With Albany gone, and an Anglophile government in power, it seemed that Henry had finally achieved his goal.

However, the stability of that government was threatened by the deteriorating relationship between its two main powers. Margaret had consistently sought to prevent the return of her husband, Angus, and now each demanded English support against the other. At the end of the year, Margaret wrote to Henry (in James's name) and to Wolsey (in her own), complaining about Angus and threatening to join with France if England continued to support him. This only served to alienate Henry, and by the end of the year, the English were actively raising support for Angus against her. When her subsequent correspondence with Albany was discovered, it can only have discredited her further in her brother's eyes. In July 1525, Margaret was formally deprived of all power of government. Instead, authority was vested in the king's council, which was to rotate its membership every three months, with Angus appointed the chief of the first group of councillors. It is a measure of the importance now attached to English support that the council informed Henry of this new arrangement, and solicited his aid, should Albany attempt to return.

This attitude was partly shaped by the temporary eclipse of Scotland's Auld Ally. François had been captured by Imperial forces in February 1525, after a disastrous defeat at Pavia. That June, the Scottish council had asked the French either for aid against England, in accordance with the treaty of Rouen, or permission to make an independent peace. In August, the French sealed the treaty of the More with England, which comprehended Scotland, without consulting the Scots. The Scots now abandoned their insistence on the inclusion of France in an Anglo-Scottish agreement. They were prepared to accept either a three-year truce, or a full alliance, to be sealed by the marriage of James and Mary. Even at this stage, negotiations were temporarily derailed by Scottish insistence that they be allowed to assist France with arms and men. But securing peace with England was now regarded as almost paramount. When Angus seized control of James, converting his three-month term of power into a permanent arrangement, his *coup* was accepted in Scotland partly because, as a longstanding ally of the English king, he was regarded as the best person to deliver this.

He duly delivered. The truce was renewed in November, and a new three-year truce was ratified in January 1526. The scene looked set for a period of Anglo-Scottish amity. But increasing cross-border lawlessness was becoming a source of concern to the English government (Chapter 9, Section i). Prime among the offenders were the Liddesdale surnames, and Angus indicated his readiness to work with Henry Clifford, Earl of Cumberland, the warden of the English West March, to destroy their power base. But Angus was no more able to control the Scottish borderers than his predecessors, while Cumberland lacked influence and resources in the region. When the Liddesdale thieves joined with English outlaws Sir William and Sir Humphrey Lisle, both sides proved powerless to halt their depredations. English demands that the Lisles and their adherents be arrested were met by Angus's protests that they had based themselves in the Debatable Lands, where neither country had jurisdiction (Chapter 9, Section ii). English border officers accused him of lying, and abetting the Lisles. When Henry Percy, Earl of Northumberland, warden of the East and Middle Marches, captured and executed Nicholas Lisle, he was said to have confessed to being maintained by the Scottish wardens.

Strained cross-border relations did not significantly affect the English government's favour for Angus's regime, which still offered the best hope for the continuation of peaceful relations. But Angus's power could last only so long as he controlled James; and in summer 1528, the king escaped. In July, he summonsed his stepfather for treason. He explained to Henry that Angus had been restored to high office to please him, but that the earl had abused his office, and defied his king. Therefore, if Angus requested English help he should be refused. But Henry ignored this, and offered his support to Angus in attempting a reconciliation with James. Notwithstanding, Angus was found guilty, and he and his brother retreated to Tantallon, holding this and other Douglas castles against James. Initially, English insistence on Angus's restoration hindered truce negotiations, but a five-year truce sealed at Berwick in December contained no mention of him. However, a separate agreement allowed Henry to receive him in England, whence he fled in March 1529, surrendering his strongholds. Henry would not commit an English army to restoring even such a reliable English agent as Angus, but his attempts to persuade his nephew to a reconciliation went on into 1531. Meanwhile, Angus, now based at Newcastle, continued to cause trouble in the Merse, in Berwickshire. Complaining that the loyalties of its inhabitants could not be relied upon while their erstwhile master remained close by, James requested his uncle to remove Angus, who, accordingly, left for London in November 1531.

Meanwhile, despite James's best efforts, the problem of cross-border disorder had not died with the Lisles. In August 1532, three months before the truce was due to expire, cross-border raids were launched by various groups of Scottish surnames, including the Liddesdale Armstrongs. Henry responded aggressively, taking Angus's homage as overlord of Scotland, and sending him back north to work with the March wardens against the Scots. James ordered southern Scotland to be put onto a war footing, and appointed his half-brother, the earl of Moray, lieutenant of the Scottish East and Middle Marches. Further raids and counter-raids followed. James pressed Henry to recall Angus to London; Henry demanded redress for Scottish raids, while countenancing similar English incursions, hoping to pressure James into reinstating Angus. Relations were further strained by James's reception of the Welsh rebel, James Gruffydd ap Powell, seeking support for another revolt; and his covert support for Alexander, chief of the MacDonald clan of the Western Isles, who was opposing the English in Ulster. In November, Northumberland reported a raid by the Scottish deputy wardens, and in December, he launched large-scale reprisals, capturing Cawmills, which he handed over to Sir George Douglas. That month, James summoned the host, and in January 1533, a large force was garrisoned in the East March – possibly intended for offensive as well as defensive action.

Henry, having no wish to involve himself in a full-scale war, stepped back from the brink, and in March, English wardens were ordered to cease raiding. At this point, Anglo-Scottish relations were once again caught up in the intricacies of the Hapsburg–Valois conflict. That April, the Emperor granted James the Order of the Golden Fleece, causing François to worry that Anglo-Scottish enmity would promote a Scottish–Imperial alliance (particularly as Henry had just divorced the Emperor's aunt, Catherine of Aragon). He therefore sent an ambassador to Scotland to broker a peace. Moray accordingly halted Scottish raids, and withdrew from the border, and English and Scottish ambassadors met in June. In May 1534, Henry and James agreed a peace treaty to extend until one year after the death of either.

The next couple of years saw both countries preoccupied with domestic affairs; James was eagerly pursuing a French marriage, while Henry was facing rebellions against his Reformation, in Lincolnshire, Yorkshire, and the North-West border counties, dubbed the Pilgrimage of Grace. In September 1537, Henry ordered Angus, who had relocated to Berwick, to remove himself from the borders. This was not the time to risk alienating James, for English rebels had looked across the border for support in the past, and shared ties of faith might now form a powerful basis for appeals to a Catholic king of Scots. From now on, Anglo-Scottish relations would be caught up in the unprecedented tide of religious reform sweeping Western Christendom.

Chapter 6: Reformations and Rough Wooing, 1537–60

i. *The Road to Solway Moss, 1537–42*

In 1537, the pope granted James V the title of Defender of the Faith.[1] He evidently hoped the Scottish king would fulfil this new role in action against his uncle Henry VIII, who had broken with Rome. In 1539, one of James's closest councillors, David Beaton, Archbishop of St Andrews, was made a cardinal, the pope expressing his hope that James would now publish his interdict calling for Henry's deposition. The Scottish clergy were intent on bringing James to war with England, for fear he should follow Henry's example. He was also exhorted to act against Henry by English Catholic rebels from the Pilgrimage of Grace, who approached him when he put into Scarborough, on his way back from France in 1537, 'weeping … [and] showing how that they had long looked for him, and how they were oppressed, slain and murdered, desiring him for God's sake to come in, and he should have all'.[2] Meanwhile, on the Continent, the Hapsburg–Valois conflict was in abeyance, for the Catholic monarchs François I of France and the Emperor Charles V had sealed an alliance in the pope's presence. By 1539 the pair were contemplating a joint invasion of England. They, too, hoped to call upon the services of the Scottish king, who had recently married François' kinswoman, Marie de Guise; and in 1541, François assured James of French support, should Henry invade Scotland.

James was thus being pressed from all sides to abandon his peace with England. From Henry's anxious perspective, there were ominous signs that he might comply. Henry urged the advantages of reformation upon his nephew; but James harboured English Catholic rebels, and allowed Irish Catholics, fresh from an attempt to invade the English Pale, to pass through Scotland on the way to Rome. And when James sailed to the

Western Isles in 1540, Henry received intelligence that he was planning to assume the kingship of Ireland (a title that Henry was to confer upon himself the following year). Henry was seriously rattled; between 1538 and 1542, he spent close to £290,000 on fortifications on the south coast and the Anglo-Scottish borders.

However, come pope, Emperor, French king, Scottish clergy or persecuted pilgrims, James had his own agenda. He had no desire for an expensive war with England, but every intention of exploiting the situation to his own advantage. He assured his uncle that he would not break their alliance, and, in 1540, requested a copy of his religious legislation. A hint that James might listen to Henry's proposals proved effective with the Scottish clergy, who duly contributed to their king's household expenses (out of gratitude, James informed the pope, for his attempts to stamp out heresy).

Given their rival interests, no Hapsburg–Valois league was likely to endure long, and by summer 1542, François had allied with the Ottoman Suleiman the Magnificent against the Emperor. The following year, French armies invaded the Low Countries, Italy and Spain. French interests now demanded Anglo-Scottish amity, for hostility between England and Scotland might provide an English ally for Charles. In 1542, François proposed a three-way meeting of the English, Scottish and French kings, but to no avail, for that summer, Henry entered the war on the side of the Emperor. The summer saw English border fortresses garrisoned, and the appointment of the earl of Rutland as warden of the English East and Middle Marches; on the Scottish side, George Gordon, Earl of Huntly, was made lieutenant of the borders, and dispatched to Kelso with a paid force. However, neither James nor Henry was anxious to rush into hostilities. For Henry, peace with Scotland was the cheapest way to secure his borders, leaving him free to campaign in France; thus Rutland was instructed to refrain from cross-border raiding save in retaliation for incursions personally ordered by James. For their part, the Scots were quick to assure Henry that Huntly's remit was purely defensive.

Nevertheless, as cross-border tensions heightened, minor incursions escalated into a series of raids and counter-raids. Henry appointed Thomas Howard, Duke of Norfolk, captain-general against the Scots, instructing him to muster the northern counties for an invasion of Scotland. Uncle and nephew exchanged reassurances of their wish to preserve the peace, but Henry now saw raids and the threat of war as a means to dictate its terms. At the end of August, Norfolk launched a large-scale raid, which ended in an English defeat when he encountered Huntly at Haddon Rig. The following day, James wrote to Henry engaging to stop all raids, and asking Henry to do the same. It was agreed that negotiations should go ahead in September, but the English continued to plan for an October invasion.

In fact, the negotiations were doomed to failure. James wished to make a perpetual peace, but would on no account renounce the Auld Alliance; Henry's principal interest in Anglo-Scottish peace was as a means to facilitate Anglo-French war. Throughout the negotiations, the English army remained on the border, and in October, Norfolk led it into Scotland. His instructions were to march on Edinburgh, or failing this, to achieve some other notable exploit that would force James to accept Henry's terms. He encountered no resistance, but, hampered by ill-health, and short of provisions, he returned to Berwick less than a week later. Meanwhile, like Edward I and Henry IV before him, Henry embarked on a search for historical evidence which would 'fully, plainly, and clearly set forth to all the world'[3] the justice of his claims to overlordship, and commissioned a report on how best to achieve the conquest of Scotland. *A Declaration, containing the Just Causes and Considerations of this Present War with the Scots*, published in early November, accused James of failing to provide either good rule on the borders or sufficient redress; of claiming the Debatable Lands and harbouring English rebels; and of refusing to ransom English prisoners from Haddon Rig. But, it proclaimed, the primary reason Henry had gone to war was the recovery of his ancient rights as overlord of Scotland.

In November, James launched what was probably intended to be the first of a series of large cross-border raids (akin to the strategy which had proved so successful for his father in 1497). He may also have intended to have the papal interdict against Henry proclaimed in an English church – a neat riposte to Henry's resurrection of the overlordship claim. The Scots entered England on the West March, and encountered its warden, Thomas Wharton, at Solway Moss. A successful manoeuvre trapped the Scots in the Esk estuary, and they were forced to surrender, with many Scottish nobles being taken prisoner. In December, their 30-year-old king died suddenly, after a short illness. James's successor was a babe-in-arms, and the next turn of Anglo-Scottish relations would be dictated by her gender.

ii. *Overlordship or Union? 1542–51*

With James V's death, a truce came into effect. As the closest male relative and heir presumptive of the new Queen Mary, the earl of Arran was named governor of the realm. He favoured peace with England, evincing Protestant sympathies; stating that he regarded the pope as a mere bishop (and a bad one at that); and announcing his intention to reform the Scottish Church. He also raised the question of a marriage between Mary and the infant Edward, Prince of Wales. Henry seized on this suggestion, and was soon plotting this new 'great affair of Scotland'.[4] In January 1543, ten of the Scottish nobles taken at Solway Moss were released, having bound themselves to Henry to support the marriage, and to keep him apprised of affairs in Scotland. They were accompanied by the earl of Bothwell, who had made the same undertaking, and by Angus and his brother George Douglas, who had reaffirmed their oaths to Henry. A final secret article bound all to aid Henry in taking the throne of Scotland if Mary died – or Scotland south of the Forth, should the marriage plans fail. Shortly after their return, Arran imprisoned Cardinal Beaton, a bitter opponent of religious reform. That spring, he requested copies of the Acts of Parliament creating Henry head of the English Church, and a copy of the New Testament in English. The Douglases were restored, and commissioners were appointed to negotiate for a marriage and peace treaty with England.

The Scottish council was not, however, monopolized by pro-English, Protestant feeling, and an opposition party soon emerged. The earls of Huntly and Argyll disliked both the marriage and religious reform. The Scottish clergy, led by a newly liberated Beaton, pledged money to the cause of defending the realm against England and warned their favoured ally, François I, of the turn of events. That spring saw the return of Matthew Stewart, Earl of Lennox, Mary's closest male relative after Arran, from his embassy in France. Along with Beaton and the queen mother, Marie de Guise, he formed the nucleus of a new anti-English faction.

In March, the Scottish parliament specified terms for Mary's betrothal to Edward. These in part reflected the personal concerns of their chief architect: Arran's place in the succession was to be secured; he was to continue as governor at least until Mary's majority; and he would control Scottish revenues without reference to Henry. More significant, however, was the emphasis on Scotland's concerns for its sovereignty (reminiscent of the treaty of Birgham, 1290, concerning the marriage of another Scottish queen to an heir to the English throne; Chapter 1, Section i). Mary would not go to England until after the marriage; no guarantees in the form of Scottish castles or hostages would be handed over; and, unless Edward and Mary had an heir, none but a Scot was to command Scottish castles. Scotland was to retain its own laws and liberties, with no appeal beyond its borders (a fear grounded in past experience). The French alliance would not be renounced. And nor, it was made clear, would the Scots at any time recognize any claim to their kingdom on Henry's part.

Although the peace and marriage treaties sealed at Greenwich in July 1543 incorporated most of these terms, they were not popular in Scotland. In early July, Huntly, Argyll and Bothwell joined Beaton's party, and Arran was forced to agree to Mary's removal to Stirling (for safekeeping from possible English seizure). Indeed, Arran himself was having second thoughts, tempted by the prospect of marrying Mary to his own son. In August, Henry offered him an alternative daughter-in-law – Princess Elizabeth – along with 5,000 English soldiers to help crush resistance to the treaty. Alternatively, Henry suggested, he might make Arran king of Scotland north of the Forth, implying both that the kingship was Henry's to dispose of, and that the other half of the country would be governed from Westminster. The Greenwich treaty notwithstanding, the overlordship claim evidently remained at the forefront of his mind.

Towards the end of the month, Arran ratified the Greenwich treaties. Henry, however, did not follow suit. He was pushing for better terms: immediate possession of Mary, and Scottish renunciation of the Auld Alliance. The latter was still of crucial importance for Henry, who had made an alliance with the Emperor the previous February, committing himself to a joint invasion of France in 1544. This obstreperousness was perhaps the final straw for the wavering Arran, who now publicly reconciled himself to the anti-English party. In September, Mary was crowned, and henceforth, her governor would be advised by a council headed by Beaton as Chancellor and by her mother, Marie de Guise. The Scottish parliament broke off the marriage treaty and renewed the Auld Alliance, and Arran received money, artillery and supplies from France. A papal legate was dispatched to collect the ecclesiastical subsidy which had been voted to James V. This would now be spent in the defence of his daughter's realm and of the Catholic faith, thus linking the two together. In January 1544, Henry's last remaining allies in Scotland, including Angus, bound themselves to resist the English.

England was now once again facing the familiar prospect of war on two fronts, against France and Scotland. In a change of tactics from the customary short sharp raids, aimed at inflicting the maximum damage before retreat, Henry's lieutenant in the north, Charles Brandon, Duke of Suffolk, was instructed to block any invasion of England by capturing and holding southern Scottish strongholds. Henry set out his stall in the Subsidy Act of 1543: he had demonstrated his just and historic title to the overlordship of Scotland – a title in no way prejudiced because kings of

England had, for a time, forborne from exercising it (see Conclusion). Thus, it followed, the Scots were his subjects, and their actions against him treasonable; he now intended to bring them to heel. Mary should indeed be married to Edward – but England would not be bound by the terms agreed at Greenwich. England and Scotland must be united, and under Henry's rule.

Internal rivalries in Scotland provided Henry with a new ally. In May, Lennox, jealous of Arran's authority, agreed to recognize Henry's overlordship; help him to capture various border fortresses; assist in promoting religious reform in Scotland; and ensure that Mary was not spirited away to another country. Although his subsequent flight to England put the latter two promises beyond his power, his claim to the Scottish succession made him a fit husband for Henry's niece, Margaret Douglas.

When Suffolk departed, to lead an English army to France, he was replaced by Edward Seymour, Earl of Hertford. Hertford considered that the proposed strategy of taking Scottish border strongholds did not pose a sufficient threat to a government based in Edinburgh. His alternative plan was now adopted. In May, Hertford led a scaled-up version of John Lord Howard's 1481 naval expedition (Chapter 4, Section ii), sailing for the Firth of Forth with an army of some 15,000 men. It was originally intended to capture and fortify the port of Leith, but in the light of the defection of Angus and Henry's other supporters, he was instructed simply to:

> burn Edinburgh town ... do what you can out of hand and without long tarrying, to beat down and overthrow the castle, sack Holyrood house, and as many towns and villages about Edinburgh as you may conveniently, sack Leith and burn and subvert it and all the rest, putting man, woman, and child to fire and sword without exception where any resistance shall be made.[5]

Scottish resistance was initially weak; Beaton and his forces fled, and Arran's army was defeated. Henry's programme was implemented, his ships burning towns and villages around the Firth. The English army marched back to Berwick a fortnight after it had set out, leaving a swathe of destruction in its wake. This was followed up by devastating border raids, which laid waste to much of Teviotdale and the Merse. Arran brought an 8,000-strong force to besiege Coldingham priory, which had been occupied by a small English garrison; but on the approach of a relieving force he abandoned his army, which promptly broke up. In September, Hertford led another large raid into Scotland, and by the end of the year, Thomas Wharton had captured several castles on the Scottish West March.

This success forced François to act to fulfil the terms of the Auld Alliance, and in 1545, he sent 3,500 soldiers to Scotland. Meanwhile, Henry's invasion strategy underwent a further development. In a move reminiscent of Edward IV's grant to his brother Richard in 1482, Henry made an open-ended grant to Sir William Eure, warden of the East March, and Sir Brian Laiton, captain of Norham, of all the Scottish lands they could take and hold. Fired by enthusiasm, the pair set off with a large force, only to be defeated by Angus at Ancrum Moor. The French now mounted a series of raids into England around Wark castle, and planned an invasion to follow. With more French support promised, Arran took sufficient heart to reject Henry's proffered negotiations, and the Scottish parliament approved a special tax to fund a force of 1,000 cavalry to guard the Merse and Teviotdale.

In January 1547, Henry VIII died, shortly after sealing a peace with France (the treaty of Camp). He was succeeded by the nine-year-old Edward VI. The appointment of Edward's maternal uncle, Hertford (now duke of Somerset), as Protector heralded a radical extension of the new approach to war with Scotland. Somerset had long argued that the traditional English methods – short raids across the border, and occasional deeper incursions into Scotland – had little lasting impact because the English always withdrew. Now it was in his power to implement a different strategy: establishing a permanent occupation of southern Scotland. Key to this was the large-scale expansion of Henry's policy of receiving Scots into the English allegiance, through assurance. A series of rapidly constructed strongholds would provide secure bases for further operations (see Chapter 8), while their garrisons fortified the assured Scots in their new loyalty.

In essence, Somerset's approach differed little from Edward I's strategy for conquering Scotland some 250 years before. However, Somerset accompanied his military campaign with a bid for the 'hearts and minds' of Scottish Protestants. The anti-heresy measures adopted by Arran's government exposed deep divisions in the country, which had erupted in the murder of Cardinal Beaton in May 1546, and the subsequent siege of his Protestant murderers in St Andrews castle. In place of English overlordship, Somerset now offered the Scots a vision of equal union with England within a 'Greater Britain', which he presented as the only hope for the survival of the reformed faith in Scotland (see Chapter 11, Section ii).[6]

In September, the first garrison was established in a new fortress at Eyemouth, up the coast from Berwick. Somerset now launched a two-pronged attack. The larger part of the English force, some 16,000 strong (including Spanish and Burgundian mercenaries, and accompanied by pioneers to construct the new forts), made its way up the east coast, supported by a fleet. As Somerset was anxious to gain Scottish support, the usual burning and ravaging was curtailed, though English tactics veered between persuasion and coercion. When Dunglass castle surrendered, its soldiers were allowed to disperse, and the town was spared. At Innerwick, however, the defenders resisted and were killed. Somerset then marched to meet up with the fleet, which was busily bombarding Leith. Arran and Huntly were encamped nearby, with an army over 30,000 strong, and the two forces clashed at Pinkie Cleugh. The English were initially taken by surprise, but naval bombardment and a cavalry charge slowed down the Scots long enough to allow the deployment of the artillery train, which fired with deadly effect on the close-packed Scottish formations. Hampered by religious and political divides, the Scottish army disintegrated and fled. Thousands were slaughtered, and Huntly was captured.[7]

Somerset was now able to proceed unhindered with the business of creating an English pale in eastern Scotland. Many East Lothian lairds had reformed beliefs, and quickly assured. English naval power established a series of forts along the east coast. The island of Inchcolm, which commanded the approach to Leith, was taken in September, and work immediately began on a fort, under Sir John Luttrell. Leith was burned, but no attempt was made to take Edinburgh. Instead, Sir Andrew Dudley was sent north, to receive the castle at Broughty Craig, near Dundee, from Patrick, Lord Gray, who had previously assured with Henry VIII after his capture at Solway Moss. The rest of the army marched back into the Scottish lowlands, where Home castle, recently modernized by French architects, was taken and garrisoned, and the ruins of Roxburgh were refortified. Somerset then returned to London, leaving William, Baron Grey of Wilton, as captain-general.

The second, smaller force was led by Wharton into Annandale, accompanied by Lennox, whose presence, it was hoped, would persuade the local population to assure. In accordance with Somerset's policy, Wharton punished those who resisted, and spared those who did not. He returned to England in October, hoping that the war could now be left to Scots in the English allegiance. Initially, this seemed a realistic prospect; Dumfries surrendered, and by mid-November, over 7,000 Scots had assured. In the south-west, at least, Somerset's plan of creating an English pale appeared to have been largely accomplished.

But winter 1547 was to prove a considerable ordeal for the English garrisons. Fortifications still under construction provided little shelter from the elements. Roads became impassable, food scarce, and men began to desert. Luttrell had difficulty extending his control from Inchcolm because he lacked ships. Further north, Dundee submitted to Dudley after being bombarded from the sea, but he was so short of ammunition that he was reduced to paying the town's inhabitants to return the shot he had fired at them. Meanwhile Patrick, Lord Gray, who was receiving large sums of money from the English, was also drawing pay from the Scottish Crown.

Arran's response to Somerset's invasion was to draw even closer into the embrace of the French. A small contingent of French troops arrived in December, along with funds to wage 10,000 Scots for a year. The price of French support was Mary's betrothal to the French Dauphin (the future François II), which would be formalized in the treaty of Haddington in July 1548. That January, Arran and his French allies re-took Dundee, and attacked Broughty. The English held out, but suffered increasing supply problems, which were only exacerbated by the arrival of reinforcements. Dundee was bombarded (again), and assured (again), but little lasting support was won among the local population. And the entire English war effort was hampered by a lack of resources. The fleet patrolling the North Sea to deter French reinforcements was disbanded in March, to save money. Pay was also becoming a serious problem; Spanish soldiers at Home, impatient for their arrears, plotted to murder their captain and sell the castle back to the Scots.

In February, Wharton led a raid on Douglas lands in Dumfriesshire, together with John Maxwell, warden of the Scottish West March. Maxwell had assured the previous November, after the family lands were ravaged, but when Angus ambushed the force at Drumlanrig, his men turned on their English fellows, who escaped only with great difficulty. The system of assurance in the region now broke down. Angus attacked those who remained loyal, and the isolated English garrisons were unable to protect them. By July, English control of the region was effectively at an end.

Meanwhile, in the east, work began on new fortifications at Haddington, intended to command Lothian with a 2,500-strong garrison – many of whom rapidly deserted, due to lack of pay. An army led by Grey devastated the area around Edinburgh, while Somerset also pressed him to act against those Scots who had reneged on their assurances. Somerset's policy was coming under increasing strain from the contradictory imperatives of deterring defections, avoiding the alienation of Scottish support, and the military necessity of ravaging the enemy.

That summer, with Mary's hand secured, and no English fleet to prevent him, André de Montalembert, Sire d'Ésse, landed in Scotland with an army of French, Italians and *Landsknechte*. However, his attack on Broughty, supported by a naval bombardment, was driven off by Luttrell (now in command of the fort); and when d'Ésse and Arran laid siege to Haddington, the two commanders quarrelled, and the Scots began to drift away. As on previous occasions, French troops aroused resentments in their Scottish hosts, causing tensions which would later erupt in rioting by Frenchmen and *Landsknechte* billeted in Edinburgh. According to an English prisoner, its citizens' response to a subsequent French defeat at Haddington was to 'rejoice as much of this overthrow as we do'.[8]

In June, Francis Talbot, Earl of Shrewsbury, was appointed lord lieutenant of the north, with orders to muster a new army to raise the siege of Haddington, establish a new fort on the coast, and engage the Scottish forces in battle. Before he could take up his post (and contrary to Somerset's instructions), Grey's forces attempted to relieve Haddington alone, but were defeated, leaving 700 slain or captured. Many of the losses were cavalry, further reducing the ability of the English to come to the aid of assured Scots. The appointment of Shrewsbury over Grey's head also caused tensions within the English command, exacerbated by the failure at Haddington. To Somerset's dismay, Shrewsbury made no move for some weeks, partly owing to the shortage of cavalry. Bowing to pressure, he crossed the border in August, with 13,200 men, including 2,000 recently arrived *Landsknechte*. Seriously outnumbered, d'Ésse retreated; Shrewsbury was able to reinforce Haddington unopposed, and to establish an ancillary fort at Dunglass (though this was of limited use, as it was too far from Haddington, and ill-suited for a harbour).

This was rather less than Somerset had hoped for. He had ordered Shrewsbury to destroy d'Ésse's forces, and deplored the enormous expense of maintaining such a large army for so long to achieve so little. Worse still, Mary had now departed for France and her future husband. The whole *raison d'être* of Somerset's campaign was gone: any hope of forcing the Scottish government to honour the treaty of Greenwich had sailed with Mary. In its stead, Somerset could only resort to the overlordship claim – which can only have further undermined support for the English.

Shrewsbury now departed, and Grey launched a series of devastating raids against lapsed assured Scots in Liddesdale and Teviotdale. Assurances continued to be agreed, but the English garrisons, penned in their strongholds, no longer had the power either to persuade or force the assured to abide by them. The Franco-Scottish forces were able to pick off English garrisons one by one, and to launch a series of destructive raids on Northumberland. A newly raised English fleet had more success, raiding Leith, keeping French ships at bay, and bringing desperately needed supplies to Broughty. But with winter approaching, the fleet sailed back home, leaving the fort as isolated as before. In January 1549, Somerset refused Luttrell's request for more light horse. Instead, he was to be left 'so few men as may be', and ordered to 'lie there as you were dead for the while ... and not intermeddle in any wise with any skirmish or attempt'[9] – a *de facto* acknowledgement that the garrison could no longer fulfil its purpose.

Events in England now began to distract Somerset's attention from the war. That January, a plot against him was uncovered, headed by his own brother; by July, he was confronting serious revolts against enclosure and his religious reforms. The most immediate consequence for the Anglo-Scottish conflict was that Grey was hastily summoned south to deal with the crisis (along with a number of his troops), and was replaced as warden by Henry Manners, Earl of Rutland, who took a force into Scotland to revictual Haddington. However, the garrison now proved too difficult and expensive to maintain, and in September, the fort was finally abandoned.

Indeed, Somerset was now facing financial disaster – the Scottish war had cost some £580,000, and Henri II of France had laid siege to Boulogne, so that England once again had to fund war on two fronts. By the time John Dudley, Earl of Warwick, seized control of the council at the end of 1549, it was obvious that England would have to come to terms with Scotland and France. In March 1550, an Anglo-French peace treaty was sealed at Boulogne, in which Scotland was included. Anglo-Scottish peace followed, embodied in the treaty of Norham of 1551, and, in accordance with its terms, all English garrisons in Scotland were withdrawn. The Anglo-Scottish war had been won by the French. And Somerset's grand dream of union was over.

iii. France Victorious, 1551–8

The majority of French troops withdrew from Scotland, but, at the request of the Scots, garrisons remained at Dunbar, Blackness, Broughty and Inchkeith castles. The Scottish queen remained in France, betrothed to the Dauphin and under the control of her future father-in-law. Under the treaty of Haddington, Scotland had become a *de facto* protectorate of France, and its government increasingly subordinate to French interests. Henri II had undertaken to 'maintain and defend this realm [i.e., Scotland] and the lieges thereof as the same as he does for the realm of France'[10]; the Scottish council addressed him as 'the sure and only defender and relief, under God, of all this realm'[11]; and he rebuked the governor, Arran, for making peace overtures to the Emperor without informing him. In December 1553, Henri proclaimed the majority of the eleven-year-old Mary. The following year, Arran resigned his governorship (being compensated with the French duchy of Châtelherault) and Scotland had a new regent: the queen mother, Marie de Guise, whose family dominated French politics.[12]

There was little prospect of any English-sponsored alternative to the French-dominated regime. The connection established by Somerset between pro-Englishness and Protestantism was terminated with the succession of the Catholic Mary Tudor to the English throne. And Mary, preoccupied with the task of returning England to the Catholic fold, did not seriously pursue schemes against Marie's regime, such as a putative plot to put the exiled Lennox on the Scottish throne. Once again, it was Hapsburg–Valois conflict that threatened the Anglo-Scottish peace. In January 1552, just two weeks after it was sealed, the peace treaty between Scotland and the Empire was threatened by Henri II's declaration of war against the Emperor. In November, the Scottish council ordered troops to be raised to go to France, with those who did not contribute men being taxed. With Mary Tudor's marriage to Philip, King of Spain, and the Emperor's heir, Anglo-Scottish relations were inevitably subsumed into the rivalry between the houses of Hapsburg and Valois. Henri offered support to the Wyatt conspiracy against Mary, and the Anglo-Scottish border proved a fertile ground for plots against her regime throughout 1554. The French ambassador was instructed to work with Marie in preparing Scotland to resume its traditional function within the Auld Alliance – splitting the English war effort. Marie began to fortify Edinburgh castle, and the following year she initiated a wider programme of repair and refortification of key Scottish strongholds. A rumour that a Spanish force was being sent to Berwick stepped up Henri's commitment, and by the end of February 1555 he had sent 3,000 troops to Scotland. Across the border, defensive preparations were also being made: Berwick, Wark and Norham were fortified and victualled, and the men of the Marches put on an hour's warning.

Marie had a clear mission: Scottish policy must be determined by French interests, up to and including engaging in war against England. However, the council had begun to drag its feet. French troops were so unpopular with their Scottish hosts that by June it was necessary to pass an Act to deal with the 'murmurs and slanders' of 'diverse seditious persons' regarding 'the most Christian King of France's subjects sent into this realm for the commonwealth and suppressing of the old enemies'.[13] Widespread resentment was caused by Marie's financial exactions, which included a tax of £60,000 for the queen's marriage, another of £48,000 to pay soldiers' wages, and, most unpopular of all, a proposed perpetual tax to fund her refortification programme. Scottish fears of an Empire-backed English invasion were sufficient to enable Marie to secure a parliamentary undertaking to support Henri – but only in the event of such an invasion.

In February 1556, Henri and the Emperor sealed a five-year truce, and most of the French troops in Scotland were recalled. But by January 1557, Henri was at war with Philip of Spain, king-consort of England, whose wife duly declared war on France in June. However, neither Mary Tudor nor the Scottish council wished to reignite Anglo-Scottish conflict. In April, Marie sent a list of border grievances to Mary, and a meeting of border commissioners was arranged in June. In order to dissuade the Scots from entering into the Hapsburg–Valois conflict, Mary offered £3,000 in damages. However, the earl of Westmorland's cynical observation that the negotiations were pointless ('we having broken with France, and you being French for your lives')[14] summed up English suspicions: Marie was simply playing for time to prepare Scotland for war.

The meeting broke up without any agreement having been reached, but a joint declaration of peace was issued until it reconvened in September. However, on the Scots' side, at any rate, this was disingenuous. Marie launched a series of small-scale raids across the border, and during August and September incursions took place on an almost daily basis. She proclaimed a general muster at Edinburgh, to be taken by Châtelherault, as lieutenant-general of Scotland. She also refortified Eyemouth, a convenient base for attacking Berwick, Wark or Norham, which had been dismantled in accordance with the treaty of Norham. To English eyes, a further provocation was offered when Archibald Campbell, Master of Argyll, led an army of redshanks and galloglasses (mercenaries from the West Highlands and Isles) to Ireland, against Manus O'Donnell of Tyrconnell. As O'Donnell held Tyrconnell of the English Crown, this amounted to an invasion of English territory, and Mary Tudor was convinced that Marie had countenanced it.[15] English suspicions of Scottish aggression seemed justified when a Scottish army marched on the border that autumn. But the Scottish nobility balked.

Increasingly resentful of French interference, and resisting a quarrel which was not in Scotland's interests, they refused to lead the army into England. However, this did little to dispel English disquiet; after Calais fell in January 1558, Mary feared that the French would use Scotland as a platform to launch an invasion of Ireland.

That spring, Scotland was bound even closer to France with the celebration of Mary Stewart's marriage to the Dauphin. In November, the Scottish parliament agreed that she might confer the crown matrimonial upon her new husband, although he was denied the customary right to succeed his wife. However, Mary had not only pledged her kingdom to her father-in-law for the money he had expended on its defence, but had secretly agreed to bequeath her crown to him, should she die without issue. Scotland's fate as a French satellite appeared to be sealed.

iv. Turning Point? 1558–60

The year 1558 saw the easing of the strains imposed by the Hapsburg–Valois conflict upon Anglo-Scottish relations. In October, France and Spain sealed a truce, followed by the peace of Cateau Cambrésis in spring 1559, in which England and Scotland were comprehended. Mary Tudor's death in November 1558 had broken the strongest link between England and the Empire. However, France refused to recognize Mary's successor, the Protestant Elizabeth I. Mary Stewart and François assumed the title of king and queen of England, and Elizabeth's none-too-secure regime feared a French attack in pursuit of this claim.

The end of the war with Spain had another consequence: Henri II was now free to turn his attention to such domestic issues as rooting out Protestantism. And, as ever, Marie adopted French policies in Scotland, abandoning her former tolerance of the reform movement. In May 1560, Perth became the centre of a rebellion by a Protestant party calling itself the 'Congregation'. In June, the rebels were joined by the earl of Argyll and Lord James Stewart, James V's illegitimate son. The Congregation claimed that their queen's marriage had imperilled Scottish independence, thus linking Protestant reform with the preservation of national sovereignty, and the Catholic government with French domination. The death of Henri the following month tied the French and Scottish administrations even more tightly together, for now François and Mary ruled France, as well as Scotland. In August and September they sent 1,800 French troops to support Marie against the Congregation. Argyll claimed that the French were:

coming in and setting down in this realm to occupy it and to put forth the inhabitants thereof, and ... to occupy all other men's rooms, piece and piece, and to put away the blood of the nobility.[16]

The Congregation now began to discuss deposing Mary and François. With Elizabeth's succession in England, Scottish Protestants could once again count a co-religionist Auld Enemy as a natural supporter against a regime dominated by the Catholic Auld Ally. In August, they wrote to Elizabeth's Secretary of State, William Cecil, suggesting that, in return for English aid for their cause, God might be pleased to transfer the rule of Scotland to Elizabeth.

It was perhaps inevitable that the Congregation should ask aid of England. It was not quite so inevitable that they would receive it. Certainly, Cecil saw Mary's claim to the English throne and French domination of Scotland as a real danger to Elizabeth and her regime. For him, a Protestant administration in Scotland, and the 'perpetuity of a brotherly and national friendship' in an Anglo-Scottish Protestant league, was England's best defence against the threat from Catholic Europe (now magnified by the end of the Hapsburg–Valois conflict, and the Counter-Reformation). Elizabeth, however, was reluctant to countenance the rebellion of subjects against their lawful monarch. In order to overcome these scruples, Cecil revived the overlordship claim. England's 'just and unfeigned title' meant that Elizabeth would not be aiding rebels against their lawful monarch, but rather acting as a 'superior king' in support of her people against an 'inferior king alone joining with strangers' (the French).[17] Elizabeth was sufficiently persuaded to send a modest £3,000 to the Congregation.

In September, Châtelherault joined the Congregation, along with his son, the earl of Arran, who had recently escaped from France and espoused the reformed faith. Their immediate aim was not, in fact, to depose Mary and François, but to put an end to Marie's regency. When she ignored their demands to resign her office and surrender Leith, where she had established herself, they dismissed her in the names of Mary and François. At the end of December, Marie's forces occupied Stirling, and Châtelherault wrote to the royal couple, offering to return to his allegiance to Marie. With the tide turning in Marie's favour, Elizabeth was finally moved to respond to the appeals the Congregation had addressed to her in November. In January 1560, an English fleet was sent north, ostensibly to deal with piracy, but in fact to cut off communications between Leith and France. Meanwhile, the duke of Norfolk, lieutenant of the north, began negotiations with Châtelherault and the Congregation. Elizabeth wanted the French expelled from Scotland, and a pro-English Protestant regime installed, but without challenging Mary and François' sovereignty.

In February, Elizabeth sealed the treaty of Berwick with Châtelherault. Its architects (Cecil, Robert Dudley, Argyll, Lord Stewart, and William Maitland of Lethington) saw it as the beginning of a new relationship between England and Scotland, for the 'joint and due preservation of both these kingdoms, thus contained in one isle as in a little world by itself'.[18] The treaty limited English intervention to preserving the Scots in their 'old freedom and liberties'; provided these liberties were not infringed, the Congregation undertook not to withdraw their allegiance from their lawful sovereigns, Mary and François. And Argyll undertook to 'employ his force and goodwill ... to reduce the north parts of Ireland to the perfect obedience of England'.[19] When, at the end of March, an English army once more crossed the border, this was a very different invasion – for, unlike her predecessors, Elizabeth required no recognition of overlordship, and was not interested in conquest. Her goal was solely to ensure the success of her favoured faction in the struggle to control Scottish government.

Marie utterly declined to negotiate with Châtelherault and the lords of the Congregation unless they returned unconditionally to their obedience to her. The English troops duly laid siege to Leith, but its French defenders held out. However, military intervention in Scotland had ceased to be a priority in France, where the Guise faced mounting domestic opposition. That summer, the English and French met at Newcastle and Berwick to settle Scotland's affairs between them, a task facilitated by Marie's death in June. The Anglo-French treaty of Edinburgh, sealed in July, stipulated that all English troops in Scotland, and all but 120 French troops, should leave the country. A series of 'Concessions' provided that Scotland should be governed by a council, selected partly by parliament, and partly by Mary and François. And the royal couple would abandon their use of the English coat of arms, thus implicitly recognizing Elizabeth as queen of England. That August, the Scottish parliament accepted a reformed Confession of Faith, and renounced papal authority. England and Scotland were now linked by a shared faith, and February's treaty of Berwick offered 'these two nations joined in one island', once 'stirred up ... by the craft of Satan to shed one another's blood', a blueprint for a future relationship of 'mutual reciprocal love and benevolence'.[20]

Chapter 7: Better Together? 1561–1603

In December 1560, François II, King of France, and husband of Mary, Queen of Scots, died. He was succeeded by his brother, Charles, and Mary returned to her native land. The Franco-Scottish bond was broken, the spectre of Catholicism and French dominance exorcized – and the Congregation promptly split into two parties. The earl of Arran and his followers favoured coercing Mary into the reformed faith and marriage with him, a policy supported by the Protestant Elizabeth I of England. A more moderate party, led by the ecclesiastically conservative George Gordon, fourth earl of Huntly, doubted the legality of thus constraining their sovereign. Both sides, however, wished to preserve the recent reforming legislation, and favoured friendship with England. Neither wished Mary to return home at the head of a French contingent. And all were agreed on rejecting French proposals for a renewal of the Auld Alliance.

The return of the Catholic Mary, in August 1561, had the potential to disrupt the new Anglo-Scottish understanding, based as it was on a common Protestant identity.[1] However, although Mary continued to observe Catholic rites in private, she made no attempt to overturn the reformation settlement, forbidding any alteration to the form of religion 'public and universally standing',[2] and eschewing the Council of Trent which launched the Counter-Reformation. She did not favour religious conservatives in her government and retained the Anglophiles Lord James Stewart (her half-brother), and William Maitland as her chief ministers. Elizabeth's secretary, William Cecil, concluded that Mary was 'no more devout towards Rome than for the contenting of her [Guise] uncles'.[3]

Of more immediate importance was the Stewart claim to the English throne, an issue which was to dominate Anglo-Scottish relations throughout

Elizabeth's reign. Elizabeth hoped to secure Mary's ratification of the treaty of Edinburgh, which relinquished her claim to be queen of England in Elizabeth's place; and Mary sought recognition as Elizabeth's heir. This was the principal obstacle to the new Anglo-Scottish amity forged by those who had devised the treaty of Berwick: Lord James Stewart and Maitland on the Scottish side, and Cecil, and Robert Dudley on the English side. That September a compromise was proposed: Mary would renounce her claim to the English throne during Elizabeth's lifetime in exchange for recognition as heir apparent. Elizabeth refused. Acknowledgement of her Catholic cousin's claim would create an instant focus for rebellion for those of Elizabeth's subjects who opposed her Protestant reforms, while it would be anathema to many who supported them. Her council feared the influence of Mary's Guise relatives, a suspicion not allayed by Scotland's studied neutrality towards the wars in France between the Catholic Guise faction and English-backed Huguenots. Opposition to Mary's claim coalesced around an English, Protestant candidate, Catherine Grey, granddaughter of Henry VIII's younger sister.

None of this prevented Elizabeth from attempting to use the succession question to manipulate Scottish politics. In 1563, proposals that Mary should marry either Archduke Charles of Austria (Cardinal Guise's suggestion), or Don Carlos, Philip II of Spain's heir, prompted a quick response. Having no wish to see Scotland succumb once again to marital dominance by a Catholic power, Elizabeth urged Mary to consider the Anglo-Scottish amity. Marriage to a Hapsburg, Valois, or any candidate of the cardinal's, would be regarded as a hostile act. However, if Mary favoured an English-approved suitor, the reward could be recognition of her claim. In March 1564, Elizabeth named her own candidate: Robert Dudley, created earl of Leicester later that year. However, negotiations ran aground over Mary's insistence on having her succession confirmed by statute, a condition which Elizabeth absolutely refused. In March 1565, Mary was flatly informed that no decision would be taken on the matter until Elizabeth had either married, or publicly determined never to do so.

Any hope of an understanding with England ended that July with Mary's marriage, by Catholic rites, to Henry Stewart, Lord Darnley (like Mary, a grandchild of Margaret Tudor). Elizabeth had permitted Darnley to follow his father, the earl of Lennox, to Scotland, after the latter's rehabilitation in 1564; however, she most certainly did not approve a marriage which joined Mary's claim to the English throne with Darnley's. The rise of the Lennoxes also threatened the existing

Scottish regime. James, Lord Stewart (now earl of Moray) and Maitland were regarded as key elements in a government sympathetic to England. Elizabeth may also have shared the fears of Moray and the earl of Argyll for the future of Scottish Protestantism under a king-consort whose religious allegiance was suspect.

Argyll and Moray now united with Châtelherault (Mary's heir presumptive) in an attempt to force Mary to repudiate her marriage. After ignoring repeated summonses to appear before the council, they were proclaimed outlaws. As the rebels gathered at Ayr, Mary mustered her army, but Moray successfully eluded her, while waiting for English aid (the affair was hence christened the 'Chaseabout Raid'). In June, before the marriage took place, Elizabeth had promised support for their cause, and had even sent money. But at the end of September, the news came that Elizabeth had countermanded her order to send troops across the border; when it came to the point, she refused to aid an outright rebellion of subjects against their anointed monarch. She also feared that sending English troops into Scotland might trigger an intervention by France or Spain on Mary's behalf. Moray fled to England; Châtelherault was exiled; and Moray and Argyll were summoned to face trial the following March.

A conciliatory attitude towards Protestantism had availed Mary little, either at home or in negotiations with England. The leading lights of the Scottish Reformation had staged a rebellion against her, and Elizabeth's involvement was undeniable. Mary now turned to Catholicism, releasing and restoring the Catholic George Gordon as fifth earl of Huntly, and announcing forthcoming legislation in favour of the old faith. She also appealed to Rome and to Philip II of Spain for money and military support in the name of its defence. Her petitions went unheeded, and merely served to lose her support among the more moderate Scottish nobles. Further resentment was created by a perceived neglect of the counsel of Scottish lords in favour of 'strangers, as have neither judgment nor experience of the ancient laws and governance of this realm',[4] in particular one David Rizzio, her Italian secretary for French affairs.

In spring 1566, the 'Chaseabout' rebels made common cause with others alienated by Mary. These included James Douglas, Earl of Morton, and Darnley himself, resentful of Rizzio's supposed influence over Mary, and her refusal to grant him the crown matrimonial. That March, Morton and his confederates had Rizzio killed in the presence of their six-months'-pregnant queen. Mary acted swiftly to divide the conspirators, condemning Morton and the other murderers, who fled across the border, but pardoning the 'Chaseabout' rebels and her husband. However, by September, she was debating how to end her marriage without casting doubt on her son's legitimacy. In February 1567, Darnley was murdered, and Mary was suspected of complicity, following her marriage shortly afterwards to the earl of Bothwell (popularly cast as 'First Murderer'). In June, Mary and Bothwell's forces were defeated at Carberry Hill by a faction of the Scottish nobility led by Moray, sworn to dissolve the marriage and bring Darnley's murderers to justice. Mary was imprisoned, and forced to abdicate in favour of her baby son (now crowned James VI) and to recognize Moray as his regent.

Mary's deposition had not originally been on the agenda of her opponents, and when she escaped in May 1568, she quickly gathered support. But following defeat in battle, she made the cardinal error of fleeing to England. As Moray's prisoner, Mary had received a measure of support from Elizabeth, who attempted to negotiate her release and refused to recognize Moray's regime. Mary hoped this would now translate into English aid for her restoration. But possession of the woman regarded by many Scots as their queen was a trump card which Elizabeth was bound to play in the English interest. She was now in a stronger position to influence Scottish politics than any English monarch since Henry V.

However, Elizabeth faced a serious dilemma. Mary's party was associated with Catholicism, although Argyll, ardent Protestant and sometime leader of the Congregation, stood alongside the Catholic Huntly as one of its leaders. Cecil feared that if Mary remained an English captive, her supporters might join forces with her Guise relatives and English Catholics to mount a rescue, regain control in Scotland, and revive the Auld Alliance. Furthermore, Argyll now threatened to use his considerable influence in Ireland to bear against the English administration there. Equally, however, an English restoration of Mary would put an end to the power of Moray, that stalwart of Anglo-Scottish Protestant amity, whom Cecil regarded as vital to his 'British alliance' against Catholic Europe. The ideal solution would be the restoration of Mary, accompanied by a guarantee of a friendly co-religionist regime in Scotland.[5]

In June 1568, Elizabeth made an offer to Mary to work for her restoration – on condition that she and Moray would submit to her judgement. Meanwhile, Cecil was working on a proposal to restore Mary to rule jointly with her son, on terms which accorded Elizabeth the role of 'umpire and principal arbiter' in Scotland,[6] an implicit recognition of her overlordship (Chapter 11, Section ii). The religious settlement of 1560 was to remain in place, and the treaty of Edinburgh to be ratified. The new regime would renounce the Auld Alliance for good and agree not to receive English rebels or fugitives. And, crucially, Mary was to rule under the supervision of a Scottish council and parliament which had the ultimate right of appeal to Elizabeth. If Mary supported any act of hostility against Elizabeth, she would not only forfeit her claim to the English crown, but would be deposed in Scotland. These conditions were to be enshrined in a tripartite treaty, to be signed by James, Mary and Elizabeth. English commissioners took this proposal to Moray in the autumn, but Cecil was also offering an alternative deal: should Elizabeth find Mary guilty of Darnley's murder, then England would endorse his regency and Mary would remain a prisoner.

By agreeing to submit their cases to Elizabeth, both Mary (arguably Queen of Scotland) and Moray (arguably King James's regent) accepted the authority of the queen of England to pass judgement upon them. Neither had much choice, for Mary's restoration was in Elizabeth's hands: Mary had to sue for it; and Moray to persuade Elizabeth against it, and to recognize James, and Moray's own administration, instead. The 'trial' took place in three stages: at York in October, Hampton Court in November, and Westminster in December. In January 1569, Elizabeth delivered her verdict: she had found nothing in prejudice of either party. In fact, her options were limited, for a judgement against Mary would have left her with the dilemma of what to do with an anointed monarch found guilty of murder, and driven the queen's party into the arms of France or Spain. Moray and his adherents left England 'in the same estate in the which they were of before they came',[7] but in possession of a loan of £5,000, which implied at least a measure of recognition for his administration, as did the limited military aid which Elizabeth also supplied.

Meanwhile, Elizabeth was facing resistance to her own religious reforms, which came to a head in November in the Northern Rising.[8] Charles Neville, Earl of Westmorland, and Thomas Percy, Earl of Northumberland, plotted to replace Elizabeth with Mary, who was to be married to Elizabeth's cousin, Thomas Howard, Duke of Norfolk. Moray proved himself a staunch ally to Elizabeth, proclaiming confederation with the English rebels a treasonable offence, and offering her 10,000 troops to aid the suppression of the rising. When their enterprise failed, Westmorland and his supporters found shelter with members of the queen's party; Northumberland, however, was arrested by Moray, who offered to hand him over to Elizabeth, in return for a guarantee of his regime and financial assistance. But in January 1570, Moray was assassinated, and another Catholic rebellion erupted in northern England. Its leader, Leonard Dacre, recruited a good part of his force from the Scottish borders, and when he, too, was defeated, he was also received by the queen's party.

Elizabeth needed to secure an Anglophile Protestant regime in Scotland, which would not ally itself with Catholic France and Spain. She regarded Mary as the principal cause of the rising, and her party's aid for English Catholic rebels confirmed that it was against Elizabeth's interests for them to triumph. But with Moray's assassination, the queen's party began to gain the upper hand; in April, they entered Edinburgh, and Argyll and Huntly moved on to besiege Glasgow castle. Elizabeth now determined on military intervention. In March, English troops were sent to aid the king's party's siege of Dumbarton castle, while the earl of Sussex marched on the Clyde valley to capture English rebels and destroy the castles of those who had supported them. In May, an English contingent escorted Elizabeth's chosen regent, the earl of Lennox (James's paternal grandfather), to Edinburgh. Elizabeth withdrew her troops in deference to French protests that their presence in Scotland contravened the treaty of Edinburgh (Chapter 6, Section iv); but they remained poised on the border until Lennox's appointment in July. As in 1560, this English army did not aim at conquest. Elizabeth's Anglo-imperialism was exercised through the manipulation of Scottish factionalism to secure a tractable regime, a time-honoured political strategy which Scottish divisions now enabled her to achieve.

In the face of such a robust response, the queen's party now attempted to conciliate Elizabeth, expressing their desire for the continuation of Anglo-Scottish peace. The English Catholic rebels were packed off to the Netherlands, and a final appeal was made to Elizabeth for Mary's restoration. Elizabeth responded with another proposal for joint rule by Mary and James, subject to an administrative set-up giving England a permanent hold over Scottish affairs. In September 1570, she orchestrated a six-months truce between the two parties, but no agreement was reached, and civil war resumed the following spring.

One thing had changed, however, and that was the mind of the earl of Argyll. Despairing of Mary's release, he became convinced that support for her cause divided and weakened Scotland, leaving it subject to

English interference. His queen's restoration at the hands of France or Spain was hardly preferable, as this would only leave Scotland subject to another power. In August, Argyll and others submitted to Lennox, as James's regent. The following month, Lennox was mortally wounded in a raid led by Huntly, the remaining leader of the queen's party. But Mary's star was sinking. Following the discovery of the Ridolfi plot, which envisaged a Spanish invasion of England and Scotland in Mary's favour, Elizabeth swore she would never again negotiate with her. The plot also alienated Catherine de Medici, regent of France, who renounced her support for Mary's restoration; and in April 1572, the Anglo-French treaty of Blois provided for the English pacification of Scotland. By February 1573, Huntly, too, was reconciled to James's rule, and to the regime of Lennox's successor, Morton, another English-approved appointment. This left only a small, stubborn remnant of the queen's party holding out in Edinburgh castle. Secure from French interference, Elizabeth sent 1,000 English troops and a siege battery to help Morton to mop them up. Having agreed that neither side would grant terms without the other's consent, English and Scottish troops co-operated in taking Edinburgh castle at the end of May. The Scottish civil war concluded with a securely pro-English regency government established in Scotland.

Elizabeth had achieved her goal. However, this satisfactory state of affairs could prevail only as long as Morton's regime. In 1578, the regent was relieved of his office, ultimately to be executed for complicity in Darnley's murder. As the twelve-year-old James began his personal rule, the tune of Anglo-Scottish relations would to a large extent be called by his new administration. The chief influence over James proved to be his French cousin, Esmé Stuart, Sire d'Aubigny, whom James created first earl, and then duke of Lennox. This abrupt termination of a regency (and regent) favourable to England was not regarded with equanimity by Elizabeth. She raged against 'that false Scots urchin',[9] vowing that James must choose between the friendship of the queen of England and that of the duke of Lennox. In 1580 and 1581, English ambassadors were instructed to covertly foster opposition to Lennox; and Elizabeth went to the extent of mustering a force on the borders, although this was disbanded without crossing into Scotland. She encouraged Archibald Douglas, Earl of Angus, to plot against the duke, and received him in England when he failed. Elizabeth also approved a palace *coup* in August 1582, led by William Ruthven, Earl of Gowrie, which proved rather more successful, as Gowrie managed to seize the king, and with him control of the government. Gowrie proposed a new Anglo-Scottish understanding, for which Elizabeth was prepared to make a payment of £2,500. While modest compared to Gowrie's original proposal (£10,000 up front, a £5,000 annuity, and the Lennox lands in England for James), it clearly indicated English support for the new regime.

Governments reliant upon possession of a reluctant king tended to have a short lifespan. In June 1583, James escaped. Elizabeth's support for the faction which had imprisoned him caused him to regard England with an unfriendly eye. Shortly afterwards, he was in touch with his cousin, Henry, Duke of Guise, promising to work against Elizabeth, and for his mother's freedom. In 1584, he wrote once more to Guise and also to the pope. Elizabeth, alarmed by rumours that James was in the hands of 'favourers' of his mother, and of the French, went on the offensive.[10] She encouraged a conspiracy against James's new chief minister, James Stewart, Earl of Arran, by Angus and others, who seized Stirling castle in April 1584. However, as before, she drew the line at offering material support to rebels against a fellow monarch, and when James mustered a force against them, Angus and his fellows fled to England.

The personal relationship between Elizabeth and James did not, thus far, augur well for Anglo-Scottish amity. However, the 1580s and 1590s saw the beginnings of more amicable relations – albeit frequently subject to strains. In 1584, in response to James's request that she expel Angus and his fellow rebels, Elizabeth ordered them to leave Newcastle for the south of England, where they could not work against his government. Negotiations for an Anglo-Scottish alliance finally flowered in the amity sealed in July 1585, and bore fruit in the treaty of Berwick of 1586. James's primary motivation was to secure the English succession; for Elizabeth, Scotland was a 'back door' to be locked against potential invaders, for England was the richest and largest Protestant country, and thus the target of an increasingly militant Counter-Reformation. The Scots came to the table requesting recognition of James as Elizabeth's successor, an English title and lands for him, and mutual naturalization of English and Scottish subjects. Elizabeth conceded none of this, but agreed to pay James an annual subsidy. Nor would she commit herself, in the treaty, to any statement about the succession; in a separate letter, she promised not to allow any claim James *might* have to be undermined, unless provoked by 'manifest ingratitude'.[11] Each realm agreed to render the other carefully specified aid in case of invasion.[12]

A scant few months after it was sealed, the amity faced its first test. In February 1587, Mary Stewart was executed for her involvement in the Babington plot, which aimed, once again, at putting her on the English throne.[13] This touched both James's dynastic honour and his sovereignty. Mary was his subject as well as his mother, and her trial and execution implied an overlordship which the Scottish Crown had been resisting for centuries. Factions at his court howled for revenge. Scottish border lords launched raids into England, and Elizabeth instructed the earl of Huntingdon, hastily appointed lieutenant-general of the North, to retaliate. James sent an envoy to France to discuss the renewal of the Auld Alliance, and to Denmark, to ask for aid against England, while he attempted to strike a bargain with Elizabeth: his acquiescence for recognition as her heir. This was the more pressing because Mary had been found guilty of treason against Elizabeth, and under the terms of the 1585 Act of Association, had thus not only forfeited her own claim but imperilled James's.[14] Elizabeth, however, conceded nothing, warning that if James intrigued with foreign nations against England he would indeed lose 'his expectation'.[15] James's appeals abroad met with no success, nor had he the resources to fight England alone, and so, in spring 1588, he began to make conciliatory noises. By the summer, normal diplomatic relations had resumed, and Elizabeth reassured James that his claim had not been prejudiced by his mother's actions.

A further strain was imposed by the resurgence of a 'Catholic' party in Scotland, led by James's favourite, George Gordon, sixth earl of Huntly.[16] In fact, Huntly's faction was defined primarily by opposition to the unpopular secretary and later chancellor, John Maitland. Nevertheless, in May 1586, Huntly wrote to Philip II of Spain, requesting military aid for the restoration of Catholicism in Scotland, through the release of James from 'the power of his enemies', into which he had fallen 'by the intrigues of his insidious sister, the queen of England'.[17] It was unlikely that Philip would commit himself to this extent, but he might be milked for money to support a Catholic faction in Scotland. Elizabeth was committed to supporting the Protestant rebellion against Philip in the Netherlands, and her alliance with Catholic France was insecure.

In 1588, the Spanish Armada demonstrated the seriousness of the Counter-Reformation threat, and from then on, Elizabeth viewed all Catholic leanings, and any contacts with Spain, as a threat. In 1589, she intercepted letters from Huntly and his confederates to Philip's governor of the Netherlands. These regretted the failure of the Armada, which they had been 'awaiting ... with forces sufficient ... to aid it against its enemies', and projected a joint invasion of England, with a contingent to be launched from Scotland, 'who will serve you no less faithfully than your natural subjects'.[18] In 1592, George Kerr, a Catholic embarking for Spain from Scotland, was discovered to be in possession of blank papers signed by Huntly and others; he confessed that it was part of a plot whereby they were to aid Philip to invade Scotland.

James treated the conspirators with a degree of leniency which baffled and infuriated Elizabeth ('Methinks I do but dream: no king a week would bear this').[19] But James was not motivated by mere partiality in maintaining Huntly and his faction. He saw himself as a 'general Christian king', a 'universal king';[20] by maintaining a balance between two factions, he limited the power of both – and thus safeguarded his own position. The continued existence of Huntly's faction also allowed James to present himself to Elizabeth as England's only bulwark against that bogeyman: a Catholic Scotland in league with Spain. As such, he might hope to gain further concessions regarding his pension and the succession.

In fact, Elizabeth responded by reducing James's pension and returning to her pre-amity policies of intervention in Scottish politics. She covertly supported the rebel earl of Bothwell, now haunting the English Marches, who should have been handed over to James in accordance with the treaty of Berwick (1586). In January 1593, James declared that if Elizabeth continued to abet Bothwell he would break the amity. Elizabeth made secret contact with 'well-affected' Scottish Protestant lords, hoping to create a faction opposing the Catholic earls; and by the end of the year, she had begun to negotiate with Bothwell to drive them into exile (though carefully stipulating that James should not be harmed). In January 1594, Elizabeth warned James in no uncertain terms that any conspiracy with Huntly and his party against her would imperil his claim to the English throne. James responded by demanding a public apology. Each expressed doubts that the amity could survive this new low in relations, and James began to make overtures to Henri IV of France. Both sides, however, stood to lose too much by abandoning the amity. That April, James wrote in conciliatory terms to Elizabeth, who responded immediately. This rapprochement was aided by Bothwell's subsequent joining with Huntly and his Catholic confederates, an association which caused James and Elizabeth to lose confidence in their respective protégés. In 1595, after Huntly attacked

Aberdeen in order to rescue his imprisoned Jesuit uncle, he was exiled along with Bothwell.

As the century drew to a close, James became increasingly impatient to secure the English succession.[21] He was not Elizabeth's only potential heir. Indeed, Henry VIII's Act of Succession had barred Margaret Tudor's line from inheriting the English throne; according to its terms, Edward Seymour, great-grandson of Henry's younger sister Mary, was the next in line. Admittedly, Seymour's claim was invalidated by bastardy, for the marriage of his parents, Lady Catherine Grey and the earl of Hertford, had been annulled. However, it would have been possible to overturn this; indeed, when Elizabeth took the throne she was herself technically illegitimate. In the face of Elizabeth's refusal to recognize his claim, James began to take steps of his own. He created his own network of supporters within England, addressing them as their future monarch; and he threatened to use force to gain recognition of his claim. In 1594, angered by Elizabeth's support for Bothwell, James cultivated a mutual understanding with her favourite, the earl of Essex. Essex was the rival of William Cecil, Lord Burghley, and his son Robert, whom James suspected of authoring the pro-Bothwell policy, and favouring Seymour's claim. James's network expanded to include English Catholics at home and abroad. In November 1599, he had his nobles swear an oath to help him pursue the throne of England, and that December, and in the following June, sought taxation to pay for an army to pursue this end.

In 1601, Essex, who had become increasingly alienated from Elizabeth over foreign policy, was executed for treason, for attempting to orchestrate a rising. If James was not privy to the plot, it seems likely the earl had designated him a part in it; two of the conspirators confessed to a plan that James should raise an army, hold it on the border, and send an embassy to England to demand recognition of his title. In early February 1601, James was indeed planning to send the Earl of Mar and Edward Bruce to put his grievances to Elizabeth; and they were, in fact, also instructed to contact Essex privately. With Essex's removal from the picture, Mar and Bruce were instructed to sound out James's 'friends' and assure them that, if they wanted him to act as their head, he would be 'as willing and ready to supply that place as they can be to desire me, only with that old reservation of the safety of the Queen's person'. If his friends were beyond help, the ambassadors were to 'use then all the means ye can to get me a party there'.[22]

In this last point, Mar and Bruce were notably successful, for they managed to reach an agreement with Robert Cecil, Elizabeth's Principal

Secretary, who began a secret correspondence with their master. James initially rebuked Cecil for having risked 'some hazards to the fortunes of both the princes [i.e. James and Elizabeth]', through his tardiness in recognizing his claim (indeed Cecil himself had confessed as much).[23] However, mutual confidence was soon established. As Elizabeth lay dying, Cecil drafted the proclamation naming James her successor, which he then sent to him for approval. On 24 March 1603, James's long wait finally came to an end: Elizabeth died. Seymour's claim received little support and was ignored by the privy council, who wrote straightaway to James, offering him the throne. James accepted, thanked the English councillors on Elizabeth's behalf for their loyal service, confirmed them in their offices, and, finally, bade them thank God for the blessing which was about to come among them.

Part 2

Chapter 8: Armies and Warfare

In 1364, during peace negotiations with England, a memorandum was composed in Scotland rehearsing the arguments for and against the proposal to make Edward III the heir of David II. Amongst the arguments in favour was the following:

> We [i.e., the Scots] are so feeble in power and strength that we are quite unable to resist [the English] in battle ... our nobles are rendered so senseless and almost lifeless as a result of the various battles, in which so many have fallen against the English, the enemy are so stout-hearted, our folk none or few, young and untrained, but the others are wise and experienced in war, that we can resist them in neither power nor war.[1]

This pessimistic assessment of Scotland's military capacity was made in the wake of a series of catastrophic defeats on the battlefields of Dupplin Moor (1332), Halidon Hill (1333) and Neville's Cross (1346), which had seen the Scottish nobility decimated, and David led away to captivity in the Tower of London.

Medieval military doctrine held that battles should be avoided whenever possible, because they were too risky. Under the leadership of Edward III, however, English armies became the most feared in Western Christendom; and although their reputation subsequently declined, the English remained eager to bring the Scots to battle throughout the period, confident that they had an advantage in equipment and tactics, and so were likely to win. As the 1364 memorandum indicates, this was a belief which the Scots had, in some degree, come to share; indeed, in 1482, James III was arrested by his own nobles to prevent him from leading them into battle against an English invasion (Chapter 4, Section ii). And the military careers of David II and James IV suggest that such wariness was – to an extent – justified. Both came to grief in the only pitched battles in which they fought: David was captured at Neville's Cross, and James killed at Flodden (1513). William Wallace and Robert I had been much more willing to risk battle, and gained some dramatic victories (notably Stirling Bridge, 1297; Bannockburn, 1314; and Byland, 1322). But after Dupplin Moor and Halidon Hill, the Scots became more assiduous in avoiding battle. This remained a preferred Scottish tactic even after deliberate battle-seeking strategies became more fashionable across Europe from the late fifteenth century.

Consequently, large-scale battles were rare. Between Humbleton Hill in 1402 and Flodden in 1513, both disastrous Scottish defeats, there was only one battle of any great size between the English and the Scots in Britain, when an English force was routed at the river Sark in 1448 (though large-scale battles were fought between English and Scottish armies in France, at Baugé, 1421; Cravant, 1423; and Verneuil, 1424 – Chapter 3, Section iii). Thus, the unfortunate Archibald, fourth earl of Douglas, one of Scotland's most active war leaders, is known to have fought in just four pitched battles, of which two were in France. Three times he was on the losing side, losing an eye at Humbleton Hill, a testicle at Shrewsbury (1403), and his life at Verneuil.[2]

Anglo-Scottish warfare was therefore predominantly a matter of raiding, small-scale skirmishes and ambushes, at which the Scots proved particularly adept. Typical was the skirmish ending in the capture of Sir Thomas Gray, the constable of Norham, in 1355. A small Scottish raiding party, laden with booty, crossed the Tweed back into Scotland just below the castle. But when Gray set off in pursuit, he was ambushed by a much larger force which had been waiting for him. This was a carefully orchestrated plan to neutralize the garrison, so that they could not interfere with the planned Franco-Scottish attack on Berwick (Chapter 3, Section i). In 1306, Gray's father had employed a ruse to escape another ambush, handing banners over to his grooms who fooled the Scots into thinking that another English force was approaching.[3] Such tactics were still the norm in the sixteenth century. In 1548, a force of Cumbrians and assured Scots was ambushed at Drumlanrig, in a pre-arranged plan which saw the Scots turning on their erstwhile allies. The English were able to fight their way back to safety, but suffered heavy losses (Chapter 6, Section ii).[4]

The particular circumstances of the Scottish wars saw tactical innovations by both sides. In the early fourteenth century, the English made great use of hobelars, lightly armoured men mounted on 'hobs' (cheap horses). Their mobility was very useful in the uplands of Scotland and the northern Marches, though their role was gradually taken over by mounted archers.[5] The Scots employed similarly equipped troops (though they did not call them 'hobelars'). When it came to men-at-arms, however, they could rarely hope to field as many as the English. Instead, they developed new tactics for their common soldiers. Axes and short spears were replaced with long spears, and the soldiers formed up in *schiltroms* (large and tightly packed formations). This enabled them to fend off mounted English men-at-arms – whose horses were understandably reluctant to impale themselves on the massed ranks of spears. These same tactics were winning unprecedented victories across Western Christendom for spearmen fighting on foot, notably at Courtrai in 1302, where Flemish townsmen inflicted a shock defeat on French men-at-arms.[6]

At Stirling in 1297, Scottish common soldiers were able to massacre an English army as it incautiously marched across a bridge. The following year, at Falkirk, Edward I used archers to devastating effect, to weaken the Scottish *schiltroms* before pressing home his attack. At Bannockburn, where Edward II failed to deploy his archers effectively:

> The Scots ... lined in *schiltroms* ... attacked the English battles, which were crushed together so that they could not move against them, whilst their horses were being disembowelled by spears.[7]

The English learned from this defeat, and within a few years, were fighting on foot themselves. Thomas Gray recalled how, in *c.*1319, his father, a veteran of Bannockburn, had led his men on foot in a successful attack on a force of Scottish horsemen. Three years later, Sir Andrew Harclay, the most successful English commander against the Scots in this period, formed his army in *schiltroms*, 'after the Scottish fashion', to crush the rebel Thomas of Lancaster at Boroughbridge.[8] In 1332, a tiny English army fighting on foot was able to inflict a catastrophic defeat on the Scots at Dupplin Moor. The following year, a much larger English army, again fighting on foot, inflicted another shattering defeat on the Scots at Halidon Hill. Crucial to this victory was the large proportion of archers now employed in English armies (Chapter 3, Section i). It was the tactics developed at these battles against the Scots that would bring the English famous victories against the French at Crécy in 1346 and Agincourt in 1415.

The Scots were never able to employ archers to the same lethal effect as the English, though Scottish kings did pass legislation such as that of 1458, ordaining 'that football and golf be utterly cried down and not used', lest they distract their subjects from archery practice.[9] Nevertheless, as their adoption of *schiltroms* demonstrates, the Scots were not averse to trying new tactics. James IV was determined to follow the latest continental military practice, preparing for his invasion of England in 1513 by purchasing large quantities of pikes, armour and handguns in Flanders. However, as Scottish armies were only summoned in time of war, there was too little opportunity for drilling them in the tactics necessary to use these new weapons proficiently. An English report of Flodden did note that the Scots 'came down the hill and met with [the English] in good order after the Almayns' [i.e., Germans'] manner',[10] but once it came to the mêlée, they proved unable to use their unwieldy pikes to good effect.[11]

A lack of training had often been a problem for Scottish armies, and may have contributed to their defeat at Falkirk, in 1298.[12] Contemporaries were well aware of this; according to a Scottish chronicler writing in the 1370s, Sir Ingram de Umfraville (who had strong connections on both sides of the border) advised Edward II to take a long truce with Robert Bruce, for then:

> most of his forces, who are just simple yeomanry ... will have to work unceasingly with plough and harrow ... to earn their crust. Thus their arms will grow old, will deteriorate, be destroyed or sold, and many who are now skilled in warfare will die during a long truce, with others arising in their place who know little of such skills.[13]

In fact, this was a potential problem for both sides, for throughout this period, neither had a standing army. One of the main methods of raising men had been the feudal summons. This had disadvantages, the chief being that service was limited to only 40 days a year. Consequently, by 1296, the English Crown was increasingly relying upon alternative methods. Foot soldiers were usually raised by commissions of array, and paid wages. These commissions did not always provide the best soldiers; many localities simply took the opportunity to rid themselves of local vagabonds and troublemakers, while unsurprisingly, men conscripted in this way frequently deserted.

By 1296, the English had begun to use contracts, known as indentures, to raise troops for some purposes, particularly garrisons. Individual captains contracted to raise specified retinues of men for a fixed term at an agreed fee. As voluntary agreements, these did not arouse the hostility which usually met compulsory recruitment. By the mid-fourteenth century, indentures had become the usual English method of recruiting armies for expeditions, in large part as a result of experience in fighting the Scots. Tactical changes in the English armies required archers equipped with horses (though they continued to fight on foot), and these were recruited largely by indenture alongside the men-at-arms. Commissions of array continued to be used for defence against Scottish invasion, with March wardens being empowered to call out the men of the counties north of the river Trent (Chapter 9, Section ii). By the late fifteenth century, English kings were becoming increasingly wary about allowing their nobility to retain large bodies of armed followers, and the indenture system was regulated by a system of licensing. Royal armies were now raised largely by retainers of the king's household (though these had always played an important role) and the stewards of royal lands, and, increasingly, by a revived system of commissions of array.

The vast expense of paying soldiers' wages regularly caused financial crises for the English Crown, and consequently, it could never afford to maintain large armies in the field on a long-term basis. For the Scottish Crown, which had far less revenue at its command, payment of wages was generally out of the question. A rare exception was the 1482 plan to pay 1,100 spearmen and archers for 90 days' service defending the borders against an expected English invasion (Chapter 4, Section ii); the cost amounted to over £11,000 Scots.[14] Throughout the period, Scottish kings relied instead on the armed followings of their nobles, and on the traditional summons to arms, by which all able-bodied men were liable to serve in the 'common army', at their own expense, and bringing their own food, for 40 days a year. In practice, the poor, who could not afford military equipment, were not called upon, while liability for service was further limited by a quota system. There is little surviving evidence to reveal how this service was organized and enforced, although by the sixteenth century, if not before, men were summoned by the dramatic gesture of sending out riders bearing a flaming cross.

The 40-day limit did restrict the ability of Scottish armies to fight prolonged campaigns. When the English invaded in 1547

(Chapter 5, Section ii), Somerset received a report from one of his Scottish supporters who told him that the governor of Scotland (the earl of Arran) 'fears your delay, for he cannot keep our [i.e., the Scottish] army together if once convened'.[15] Nevertheless, this limit was not usually a major disadvantage, given that large-scale English expeditions into Scotland generally lasted only for a few weeks before retreating south of the border. Scottish invasions of England tended to be equally brief, and the prospects of plunder, ransoms and blackmail money were a strong inducement for service on such expeditions.

Both sides relied on foreign mercenaries or allies. Edward I and Edward II employed large numbers of Anglo-Irish soldiers, and some Gascons, particularly crossbowmen (though these were, of course, subjects of the kings of England). The army which the youthful Edward III led to Weardale in 1327 included a contingent from the Low Countries, previously employed to overthrow Edward II (Chapter 2, Section i). Their relations with the English were not entirely happy, for even before the campaign began, a fight broke out in which several English archers were killed. The Fleming John Crabbe, a notorious pirate and siege engineer, was employed first by the Scots, and then by the English, after they captured him in 1332.[16] The French sent a contingent of knights to Scotland to assist King David's supporters in 1339, helping at the siege of Perth. Sizable French forces were dispatched in 1355 and 1385; and on both occasions, the English were sufficiently alarmed to mount full-scale royal expeditions north of the border in response (see Chapter 3, Sections i and ii). In fact, in 1385, the French fell out with their Scottish hosts, accusing them of being overly cautious, while the Scots resented the many bills left unpaid by their French guests. Very much the same problems would recur when a French army came to assist the Scots in 1548.

The use of foreign troops was becoming much more common by the end of the fifteenth century. Edward IV employed at least 1,800 Burgundians, Germans and Swiss for his Scottish campaign of 1482, along with many gunners and engineers from the Continent.[17] In particular, the armies which fought the war of 1547–50 had a distinctly international flavour; the English employed Spaniards and Burgundians, including cavalry, arquebusiers and engineers, the Scots were supported by substantial French forces, and both sides employed companies of Italians and German *Landsknechte*. This was in keeping with military trends across Europe, which saw increasing reliance on foreign mercenary troops. Indeed, the Italians and *Landsknechte* who fought with the Scots were part of the French contingent – most of the mercenaries employed in the Scottish wars were in the service of the English or of Scotland's French allies, for the Scottish Crown lacked the revenues to cover the huge costs of hiring them. When James IV had deployed pikemen for his invasion of England in 1513, he could not afford to employ professionals from the Continent, and so had to rely on his own men – with less than successful results.

In those periods when the English held lands in Scotland, they needed to maintain permanent garrisons in Scottish towns and castles, in order to defend and administer them (Chapter 9, Section i). These performed a vital wider defensive function, providing a standing force to defend England against Scottish incursions. This role is clearly demonstrated in a letter to Edward III of *c*.1340, informing him that the garrison of Roxburgh had ambushed a large Scottish raiding party as they were returning from Northumberland. They killed or captured many of the raiders, and recovered the booty which the Scots had plundered.[18] In the war of 1547–50, fortifications were also used to provide secure bases for operations deep inside Scotland.

The Scottish Crown made far less use of fortifications. Robert I's usual policy was to demolish all the castles he captured. His armies relied on mobility, wearing down his enemies, both English and Scottish, by raiding; when faced by an English army, he generally retreated, preferring to avoid battle and adopting a policy of 'scorched earth', removing or destroying all supplies so that the English were forced to turn back, unable to feed themselves. Castles were worse than useless for such a strategy; a besieged castle could not usually hold out for long without being relieved, and relieving armies could become embroiled in battle – as would happen at Halidon Hill. In any case, Bruce did not have the money to pay for garrisons, and there was no point in leaving castles intact to be re-occupied by the English.[19]

Siege operations (in which an encamped army surrounded a fortification, and attempted to capture it by force) were thus fairly rare in the Scottish wars, perhaps more so than in other wars in this period. The Scots seldom attempted to hold castles against the English; and lacking the resources to conduct close sieges, they preferred to take English-held castles by surprise or by ruse, or to blockade them and starve the garrisons out. The customs of war allowed for terms for the defenders to surrender on a fixed date if they had not been relieved. Just such an agreement was made when Berwick was besieged by Edward III in 1333 (Chapter 2, Section ii). A fifteen-day truce was agreed, at the end of which the town was to be surrendered if not relieved. The town's captain, Alexander de Seton, handed over one of his sons as a hostage, to guarantee fulfilment of the terms. On the evening the truce was due to expire, a small party of Scottish men-at-arms managed to get into the town across the Tweed from Northumberland; Seton therefore refused to surrender, claiming that the town had been relieved. Edward disagreed, and hanged the unfortunate son in full view of his father. This persuaded Seton to negotiate again, leading to a new truce of just five days. Unsurprisingly, very precise conditions were now specified as to exactly what would constitute the relief of the town, and were committed to writing. It was the Scottish attempt to relieve Berwick under these new terms which led to their disastrous defeat at Halidon Hill. Such disputes were, however, the exception; usually, there was no doubt whether or not a siege had been lifted, and agreements were generally honoured without question.

Sieges became more common with the gradual adoption of gunpowder artillery. The English first started to use handguns and bombards (an early form of cannon) in the mid-fourteenth century. By the 1380s, they were routinely being issued to the English-held fortresses of Berwick and Roxburgh from the king's armoury at the Tower of London. At the same time, an 'instrument called a gun' was installed by the Scots in Edinburgh castle, while the French expedition which came to Scotland in 1384 was equipped with some handguns.[20] Gunpowder artillery was first successfully employed in a siege in the Anglo-Scottish Marches (and indeed, in Britain) in 1405, when Warkworth castle in Northumberland, held by English rebels, was rapidly bombarded into submission by Henry IV. He immediately went on to Berwick, which had been handed over to the Scots, and stormed the town after breaching the walls with his guns (Chapter 3, Section ii). For years afterwards, its English captains complained because the ruinous damage had never been repaired. The Scots do not seem to have employed guns on any significant scale until James I attacked Roxburgh in 1436, with gunners hired from Germany; the siege was, however, an abject failure, and the guns had to be abandoned (Chapter 3, Section iii). James II was famously killed when one of his own bombards misfired during another siege of Roxburgh in 1460, although the siege was carried to a successful conclusion anyway (Chapter 4, Section i).

Castles were by no means rendered obsolete by the advent of gunpowder weapons; rather, castle design was developed, and existing castles were modified, to withstand them. James IV had his huge gun, Mons Meg, hauled from Edinburgh to bombard Norham in 1497, but the castle withstood the cannonade, despite suffering extensive damage. He had more success in 1513, when it was bombarded into submission. But on both occasions, the castle was rebuilt, and provided with extra gun casements of its own. Wark castle was also captured in 1513, but was rebuilt with platforms for 'great bombards', and successfully withstood a Franco-Scottish attack in 1523.[21] Similarly, Cessford castle, Roxburghshire, was reinforced with earthworks which enabled it to withstand an intensive English bombardment in the same year. It fell only because its absent owner, Sir Andrew Kerr, returned and agreed to surrender the place. The English commander subsequently reported that if Kerr had not turned up, he doubted that he would have been able to take it by force.

The fortresses constructed by the English during Somerset's campaign of the late 1540s were built according to the latest continental principles, the *trace italienne*, with low and very thick walls, protected by wide ditches and ramparts, and equipped with projecting gun platforms to provide flanking fire. Eyemouth fort, north of Berwick, constructed at the outset of the campaign, was the first in Britain to be built along these lines. Such forts could be built very quickly from earthworks, which were as resistant to guns as stone masonry (though unlike stone, they did tend to collapse under heavy rain). The earthwork forts thrown up at Haddington and Broughty were able to hold out against prolonged heavy bombardment and repeated assaults (see Chapter 6).[22] In 1558, Mary Tudor ordered the refortification of Berwick, with state-of-the-art fortifications on a vast scale. The work carried on after Elizabeth's succession in the same year, and although work eventually ground to a halt unfinished in 1570, it had already cost the prodigious sum of £130,000 – the single most expensive building project of Elizabeth's reign. This was besides the costs of maintaining the garrison of over 650 men, including 70 gunners.[23] Unsurprisingly then, a proposal, made late in Elizabeth's reign, to fortify the entire line of the Anglo-Scottish border with a rampart, ditch and artillery bastions, was not taken up – despite its anonymous author's assurance that the scheme could be funded for no more than £30,000.[24]

From the late fifteenth century, guns were also increasingly employed in the field. By the 1480s, artillery trains were a standard part of any invading army, English or Scottish. The artillery train which accompanied

James IV's ill-fated invasion of England in 1513 was described by the bishop of Durham as 'the finest and best that lately has been seen'.[25] Nevertheless, it was the English gunners who got the better of the artillery duel at the battle of Flodden, possibly because the Scottish guns were heavy pieces better suited to sieges than the battlefield. They fell into English hands after the battle, and were valued at 1,700 marks (£1,133 6s. 8d.); they were subsequently put into service defending Berwick against their previous owners. Nor was their use restricted to large-scale expeditions. By 1528, the earl of Northumberland, warden of the East and Middle Marches, had at least 'six pieces of small artillery of his own' at Alnwick castle, which he lent to William, Lord Dacre (warden of the West March) for 'the conflict that has been between him and the Scots'.[26]

One area where guns undoubtedly had a huge impact was naval warfare.[27] Shipping had always been vital to the English for the transport of supplies and troops. The Disinherited had invaded Scotland by sea in 1332; and in 1481, Edward IV used his ships to land large raiding parties to support a cross-border invasion (Chapter 4, Section ii). But by the sixteenth century, advances in the design and manufacture of artillery enabled ships to act as floating gun platforms, and they were increasingly used tactically in conjunction with land forces. During Somerset's campaigns of 1547–50, English ships repeatedly bombarded Dundee and Leith, and they were even employed at the battle of Pinkie, fought by the coast. Similarly, French ships bombarded the English fort on the island of Broughty (Chapter 6, Section ii). However, there were never any major naval battles between England and Scotland.

Naval forces were not usually maintained on a permanent basis until the late fifteenth century, and then only on a relatively small scale. Instead, the English generally preferred to impress merchant ships into royal service according to need. For service in the Irish Sea, Scottish kings employed the galleys used by the men of Argyll and the Isles; Robert I made a number of grants of land in return for such service. James IV, a keen shipbuilder, did attempt to create a strong navy with up-to-date ships, partially financed by the French. The *Margaret*, built at Leith in 1504–7, weighed 600–700 tons. This may in turn have inspired Henry VIII to begin construction of the *Mary Rose*, in 1509.[28] James went on to build, at colossal expense, an even more enormous warship, the *Great Michael* – at 1,000 tons, one of the largest ships in Europe. But its only service against the English was to support a raid on Carrickfergus in Ireland, in 1513, before it was sold off to the French, because James could not afford the prohibitive costs of maintaining and crewing it.[29] Rather, the war at sea was conducted mainly through Crown-sponsored piracy, usually on a private enterprise basis. This could often yield great prizes, of which the capture of the young prince James (soon-to-be James I) by English pirates in 1406 (Chapter 3, Section iii) was only the most spectacular.

Writing in the late fourteenth century, the French canon lawyer Honoré Bouvet commented with bitter irony that 'the man who does not know how to set places on fire, to rob churches and usurp their rights and to imprison the priests, is not fit to carry on war'.[30] Although writing about France, his comment was equally true of the Scottish wars. Invading armies almost invariably set about the calculated and deliberate devastation of the lands they passed through. This had several motives. On a basic level, it was always difficult to feed armies; and in enemy territory, they could feed themselves by simply plundering food. But it was also a form of economic warfare, for regions which had been devastated were unable to contribute towards their king's war effort. The English border counties were excused taxation for much of the fourteenth century, on the grounds of poverty due to war damage inflicted by the Scots (see Chapter 9, Section i). Politically, plundering and ravaging were intended to undermine the authority of the opposing king, by demonstrating his inability to protect his subjects.

For the plunderers, ravaging could bring great profits – a particular incentive for Scottish armies, who were not paid for their service. The English chronicler John Hardyng approvingly described the vast and varied plunder acquired by his Northumbrian compatriots in a naval raid in c.1409. As well as commodities such as woollen and linen cloth, pitch and tar, flour, oatmeal, rye, timber, wool, hides and iron, the haul offered some rather more valuable spoils, including cloth of gold, spices, jewels and precious stones, and sweet wine.[31] Similarly, in 1542, an English cross-border raid netted 80 prisoners, 60 horses, 280 cattle, 3,000 sheep, and 'a great substance' of household goods, 'which as it is thought, was the best booty that has been gotten by any man's remembrance in these parts', as the earl of Hertford proudly reported to the king's council.[32]

For the victims, the devastation could be appalling. During the 1330s, for instance, many unfortunate Scots were ravaged by both sides. In particular, the adherents of David II deliberately caused local famines, as a means of terrorizing regions into submission. Lurid tales were told of cannibalism, including 'a certain peasant called Christy Cleke with his fierce wife', who 'lay in wait for women [and] children' and 'lived on their flesh'.[33] However, custom did allow for invading armies to be bought off. Typical was the agreement reached in October 1314, by which the community of the Bishopric of Durham paid 800 marks (£533 6s. 8d.) to buy immunity from Scottish raiding until the following January. Such agreements spared the English from having their homes plundered and burned, while guaranteeing the Scots large quantities of easily portable wealth, for a minimum of trouble.[34] Indeed, for most of the 1310s, the border counties were effectively paying tribute to Robert I instead of taxes to Edward II.

This practice continued throughout the period, and was common to both sides. Even as late as 1542, the prioress of Coldstream nunnery arranged to pay off an English army; however, the agreement broke down, and the nunnery was put to the flame. Consequently, the townsmen of Coldstream lost their goods, 'for by reason the prioress took herself to be *patised*, all they of the country had conveyed their corn and goods to her' (payments to buy off enemy forces being known as *patis*).[35]

Throughout the period, these wars were fought broadly according to the conventions that pertained across Western Christendom; the same customs of war generally applied in Scotland as in France. French soldiers fighting in Scotland may have regarded their hosts as uncouth, and overly cautious in war, but their strategy, tactics, equipment and outlook were not fundamentally different. Nevertheless, the conduct of Anglo-Scottish warfare was undoubtedly shaped by distinctive factors and priorities, in part because of the disparity of resources between the two sides. In particular, the Scots adopted *schiltroms*, close formations of spearmen, to counter the English strength in mounted men-at-arms; and invading Scottish armies moved very rapidly to prevent the English from gathering forces to oppose them. In response, the English were forced to adopt new tactics and methods of recruitment, developments which have been characterized by historians as contributing towards a 'military revolution'.[36] It was these new tactics, developed from the experience of fighting the Scots, which proved so successful for the English against the French. By the end of the fourteenth century, however, Anglo-Scottish warfare tended to follow continental trends, rather than setting them.

Chapter 9: The Marches

i. Border Society

At Easter 1296, a Scottish raiding party defeated a force of English borderers near Wark on Tweed in Northumberland. According to an English chronicler, the Scots had arranged a password, to distinguish friend from foe; but many of the English were able to escape, pretending to be Scots by repeating the password themselves. Some eighty years later, another force of northern Englishmen was overwhelmed at Otterburn, in Northumberland (Chapter 3, Section ii). According to a contemporary account, the English were defeated:

> because the darkness deluded our Englishmen so much that when they struck carelessly at a Scotsman, due to the chorus of voices speaking a single language, they struck down an Englishman.[1]

As these events demonstrate, people on both sides of the border spoke a similar northern dialect of English, so much so that the Englishmen and Scotsmen of the Marches were sometimes indistinguishable, even to each other.

The Anglian kingdom of Northumbria had, at its peak, extended as far as the Firth of Forth, and a considerable degree of social unity had survived its demise; in 1296, therefore, the border marked a political boundary, but not a cultural one. These cross-border links were both reflected and reinforced by cross-border landholding (Introduction, Section ii).[2] Many English and Scottish magnates held estates which straddled the border, as did many lesser landowners. The Dunbars, Scottish earls of March, were descendants of the Anglian earls of Northumbria, and still held the Northumbrian barony of Beanley. The Umfravilles had acquired extensive lands in Northumberland and Scotland in the early twelfth century; in 1243, marriage brought them the Scottish earldom of Angus. Various branches of the Comyn family, the pre-eminent Scottish magnates during the thirteenth century, held lands in Northumberland. And the kings of Scots held the liberty of Tynedale in Northumberland, and the lordship of Penrith in Cumberland, granted to them in 1237.[3]

Many religious houses in the Marches had close links with houses across the border. Durham priory had acquired lands across the old kingship of Northumbria, including Coldingham, north of the Tweed. More recent foundations created new links, particularly during the monastic revival of the twelfth century. Melrose abbey in Roxburghshire was a daughter house of Rievaulx in Yorkshire, and was in turn the mother house of Holm Cultram in Cumberland (founded by David I's son, Henry, while Cumberland was in Scottish hands). Similarly, Dryburgh abbey in Berwickshire was a daughter of Alnwick abbey in Northumberland.

The border itself was long-established by 1296, and its broad course had been formally recognized under the treaty of York, 1237. Its precise line was subject to the occasional squabble (such as the long-running controversy over the 'Debatable Lands');[4] but whatever other issues were at stake, the Anglo-Scottish wars were not border disputes. When Edward III took over the lands granted him by Edward Balliol in 1334, these lands remained Scottish. Even Berwick, which remained in English hands for most of the period, was not incorporated into the kingdom of England, but remained part of 'the king's lands and lordships in Scotland'.[5]

The Anglo-Scottish Marches were shaped by geography, both physical and political. In the east, the border followed the river Tweed and the Cheviot hills; in the west, the Solway and the Esk. Easily traversed coastal plains lay at both ends of the border, but communications across the middle were restricted by uplands. South of the border, Northumberland was cut off from Cumberland and Westmorland by the Pennines, with the Tyne valley providing the only easy route across (a route frequently employed by invading Scottish armies). These three counties were remote from the seat of English government at Westminster, a good week's journey away. By contrast, the Scottish border counties were much closer to the centres of Scottish royal government, and Lothian in particular was an area which had long been closely tied to Scotland's kings. On the other hand, the valleys of Liddesdale, Eskdale, Annandale and Nithsdale in the West and Middle Marches were isolated from each other, and from Edinburgh, by uplands. Further west, Galloway was culturally distinct, being mostly Gaelic-speaking, and had historically been much more peripheral to the Scottish kingdom.

The border uplands were comparatively unproductive, thinly populated and mainly devoted to livestock farming. However, the borders were by no means devoid of wealth; the coastal plains were much more fertile, while Newcastle on Tyne was one of the wealthiest towns in England, in part due to the coal trade. And Berwick had been Scotland's main port – until it was taken by Edward I.

Inevitably, the outbreak of war had a huge impact on the Marches. Medieval warfare was conducted by means of deliberate and calculated ravaging, which could be utterly devastating (see Chapter 8). The English borders suffered a succession of large-scale Scottish invasions in the decade after 1311, and the effects of these repeated attacks are starkly revealed by the financial records of Durham priory. In 1292/3, before the outbreak of war, it received an income of over £420 from its parishes at Norham and Holy Island, hard by the border. In 1321/2, this income had been reduced to less than £22.[6] Other English accounts from the same period (both financial and literary) recite a sad litany of destruction; inquests from the English border counties record many estates as worthless, such as the manor of Linmouth, Northumberland, which 'now renders nothing because devastated by the war' (from 1322), or the Northumbrian barony of Bolam, 'worth nothing because now lying waste by the devastation of the Scots' (1324).[7]

There is far more surviving evidence of the impact of Scottish raiding on England, than of English raiding on Scotland (see Introduction, Section i). But occasional glimpses are provided by Scottish records, such as the accounts for the earldom of March, following the forfeiture of George Dunbar in 1435; these record a number of reduced rents in 1453 and 1454 'on account of devastation', and, in 1466–7, a shortfall of £229 from lands 'burned and devastated by the English after the siege of Norham castle' (some three years before; Chapter 4, i).[8]

Warfare undoubtedly did have some severe long-term economic impacts. Berwick, for instance, cut off from its natural Scottish hinterland, never recovered its pre-war prosperity. Nor did the continuing threat of war instil confidence for the future amongst borderers. Writing in the late sixteenth century, the Scottish historian John Leslie said of the Scottish borderers that 'in time of peace … fearing that shortly the wars [will] oppress them, they utterly disdain to till'.[9] Such fears are reflected in the numerous property deeds from both sides of the border which make allowance for war damage. In 1454, for example, when Andrew Kerr granted lands near Jedburgh to Robert Thomson in return for his service, Kerr promised to pay him £5 a year, if he was unable to have the use of the lands, 'for open war of Englishmen'.[10]

Nevertheless, records indicate that in general, recovery from ravaging was remarkably rapid. Usually, devastated estates would recover to nearly their full value within five years or less – always assuming the devastation was not repeated. There was a region along the border itself, and for a few miles either side, which was more permanently depressed by the round of small-scale raiding that carried on largely irrespective of truces. But outside of this narrow frontier zone, over the long term, warfare had only a comparatively marginal effect on the economy of the Marches.[11]

In fact, natural disaster in the shape of bad weather and disease had a much more profound long-term impact than the man-made disaster of war. As well as invasions by the Scots, the 1310s saw harvest failures and epidemics of disease amongst sheep and cattle, leading to famine across Western Europe. Changing climatic conditions forced the abandonment of marginal, less fertile lands across much of Britain, which were increasingly given over to animal husbandry instead of agriculture, and the border uplands were particularly affected by these developments. These difficulties were exacerbated by the Black Death of 1348–9, which killed perhaps a third or even a half of the entire population of Britain. Successive outbreaks of plague prevented the population recovering to its pre-1300 levels until the end of the sixteenth century.

Contemporaries were well aware that economic decline in the Marches was not just the result of war. In 1420, the bursar of Durham priory sought to explain the drastic fall in the priory's income since 1293. He suggested four factors: firstly, the priory no longer received anything from its churches in Scotland, 'because the Scots have not permitted'; secondly, 'the war between the kingdoms'; thirdly, because many of the arable lands from which the churches had received tithes of wheat had been put to pasture; and fourthly, 'because of frequently happening plagues, because of which many places are deserted'.[12]

Nevertheless, the onset of war in 1296 did bring about permanent and fundamental changes in border society. It posed a particularly acute problem for cross-border landholders. Even before the fighting began, Edward I confiscated the English estates of all Scots remaining in the allegiance of King John. The settlement of 1304 (Chapter 1, Section ii) promised the restoration of forfeited lands, offering the prospect of a return to the pre-war *status quo*; but Robert Bruce's *coup* of 1306 was swiftly followed by a new round of confiscations, and Robert himself forfeited the Scottish lands of all those who refused to come to his allegiance after Bannockburn (Chapter 2, Section i).

By the time of the 1323 truce, cross-border landholding had been almost completely eliminated. The rapid dismantling of a cross-border society, which had flourished for two centuries, left something of a vacuum of power, as border magnates such as the Umfravilles (who sided with the English, despite their Scottish title) and the Dunbars (who went over to the Scottish allegiance after Bannockburn) were left weakened by the loss of their cross-border estates.

The recurrent bouts of warfare also led to the rapid militarization of society on both sides of the border, as locals had little choice other than to take up arms against enemy invasion. Thus a 1324 survey by the English Crown of knights and men-at-arms recorded proportionately far more men-at-arms in the border counties than elsewhere in the country. And, on the English side of the border at least, militarization was marked in stone by the proliferation of castles, built to highlight the military status of their builders, as much as to defend against the Scots.[13]

There were plentiful opportunities for militarily active magnates who were able to adapt to this new environment. Noble families such as the Percies, the Nevilles and the Cliffords in the English Marches, and the Douglases across the border in Scotland, flourished by providing dogged – if not always successful – leadership in war. All of these families held extensive estates outside the Marches, which were less vulnerable to raiding: the Percies and Cliffords in Yorkshire, the Nevilles in the bishopric of Durham, and the Douglases in Clydesdale. They were established in the Marches partly at the expense of the old border nobility; when, for instance, the Dunbars lost their Northumbrian lands for good in 1335, these were granted to the Percies, who thereby significantly increased their estate in the county. Similar opportunities extended further down the social scale, enabling many of the knights and gentry of the Marches to advance themselves through military service.[14]

The rapid promotion of successful war leaders, and particularly of those who lacked social eminence, frequently generated social tensions and rivalries which could erupt into violence. In 1342, David II appointed Sir Alexander Ramsey sheriff of Roxburghshire, as reward for capturing Roxburgh. This was regarded by Sir William Douglas of

Liddesdale as an intolerable intrusion into his sphere of influence, and he reacted by kidnapping Ramsey and starving him to death (Chapter 3, Section i). Douglas was in turn ambushed and killed in 1353. His killer was his godson and namesake William Douglas, from the senior branch of the family, from whom he had seized the lordship of Liddesdale. The minor Northumbrian esquire John de Coupland made his fortune by capturing David II at Neville's Cross in 1346, and was rewarded with a £500 annuity by a grateful Edward III. He exploited his new-found influence to grab lands by dubious methods, and to persecute his neighbours through legal chicanery. Consequently, in 1364, he was murdered by his fellow Northumbrians.[15]

During the fourteenth century, the repeated – if intermittent – bouts of open war underlined the importance for both sides of maintaining their Marches in a state of military readiness. The resources and (at least in the case of the English Crown) money that poured into the region also had the effect of keeping the political communities of the borders, both English and Scottish, in close touch with their respective governments. In particular, border magnate families such as the Percies and the Douglases came to wield considerable influence in national politics.[16] However, as open war became less common in the fifteenth century, so the defence of the borders became less of an immediate priority, particularly for the English. Consequently, both the English and Scottish Crowns were less reliant on powerful, militarized border magnates. At various times, the Percy, Clifford and Dunbar families, and the leading branches of the Neville and Douglas families, all forfeited their lands for rebellion against their respective kings. Though some of these families were subsequently restored, by the sixteenth century, the power and authority of the great Marcher magnates had been considerably restricted, particularly on the English side of the border.

Despite the hostilities, some cross-border links survived the outbreak of war, or indeed were created by it. English administrations were established in Scotland in 1296, when Edward I abolished the kingdom; they were re-established in southern Scotland in 1334, when Edward Balliol ceded parts of it to Edward III; and again in 1347, when the English invaded the Scottish borders in the aftermath of Neville's Cross.[17] The most important and long-lasting were those based in Berwickshire, Roxburghshire and Dumfriesshire, centred on the castles of Berwick, Roxburgh and Lochmaben respectively. Lochmaben was captured by the Scots in 1384, and demolished, but

Roxburgh did not finally fall until 1460. Berwick was surrendered in the same year, but was retaken in 1482, and remained in English hands thereafter (Chapter 4, Section ii). A degree of English control over the Scottish borders was also imposed during Somerset's campaigns of 1547–50. A number of fortresses were constructed, while Roxburgh castle was refortified, and large numbers of Scots were received into the English allegiance, as 'assured Scots' – though in the event, the English occupation proved short-lived (Chapter 6, Section ii).

These administrations accounted to the Exchequer in Westminster, and were often led by English officials, many of them from the Marches. However, they remained jurisdictionally entirely separate from England; the king's lordships in Scotland were subject to Scottish law, administered according to Scottish custom. Thus, although most Scots in these areas came into the English allegiance (albeit often very reluctantly), they were never integrated into English political society. Consequently, the imposition of English rule in the Scottish borders had a minimal impact on perceptions of national identity. Scots under English rule continued to think of themselves as Scots, and were regarded as such by English officials.[18]

Scots who held lands in these areas of English control did, however, require a degree of flexibility in their loyalties; they needed to be able to make timely changes of allegiance to avoid losing them, as the boundaries of English lordship waxed and waned. However, neither the English nor the Scottish Crowns could afford to alienate potential supporters by too ruthless a policy of forfeiture. Consequently, Scots who changed sides were not generally penalized for their previous adherence to the enemy, provided they jumped at the right moment. Families such as the Kerrs of Selkirk Forest thus managed to carve out a lasting prominence for themselves in Teviotdale society through a series of well-judged switches of allegiance.[19]

Although the English occupation of these lands was inevitably a major cause of Anglo-Scottish conflict, there was occasionally a degree of co-operation over their administration. In 1360, the earl of Hereford, the English lord of Annandale, reached an agreement with David II to share the rents from the lordship, an agreement which was still working in 1373. And even after the Scots had recovered most of Berwickshire in the 1370s, Durham priory was able to hang on to its cross-border dependency, Coldingham priory, along with its Berwickshire estates. Though threatened with confiscation on numerous occasions, the

Durham monks were able to call on the support of such eminent Scottish border magnates as Archibald, Earl of Douglas, William Douglas, Earl of Angus, and George Dunbar, Earl of March, until they finally lost control of Coldingham in the 1470s.[20]

Co-operation between Englishmen and Scots also extended to commerce. Until 1296, the Anglo-Scottish border had little economic significance, and was no barrier to trade, which flourished during the thirteenth century. Though the outbreak of war disrupted this trade, it did not halt it altogether (Chapter 10). Scottish merchants continued to trade through Berwick, even while it was in English hands. In 1389, for instance, the monks of Melrose were granted a licence by Richard II to export 1,000 sacks of wool through Berwick, at a reduced customs rate, 'as alms for the destruction and burning sustained by the abbey when the king was there with his army' (in 1385).[21] However, the licence was revoked after just a year, because the monks, undoubtedly acting as agents for other Scottish wool-producers, had already exceeded the limit, exporting some 1,200 sacks. The monks also traded across the border in England; in the same year, a licence was issued allowing their servants to go into Northumberland and Cumberland to sell their beasts and produce, and to buy supplies and wine.[22]

The English garrisons of Roxburgh and Berwick obtained much of their food and fuel from Scottish merchants. Thus in 1403, the captain of Roxburgh was permitted to grant safe-conducts for Scots coming to supply the castle from Teviotdale, which was in the Scottish allegiance. Indeed, in 1455, when James II was bent on retaking these English outposts, he found it necessary to issue a statute in parliament, forbidding any Scots from supplying them under pain of treason. At the same time, statutes were passed forbidding any Scottish man or woman from crossing into England without permission, again under pain of treason; while Englishmen coming to Scotland without permission, 'to church or market or any other place', were to be arrested.[23] This was just the latest in a long series of attempts to limit and control cross-border contacts; and like the preceding measures, it had little practical effect.

Indeed, many Scots took up residence in the English borders. Tax records suggest that, unsurprisingly, Scots were far more common in the borders than elsewhere in England; the returns for the 1440 tax on foreigners listed 740 in Northumberland alone; and there were undoubtedly many more who managed to evade the taxation, or who were exempted (Chapter 10). The English authorities regarded these

Scots with some suspicion. In 1490, proclamation was made in Yorkshire, Northumberland, Cumberland and Westmorland that:

> whereas great numbers of Scots and other strangers applying themselves to idleness and begging have over-run the realm and specially the above places to their likely impoverishing, under pain of imprisonment, all such shall return to their own countries, except those who are householders or menial servants, and of known good reputation and allegiance.[24]

Nevertheless, Scots were resident in English Marches in even greater numbers a hundred years later. In 1587, Lord Hunsdon, warden of the English East March, wrote a letter complaining that they were making his job difficult; but at the same time, he had to concede that they were vital for the local economy:

> There are so many Scots planted within Northumberland, especially upon the very borders, as no exploit or purpose can be so secretly resolved upon, but ... the Scots have straight warning. For in many English towns there are more Scots inhabitants than English, and some have 1,000 sheep going in England, and corn worth £200 or £300 in one town. ... And truly the only way to help this is to have a commission sent down for the making of denizens, which if it may please Her Majesty to let me have, I will rid the country of 2,000 or 3,000 Scots, and leave sufficient necessary men as colliers, fishers, herds, and shepherds.[25]

Nevertheless, despite their importance to the local economy, mistrust of Scottish immigrants remained endemic, and many of the trade guilds in Newcastle, Carlisle and Durham refused to accept men born in Scotland as apprentices.

This mistrust stemmed in part from another form of cross-border co-operation: crime. The border, which marked out separate legal jurisdictions, served to exacerbate problems of law and order. Those who committed a crime and then escaped across the border could not be pursued. Due to the nature of the records (Introduction, Section i), there is much more evidence of crime from the English side of the border, which reveals that it was common for English thieves to co-operate with Scots, taking their ill-gotten gains into Scotland, where they could be sold with relative impunity. Cattle and sheep were often stolen and driven across the border, and there was a thriving trade in cross-border kidnapping and ransoming.

Typical were the activities of men such as the Northumbrian William Davison, charged with meeting up with some Scots at Ingram in Northumberland, and helping them steal a horse. He was also accused of meeting some Scots at Lowick, in 1408, in a plot to betray Roxburgh castle, for which he was hanged. A rather more dramatic example of criminal cross-border co-operation came in 1409; 200 Scots were employed by Sir Robert Ogle to help besiege Bothal castle in Northumberland, in a dispute with his brother over the family inheritance. English criminals were also active in Scotland; in 1530, for instance, the Scotsman William Cockburn of Henderland in Selkirk was hanged for associating with English thieves.[26]

Perhaps the most notorious cross-border crimes, however, arose from the border 'surnames', during the sixteenth century. The first documented use of the term 'surname' in a border context is from 1498, in an English royal writ ordering the arrest of a number of men from Tynedale and Redesdale, including a number of men with the surnames Hedley, Rede, Charlton and Wilkinson: 'inasmuch as all persons of the said surnames are banded together ... all persons of the said surnames are to be arrested by the sheriff as the king's traitors, outlaws and banished men'.[27]

The 'surnames' were bound by ties of extended – and sometimes fictive – kinship, looking to the heads of their kin-groups to provide protection and maintenance. They were not dissimilar to the clans of highland Scotland; and indeed, by the end of the period, the Scottish Crown was adopting similar policies for dealing with both. An act of 1587 concerning 'the wicked inclination of the disordered subjects, inhabitants in some parts of the borders adjacent to England and in the highlands and isles' referred to 'the captains, chiefs and chieftains of all clans, as well on the highlands as on the borders'.[28]

Though some of the surnames inhabited the East Marches, such as the Taits and the Davisons, it was the surnames of the central uplands of the Middle and West Marches, particularly Liddesdale, Tynedale and Redesdale, who were considered the real problem, and especially the Elliots, the Grahams and the Armstrongs. Certainly, some of the surnames were heavily involved in cross-border crime, as notoriously illustrated by the exploits of William Armstrong of Kinmont, a Scot known, and feared, by the soubriquet Kinmont Willie. He was accused of leading a cross-border raid in the midsummer of 1579, with 400 men, in which Oswald Dodd, one of the English surnames, was killed, and 800 cattle and 1,000 sheep were stolen. In another raid in August 1583, he and 300 followers were alleged to have committed six murders, and to have rustled 400 cattle, 400 sheep and 30 horses.[29] Disorder was sufficiently endemic that many of the inhabitants of Tynedale and Redesdale resorted to building bastle houses, small stone-built (and so fire-proof) dwellings designed to be defendable against raiding parties.

This lawlessness stemmed from economic problems, combined with failures of governance exacerbated (rather than caused) by warfare. The upland economies were becoming increasingly marginal; a 1541 survey of the borders for the English Crown reported that Tynedale was 'overcharged with so great a number of people more than such profits as may be gotten and won out of the ground within the said country are able to sustain and keep'; and consequently, 'for lack of living', its inhabitants were 'constrained to steal or spoil continually either in England or Scotland for the maintenance of their living'.[30] Furthermore, Tynedale and Redesdale were liberties, and so in large part removed from the Crown's jurisdiction. Thus, a petition from the 'commons of the county of Northumberland' to parliament in 1414 complained that:

> numerous murders, treasons, homicides and robberies and other crimes are daily committed against the said commons by various people of the franchises of Tynedale, Redesdale and Hexhamshire ... because they are thus enfranchised; and also some of the said people harbour and support numerous people from Scotland.[31]

These difficulties were heightened by an absence of lordship, for Tynedale had been confiscated from the kings of Scots in 1296, and granted out by the Crown to a series of absentee lords; while the Umfravilles, lords of Redesdale, died out in 1437, and were succeeded by lords whose main interests lay elsewhere. The liberty status of Tynedale was abolished in 1495, and that of Redesdale in 1536, but this had little impact, for local Crown officials were unable to impose their authority.

These difficulties were compounded by the fact that both sides relied on the surnames to provide troops. The extent of this reliance is revealed by a muster of arrayed men in Northumberland taken in 1538, which listed 391 men as 'North Tynedale thieves', all 'able with horse and harness' (unlike many of those from more law-abiding parts of the county, who were annotated as having 'neither horse nor harness'). They included no less than 69 men with the surname Robson (including one Mickle Jock Robson of the Nook), 51 Charltons and 41 Dodds. Another 185 were listed for Redesdale, 'able men with horse and harness, beside all the foot thieves'; 35 of these bore the surname of Hall.[32] Royal officials charged with maintaining law and order were frequently also charged with defending the borders, leading to a conflict of interests (see below, Section ii).

In fact, the 'problem' of the surnames was, at least in part, one of perception. To the English Crown, the surnames were anomalous, for they did not fit the model of local government and society in the English shires which was now regarded as normative. This was of a piece with southern English views of the Marches more generally. When the long truce of 1389 brought an end to campaigning in France, England became increasingly demilitarized, as fewer of the gentry took up arms, a trend which continued even after the renewed outbreak of war with France in 1415. Of necessity, however, the Marches remained far more martial. This was reflected in measures such as the prohibition against granting livery announced at Edward IV's first parliament in 1461; specific exception was made for 'the wardens of the Marches of Scotland, whose livery, mark or token may be given, borne and used from Trent northward, at such time as is necessary to raise people for defence of the Marches'.[33] Increasingly, the region was perceived by southern Englishmen as warlike and mired in lawlessness, and was correspondingly looked down upon as wild and uncivilized.[34]

From the perspective of the less centralized Scottish government, however, kin-groups based in economically marginal uplands were hardly an unusual phenomenon. The borders were not seen as particularly distinctive, partly because they were so much nearer the centres of government, and partly because the Gaelic-speaking Highlands and Islands provided the main target for the cultural condescension of the Scottish ruling elite (Chapter 11, Section i). As government became more centralized, however, attitudes hardened against regional lawlessness, both in the Highlands and on the borders. And as the prospect of James VI's succession became increasingly likely, so the Scottish Crown became increasingly concerned about the potential for cross-border crime to cause problems with England.

There was, to a certain degree, a distinctive borderer culture, notably the famous border ballads which celebrated the feuds and raids of English and Scottish surnames. As John Leslie noted, the men of the borders 'delight much in their own music and harmony in singing, either of the acts of their forebears they have learned, or what themselves have invented of an ingenious policy to drive a prey and say their prayers'.[35] Nevertheless, these ballads retained a strong element of national identity. And strong national sentiments were revealed by the brawling that broke out at a football game between English and Scottish borderers at Bewcastle in 1599.[36]

Unlike many medieval border societies, such as the English in Ireland, 'acculturation' – in the sense of the opposing sides picking up and identifying with facets of each other's culture – was not an issue in the Anglo-Scottish Marches; by 1296, the two societies, English and Scottish, were already thoroughly and comprehensively acculturated. Allegiance was therefore a question of (more-or-less) straightforward political or familial loyalty, uncomplicated by side-issues of cultural identity; there was, for instance, little chance of English officials in Berwickshire or Teviotdale 'going native'. Nor did the occasional English occupation of southern Scotland do anything to break down notions of separate national identities, because the border remained fixed, and the English lordships on its northern side remained entirely separate from England, both legally and politically. The inhabitants of these lordships were subjects of the king of England, but they were still Scots. Indeed, the almost permanent state of Anglo-Scottish hostility worked to reinforce national identities, for all that large-scale campaigning was comparatively rare. The Debatable Lands aside, the line of the border was clear cut; and while borderers from both sides had a great deal of contact with each other, and might co-operate together, there was no doubt as to their nationality. Borderers they may have been, but they were still English or Scottish borderers.[37]

ii. *The March Laws*

Apart from the (very) brief periods when Edward I was able to put into effect the longstanding English claims to overlordship, England and Scotland had entirely separate legal jurisdictions. Inevitably, this raised problems when the subjects of one realm were accused of crimes against the subjects of the other, or when criminals fled across the border. Consequently, a body of law gradually evolved in the Marches to deal with cross-border disputes. Known as March law, it was first codified in 1249, though elements of it appear to have developed before the Norman Conquest.[38]

Edward I, however, took a dim view of March law. He was intolerant of any exception to the jurisdiction of English common law; and after 1292, in his eyes, English overlordship rendered the distinction between English and Scottish jurisdictions redundant.[39] With the outbreak of war in 1296, March law became irrelevant, and neither side made any great effort to revive it until the 1340s, when the collapse of Edward Balliol's regime left David II unopposed in Scotland. As Edward III's attentions were now concentrated on France, he was anxious to avoid hostilities with the Scots. March law offered a means of settling cross-border disputes peacefully, preventing their escalation into war.

As March law was a separate jurisdiction from the English and Scottish common laws, it required separate administration, and this came to be exercised by the wardens of the Marches. This office was originally created by the English Crown for the defence of the English border counties after 1296; the wardens were northern magnates appointed to raise men from within the Marches against the threat of Scottish invasion, by commission of array. Thus, their role was initially purely military, with no judicial functions. Breaches of the truce by Englishmen – when there was any truce to be broken – were dealt with by specially appointed commissions, under the English common law. The wardens acquired their judicial role from the late 1340s, when they were given responsibility for punishing such breaches. Around this time, the March law was revived, and the wardens were charged with its operation. The Scots began to appoint March wardens of their own, and wardens' courts, held jointly by the English and Scottish wardens on March days, had begun to operate by the end of the 1340s.[40]

The power and authority of the English March wardens developed markedly in the late fourteenth and fifteenth centuries. For most of the fourteenth century, it was usual for the Crown to appoint two groups of wardens, for the East and West Marches respectively, with new commissions being appointed every year or so. The wardens were usually northern magnates, though sometimes the commissions included knights and esquires from the Marches, the bishops of Carlisle and Durham, or magnates from southern England. With the renewed outbreak of raiding and fighting after 1369, it became increasingly common to pay the wardens substantial fees, to cover the costs of raising military retinues to serve on a long-term basis. After the 1389 truce, it became usual to appoint just one warden for each March, for a period of several years. The Percy family, which held extensive lands in Yorkshire and Northumberland, had always been prominent as March wardens, and they now increasingly came to dominate the office.

By this stage, the fees were enormous; when Henry 'Hotspur' Percy was appointed as warden of the East March in 1393, he was to receive £3,000 a year while the truce lasted, and £12,000 a year if war broke out. The appointment was renewed for another ten years in 1396, on the same terms.[41] It is hardly surprising, then, that the Percies were determined to hold on to the offices, which allowed them to support large retinues at the expense of the Crown, while increasing their authority through the exercise of March law. Richard II's attempts to break their monopoly on the office by promoting his own candidates were an important factor in persuading the Percies to support Henry Bolingbroke's *coup* in 1399. But the regular payment of these vast sums presented huge difficulties, particularly for the cash-strapped government of Henry IV. His failure to keep up payments, combined with his promotion of the Neville family, who held estates in Durham and Westmorland, led the Percies into rebellion against him in turn. Thereafter, the level of fees was greatly reduced, and they were habitually paid in arrears. Nevertheless, the office remained a powerful one, and for much of the fifteenth century was dominated – and contested – by the Percies and Nevilles. Richard, Duke of Gloucester, appointed warden of the West March in 1470, used it to help build up a power base which enabled him to seize the throne as Richard III in 1483. Consequently, Henry VII and his successors kept their wardens on a tight leash and a tighter budget.

Evidence for the development of the Scottish wardenships is much more scanty, but it is clear that although Scottish wardens performed a similar role to their English counterparts, their office took a distinctively Scottish form. From the start, the office was usually exercised by individual magnates, rather than commissions. Scottish kings generally worked with existing power structures, and the division of the borders into three Marches (East, Middle and West) reflected existing territorial interests. These were associated with powerful border lordships (even more so than in England), with border magnates acting as wardens almost by hereditary right. Increasingly, the office was dominated by the various branches of the Douglas family, the most powerful of the Scottish marcher nobility – particularly after the Dunbar earls of March lost much of their influence following the temporary defection of the ninth earl to the English in 1400. Just as in England, the office was viewed by local magnates as a vital adjunct to power in the Marches, and rivalry over appointments could lead to contention. In 1430, the appointment of William Douglas, Earl of Angus, as warden of the East March, led to a bout of violent feuding with George Dunbar, tenth Earl of March.

The bulk of Dunbar's lands lay there, and he resented Douglas' appointment as an intrusion into his country. Increasing disorder culminated in Dunbar's forfeiture, in January 1435. He responded by going over to the English allegiance – just as his father had done in 1400.

Scottish wardens were not usually fee'd during the fourteenth century, although they were paid expenses on an occasional basis, for attending March days. These varied from the 50 marks (£33 13s. 4d.) paid to the earl of Douglas in 1388, to the rather more generous payments totalling over £800 made to the duke of Rothesay for a March day in 1398.[42] It only became usual for Scottish wardens to be paid a fee after the Douglases' monopolistic grip on the office was broken in 1455. Their dominance of border society had prevented any other families from attaining a similar stature. Scottish governments therefore tended to employ local lairds and minor lowland nobles, few of whom possessed the wealth and resources necessary to retain a sufficient following for the job – and so they had to be paid. The usual fee was £100 a year, though payments for wardens of the West March rose markedly during the late sixteenth century. Nevertheless, payments tended to be tardy, and were usually inadequate. Therefore, Scottish wardens had to rely on their kinsmen and followers to maintain their authority and standing.

And this highlights the conflict of interest between the judicial and military functions of the warden's office: wardens who were dependent on a restricted group of kinsmen or followers to exercise that office could hardly pursue cases brought against their followers without undermining their own authority. On the English side of the border, such problems were exacerbated by the determination of Henry VII and his successors to prevent any magnate from using the office to build up too strong a position in the borders. Wardens were kept on a shoestring budget, which hindered any attempt to build up an effective military following. But military followings were necessary for the defence of the Marches. The Cumberland magnate Thomas, Lord Dacre, was appointed warden general of the Marches in 1511. Having little land and few supporters in Northumberland, he was unable to rely on the men of the county to serve against the Scots. He had, however, made contacts with the men of Tynedale and Redesdale, when he had been appointed as lieutenant of the Middle March in 1502, and constable of Harbottle castle in Redesdale; and after 1511, he had little choice but to rely on these men, who were willing to serve him – so long as their misdemeanours were overlooked.[43]

Similar considerations affected Scottish wardens. In 1596, Ralph, Lord Eure, the English warden of the Middle March, complained of his opposite number (Sir Robert Kerr of Cessford) that his 'mean estate of living ... forces him to befriend his clan, overlook outrages, and support lawless men about him who serve him without charge'.[44] In the same year, in one of the more celebrated incidents of border history (subsequently commemorated in ballad form), Sir Walter Scott of Buccleuch broke into Carlisle castle to rescue the notorious Scottish reiver Kinmont Willie.[45] Scott was undoubtedly motivated in part by anger at the breach of border custom involved in Kinmont's arrest (see below). But more importantly, Kinmont was one of his followers, and he needed to act to protect him, in order to maintain his own standing. In this, he was successful; as the English warden William Bowes commented in the following year, both Buccleuch and Kerr of Cessford 'have got great reputation with the inland lords and gentlemen, for their valorous defence of their charges'.[46] In the same vein, an English report of 1602 claimed that 'disorders' on the borders often arose from abuse of office by the Scottish wardens, who were concerned 'to maintain their private greatness by working a dependency of such persons as will the rather at any time follow [them] in all their private quarrels, when they are winked at in their own disorders'; the same report went on to claim – with unwarranted complacency – that English wardens were not so constrained, 'both because those quarrels and feuds are here unusual, and that their entertainment [i.e., fee] from the Queen is such and so great as they have no such need to make any other profit by their office'.[47]

The operation of March law continued to be subject to changing diplomatic and political imperatives in both realms. Henry IV took a decidedly bellicose stance against the Scots – albeit more in rhetoric than in practice – and was not willing to make the diplomatic effort to maintain the mechanisms of March law. Its workings were also hampered by the loss of the most authoritative and experienced wardens on both sides of the border: George Dunbar, Earl of March (defected to the English in 1400); Archibald, Earl of Douglas (captured at Humbleton Hill in 1402); Hotspur (killed in rebellion in 1403); and his father, the earl of Northumberland (forfeited for rebellion in 1405). However, the minority government of Henry VI, wrestling with the problems of war with France, was bent on improving relations with Scotland, and the seven-year truce sealed after the release of James I in 1424 made full provision for the resumption of the wardens' courts. Thereafter, as bouts of open warfare became less frequent, there were fewer interruptions to the functioning of March law, although its operation could still be hampered by strained relations between the English and Scottish governments. More localized disputes and squabbles could also pose an impediment; the Debatable Lands, for instance, were effectively left lawless, because neither realm could recognize the jurisdiction of the other's wardens there without implicitly recognizing its claims. As William, Lord Dacre, put it, in a letter to the privy council in 1550:

> ... neither I will suffer the warden of Scotland to answer for it, because I will not affirm it to be Scotland, nor will they on the contrary consent that it shall be England, which, unprovided for, shall bring the Marches in great misorder, and be occasion that no redress shall be had, nor punishment for them which be notable offenders.[48]

The form of March law evolved continuously, as an amalgam of customary law, based on the experience of the wardens and their deputies, and written law, incorporated and recorded in treaties and truce agreements made between the two Crowns. It had first been reduced to written form as early as 1249, when juries drawn from both sides of the border were called upon to record existing custom. However, as late as 1579, James VI's government directed one of his March wardens that a disputed point of March law was to be left until it could be decided 'either by the written law or the meeting of commissioners or until the laudable custom be verified by the most knowledgeable borderers of both the realms'; and in 1593, William Kerr of Cessford could argue that 'the custom of the Borders' outweighed the written authority of 'the treaties'. On the other hand, by this date, the wardens on both sides kept 'law books of the border', and on occasion, both sides' books might be compared and collated, to ensure that they conformed with each other.[49]

Two such law books survive, both from the English side of the border. The March warden Sir Robert Bowes wrote a treatise in 1551, *The Form and Order of a Day of Truce*, referring to practice on the East and Middle Marches, which was 'grounded and taken forth of the articles of the last treaty of peace'.[50] Some fifty years later, Richard Bell, clerk to the warden of the West March, wrote a treatise recording practice, *The Manner of Holding a Day of Truce*, containing copies of the March laws and treaties from 1249 to 1597 (though some of the texts are muddled). The need for such careful record keeping was well appreciated by contemporaries; in 1576, the Scottish privy council noted the 'daily experience [of] what harm and inconvenience occurs upon the borders of both the realms through ignorance of the laws and laudable customs thereof'.[51]

By the end of the sixteenth century, March law covered a variety of offences, ranging from the serious – including murder ('slaughters'), wounding, arson, the capture of castles and forts, the unlawful taking and ransoming of prisoners, and receiving fugitives from across the border – to the rather more mundane, such as hunting or pasturing cattle across the border, or impeding fishing in the river Tweed. Other offences concerned attempts to subvert the workings of March law itself, such as committing perjury at a day of truce, overstating the value of stolen goods ('overswearing'), or unauthorized reprisals.[52] In the fourteenth century, acts of piracy at sea were also included within the wardens' jurisdiction, as truces usually covered the sea as well as land. By the sixteenth century, however, it had become usual for piracy cases to be dealt with at the royal courts of both kingdoms, through the agency of ambassadors.

March law allowed raiders to be pursued across the border and summarily punished, providing this was done openly, and with due form, and the raiders were caught red-handed, or with stolen goods or livestock still in their possession. Immediate pursuit was known as 'hot trod', while 'cold trod' allowed for a pursuit to be mounted within six days. Any form of reprisal raid was illegal, except when authorized by a March warden, and then only after all other avenues of legal redress had failed. Rather, the victims of breaches of the truce and cross-border crime were expected to seek redress from the March wardens. Cases were dealt with at wardens' courts, held on March days. Complaints could be lodged with the wardens in advance, and they were responsible for ensuring that fellow countrymen accused of breaches of the truce or the March law turned up on the day. Cases were heard before mixed juries, comprising Englishmen and Scots. When accusations were upheld, the accused would be required to pay reparations, in the form of the restoration of goods or monetary compensation; and the wardens were required to enforce judgements made against their compatriots.

A good example of the workings of these courts is provided by the case of the Cumberland lord Sir Hugh Dacre, accused of depredations against the earl of Douglas in 1370. At the next March day, a jury found against Dacre, and he was ordered to pay £100 compensation. When he refused, Henry Percy, one of the English March wardens, paid Douglas out of his own pocket, so as to keep the peace. He then set about recovering his money by obtaining a writ from the English Crown, authorizing Dacre's arrest and the seizure of his goods. Further light is shed by a letter sent to the Northumbrian Sir William Swinburne by Henry Percy at some point after 1377 (by which time he had been created earl of Northumberland):

> Dear Companion. We have heard through John de Mitford that you say you are unable to come to Kershope Bridge next Monday on the double day of the March which will be held there between the deputies of the earl of Douglas and ours for Annandale and Tynedale at which we are astonished. And we charge you on behalf of the king ... to be there on the said day to do and receive as right requires, because whatever will be determined there about you and your men, by the said deputies, will guide us and we wish to compel you to do right and justice. And take this to heart.[53]

Mitford was a lawyer, and one of Percy's most prominent retainers. As this letter reveals, much of the routine work of the wardens was actually carried out on their behalf by deputies, relying on the authority of the wardens to enforce their decisions. To reinforce the point, Percy sent a second letter to Swinburne, threatening him with the seizure of his goods if he failed to turn up.

March days were held under strict conditions of truce, with all those present being granted immunity from arrest, 'from the sunrise of the one day till sunrise of the next, that every man may likely be returned safe to his dwelling as he came to the place of meeting'.[54] This was necessary to ensure that those suspected of offences should not be deterred from attending for fear of being arrested by the other side. Violations of the March day truces were taken very seriously. An alleged assault by an Englishman on one of the retainers of George Dunbar at a March day led him to mount a particularly destructive retaliatory raid on Roxburgh market in 1377, in breach of the general Anglo-Scottish truce in force at the time. Some two centuries later, in 1596, a similar breach of the March day truce led to the notorious episode of Kinmont Willie's rescue from the dungeons of Carlisle castle.[55] Returning from a March day at Kershope, Kinmont was seized by Thomas Salkeld, deputy of Thomas, Lord Scrope, warden of the English West March. Sir Walter Scott of Buccleuch, the Scottish keeper of Liddesdale, complained to Scrope, demanding Kinmont's release. When this was not forthcoming, Scott took matters into his own hands and led an audacious raid to spring him from Carlisle. Kinmont's rescue caused a major row between the

English and Scottish governments, for the Scots refused to punish Scott or hand over Kinmont, on the grounds that his arrest had been illegal in the first place.

On occasion, cross-border disputes might be settled by judicial duel, rather than in the wardens' court. The Northumbrian Sir Thomas Strother fought two such duels against Scotsmen, the first in 1380, against Robert Graunt; and the second in *c.*1393, when he was killed fighting William Inglis, who had attacked Jedburgh castle (of which Strother was the constable) in time of truce. Trial by combat was a procedure which, by the start of the period, had already become very restricted under the common law, although it remained a feature of the law of arms. Such duels were never frequent, however, and by the sixteenth century, were increasingly disallowed. In 1560, the wardens refused the laird of Ormiston permission to settle a dispute by combat, when he challenged his accuser at a March day. Similarly, the Burns and Collingwood families were forbidden from settling a dispute by judicial combat in 1586.

Over the three centuries after 1296, the operation of March law was undoubtedly partial, frequently chaotic and often ineffective. Inevitably, it was subject to the vicissitudes of relations between the two Crowns; and, as cross-border raids and plundering were deliberately encouraged as a military strategy, it was hard to prevent them once war had ceased. However, March days did provide a regular forum where disputes between Englishmen and Scots could be settled without recourse to violence, and as such, did a great deal to limit conflict. Indeed, given the frequency of Anglo-Scottish warfare, and the legacy of bitter mistrust and hostility inevitably left in its wake, it is perhaps surprising just how well the March law functioned.

Chapter 10: Relations between Peoples

For the greater part of the period 1296 to 1603, England and Scotland were formally at war. Yet for much of this time, truces were in force. While Englishmen and Scots frequently regarded each other with open hostility, or at least wary suspicion (Chapter 11, Section i), this was not invariably the case, and despite the conflict, there continued to be a considerable degree of peaceful interaction between the two countries. Certainly, the intensity of warfare in the first half of the fourteenth century greatly hindered such contacts, but the long truce following David II's capture in 1346 allowed for the resumption of more peaceable relations, which the intermittent bouts of open war in the 1370s and 1380s did not entirely interrupt. Thereafter, full-scale open war was comparatively rare.

England had been one of Scotland's main trading partners during the thirteenth century, and while the outbreak of war in 1296 disrupted this trade, it did not end it, despite a persistent problem of piracy at sea (goods were usually shipped, as this was far cheaper than transport by land). One of the major commodities was grain, for Scotland's climate was not well suited to the cultivation of cereals. Interrupted during the first part of the fourteenth century by poor harvests as well as war, the corn trade soon revived, with Scottish merchants to be found in many ports on the east coast of England, particularly Hull and Lynn (now known as King's Lynn), buying malt, wheat and barley. Even in times of open war, English grain might be imported as a form of ransom payment for English prisoners of war. More upmarket commodities, such as wine and spices, were also imported, sold on to Scotland from English ports. Indeed, there was a certain amount of dumping; wine un-saleable in London, 'on account of its poor quality', was shipped to Scotland in 1366, as was 'weak wine' from Gascony, via Yarmouth, in 1374.[1]

The food trade was not all one way. Scotland produced an abundance of fish, much of which found its way south of the border. There was a thriving market for Scottish oysters in Newcastle throughout the fifteenth century, and earlier; they were being imported in 1390–92, just a year or so after the Scots had raided Northumberland. A couple of years later, herring was being sent from Newcastle to Scotland. London traders sought licence to buy fish in Scotland during periods of truce in the later fourteenth century, and from then on Scottish ships are regularly recorded bringing cargoes of fish to English east-coast ports, even as far south as Dover. As now, Scottish salmon were prized in England. In 1433, the London fishmonger Thomas Weston obtained a safe-conduct to allow a Scottish ship to bring salmon, while the alderman Thomas Barnwell obtained similar safe-conducts in 1435 and 1438, going to Scotland himself in 1437, to purchase salmon for the London market.

As well as food, there was a considerable trade in raw materials. Although Scotland produced and exported large quantities of wool, it was generally fairly poor quality, and so higher-grade wool was imported from England. Some Scottish wool did find its way to England, such as the load sent to Yarmouth in 1464–5, but it may have been intended for re-export. Rather more Scottish cloth went to England, with linen being exported to east-coast ports such as Newcastle, Hull and Boston. In return, mid-quality cloths, such as russets and worsteds, were imported from all across England. Minerals were also traded, including coal, exported to Scotland from Newcastle, although the trade fell off from the late fifteenth century, as Scotland's own coal production increased. And large quantities of Scottish salt were sent to England, much of it going through Hull, Boston and Lynn; in 1586–7, no less than 39 Scottish vessels made a total of 54 voyages carrying salt to Lynn.

Nevertheless, trade was subject to frequent attempts at curtailment by the governments of both realms, usually for political reasons. In 1514, for instance, six months after James IV had been killed at Flodden, the Scottish council decreed that 'no Scottish man take upon hand to pass in England with no manner of victuals, fish or other stuff'.[2] There were also attempts to control trade for economic purposes. In June 1535, the Scottish parliament passed statutes forbidding the sale to Englishmen or export to England, of horses, and of cattle, sheep, victuals, fish or salt, ostensibly because such sales were causing shortages, 'whereby all manner of stuff has grown to a great price and dearth'.[3] This seems to have had little impact; salt was being taken in Scottish ships to Hull in 1542, the same year that an English army invaded Scotland.

Smuggling was rife throughout the period. In the late fourteenth century, for example, wool from northern England was regularly smuggled to Scotland for export, because Scottish customs duties were lower. These customs were one of the main sources of income for the Scottish government; and so wool smuggled from England helped to pay for David II's ransom. Such smuggling was common even in times of war, which saw a flourishing cross-border arms trade. In 1342, at the same time that an army was being recruited to defend the Marches against Scottish invasion, the sheriff of Yorkshire was ordered to arrest 'all those found taking armour and victuals to the king's enemies [in Scotland]'.[4] Such orders were issued with monotonous regularity, a telling indication of their lack of effect.

Anglo-Scottish trade – whether legitimate or not – was initially easy to transact because Scottish and English coinage had long been recognized as equal and interchangeable, and circulated freely in both realms, the outbreak of war in 1296 notwithstanding.[5] Indeed, during the later thirteenth and early fourteenth centuries, English coinage was used far more widely in Scotland than Scottish. This situation lasted until 1355, when Edward III ordered that a recent Scottish recoinage (issued under the orders of Robert Stewart) should be accepted only as bullion, because it had been debased. After his release in 1357, David II ordered another recoinage, and successfully petitioned Edward for Scottish coins to be accepted on parity with sterling again. However, financial difficulties, stemming in part from the payment of David's ransom, led to further debasement, and parity with sterling was lost for good. By 1502, Margaret Tudor's dowry of £10,000 sterling was reckoned to be equivalent to £30,000 Scots. A hundred years later, the exchange rate had slumped to twelve Scottish pounds to one pound sterling.

Warfare might occasionally disrupt trade – while providing openings for less scrupulous merchants – but it did provide opportunities for employment, and many Scots in the English allegiance served in English garrisons on the Scottish side of the border.[6] During the fourteenth century, some were also willing to serve with the English in France. In 1345, Edward III granted a safe-conduct for 100 Scottish men-at-arms coming to serve him overseas, though how many of them actually turned up is not clear. One who certainly did was the Balliol supporter Patrick McCulloch, from Galloway, who served in Brittany.[7] And this was at a time of high tension on the Scottish borders, culminating with the battle of Neville's Cross. Truces gave greater scope for overseas service. After the outbreak of peace in 1357, a number of Scots in the English allegiance served on Edward III's expedition to France in 1359–60, such as the Berwickshire landholder Thomas Bisset. But some Scots in David II's allegiance also contracted to fight for the English on this campaign, notably Thomas Stewart, Earl of Angus. And the chronicler Froissart recorded the deeds of a Scottish mercenary captain Hagre l'Escot who fought for Edward III in 1360, and on the Black Prince's expedition to Castile in 1366.

After the renewal of Anglo-French war in 1369, considerable numbers of Scots found employment in the English garrison of Calais, despite the increasing tension on the Anglo-Scottish Marches. The Franco-Scottish treaty of Vincennes in 1371 served to reduce these numbers, but John of Gaunt was still able to recruit many Scots for his *chevauchée* in France in 1373; and in 1386, just a year after leading his retinue in Richard II's invasion of Scotland, he still hoped to call on 'the flower of Scotland's chivalry' for his own expedition to Spain.[8] Among his retainers was the Lothian landholder Sir John Swinton, who made a lucrative career as a soldier in English service from 1370. Retained by Gaunt in 1372, and knighted in 1373, he remained in Gaunt's service until the breakdown of the truce in 1384. He then returned to Scotland to take up arms against his former employers, fighting at Otterburn in 1388, before being killed at Humbleton Hill in 1402.[9]

Few Scots fought alongside the English when war with France broke out again in 1415, probably because of the intensive recruitment in Scotland by the French, although amongst those who did was the captive James I (Chapter 3, Section iii). Another was Stephen Hart, a Scotsman in French service who was captured at Verneuil in 1424, by the English squire William Champaigne. Unable – or unwilling – to pay a ransom, he swore to become 'the liege man and subject' of Henry VI, and served in Champaigne's company for at least five years.[10] Even after the end of the Hundred Years War, lingering Anglo-French hostility provided occasional opportunities for military service with the English. In 1474–5, the Scottish exiles James, Earl of Douglas, and Robert, Lord Boyd, both raised retinues to serve with Edward IV's expedition to France; and Scots were recorded as being amongst the 'depraved, brutish soldiers from all nations under the sun' who were serving in the Calais garrison in the 1540s.[11]

A rather more peaceful arena for Anglo-Scottish contact was provided by higher education. Until the founding of St Andrews in 1413, Scots wishing to study at university had to go abroad, and although the majority went to France, some did go to Oxford or Cambridge. One of these was Walter, a younger son of the earl of Ross, granted ten marks (£6 13s. 4d.) by Edward I, while studying at Cambridge in 1305. Opportunities for Scots to study in England were curtailed by the prolonged hostilities that broke out in 1306; however, the situation improved with the thawing of Anglo-Scottish relations in 1357, and by the end of the century, 90 Scottish students had received safe-conducts to attend university in England.

These contacts often fostered a degree of goodwill. During peace negotiations in 1401, one of the English negotiators, Richard Young, bishop of Bangor, made a light-hearted allusion to having known one of his Scottish counterparts, John of Merton, a doctor of canon law, when they were at Oxford together.[12] The Scottish theologian, philosopher and historian John Mair was at Cambridge in 1492–3, and later recalled his time there with some fondness. He dedicated one of his works to Cardinal Wolsey, who had offered him a teaching post at Christ Church, Oxford, referring to the frequent hospitality he had enjoyed in England.[13] English universities became particularly attractive for Scottish Protestants after the Reformation. Two of the sons of John Knox, the celebrated Protestant preacher, were educated at Cambridge, and became fellows there.

Many Scots settled in England on a long-term basis, particularly after the end of full-scale war in 1389. Records for the 1440 poll-tax on foreigners reveal that well over 1,000 Scots were then living in England; and this represents only a fraction of the real total, for the tax was widely evaded, and did not apply to Scots who had been naturalized. Most of those taxed lived north of the Trent, where they accounted for a clear majority of foreigners. However, there were Scots living as far south as Cornwall and Devon; and in 1483, 161 Scots paid this tax in London alone (just over ten per cent of the foreigners recorded there). Many of these Scots were unskilled, being described as labourers, porters or servants; but there were some artisans, including a brewer, a carpenter, a tailor and cook, as well as James Ramsey, a surgeon; John Gurdon, an armourer; and Roger Broun, a fiddler. Where their place of origin can be identified, most seem to have come from the east coast, and mainly from burghs such as Edinburgh, Aberdeen, Dundee and Arbroath; and certainly, the vast majority were from English- rather than Gaelic-speaking areas.

There were periodic attempts to limit, or at least control, this migration, usually at times of Anglo-Scottish tension. In 1430, and again in 1455, the Scottish parliament enacted statutes declaring that any Scot who resided in England without the permission of the king (of Scots) would be considered a traitor. On the other side of the border, a statute was enacted in the Westminster parliament of 1491–2, ordering that all Scots who were not denizens (or who did not immediately acquire such status) should leave the realm within 40 days. In 1497, when Henry VII was preparing to lead his expedition to Scotland, it was again decreed that all Scots should leave the realm; those wishing to remain were to obtain licence – at the cost of half their goods, and a year's income.

Nevertheless, Scottish migrants were not always regarded with hostility. In the parliament of 1369, the Commons petitioned the king, questioning why commissions had been issued to enquire into the identity of 'Scots and other aliens who have married and inherited or are living and working within the land ... since it seems to the said Commons that to have such people dwelling in ... the realm is to the common profit'.[14] The king responded by cancelling the commissions. This was a period, in the aftermath of the Black Death of 1348–9, when England was suffering from a shortage of labour, so incoming Scots would have found plenty of opportunities for employment, particularly on a seasonal basis.

Many incomers obtained licence to remain in England on a permanent basis. Between 1400 and 1560, some 300 Scots are recorded as taking out letters of denization (granting them the status of Englishmen), while others swore oaths of allegiance to the English Crown. Significantly, most of these did so at times of particular tension, such as the outbreak of war in 1480–81, or during the wars of the 1540s; and most of them were living in southern England. Clearly, the vast majority of Scots in the realm, and particularly those living in the north, were able to manage without acquiring any such official recognition of their status (indeed, for most, the cost would have been prohibitive). Certainly, the Scotsman John Killingworth claimed to have been living in England for 58 years when, in 1440, he was granted licence for him and his English-born son to remain. Of those who did bother to regularize their status, many were clergymen. The Scots Cuthbert Karre and Adam Ridley had been able to acquire substantial livings, as the rectors of churches in Essex and Kent respectively. Indeed Ridley held two livings in plurality, and had lived in Kent as a beneficed priest for 21 years before he felt the need to acquire any licence to remain in England, which he did in 1481. Other Scottish churchmen led a rather less settled existence south of the border; the Scottish poet William Dunbar (d.1513?) wrote a poem depicting the life of a (supposedly) typical Scottish friar who had travelled 'into every lusty [i.e., pleasant] town and place of all England, from Berwick to Calais'.[15]

There is much less evidence for Englishmen migrating to Scotland. After his release from captivity, David II paid for the services of an English doctor, probably to treat the arrow wound he received at Neville's Cross; and a team of English craftsmen was employed to make his tomb, in 1372. When Melrose abbey was burned down by the English in 1385, the monks brought in a Yorkshire mason to take charge of rebuilding it. And an agreement of 1398 for the maintenance of the truce suggests that many Englishmen had settled on the Scottish side of the border by that date (see Chapter 9, Section i). Taken together with the Scots who had settled in England, this was considered to be 'the principal cause of disturbance of the quiet of both the realms'. However, although it was agreed that no more such cross-border settlement should be permitted, there was no suggestion that the existing immigrants should be expelled; rather, it was agreed that Scots in England should 'dwell and make residence on the south side of the water of Tyne', and Englishmen in Scotland should 'dwell and make residence as far from the Marches as Edinburgh'.[16]

Pilgrimage was another activity which took people across the Anglo-Scottish border. David II made a pilgrimage to Canterbury just before his release in 1357, and he subsequently obtained safe-conducts to make five more such pilgrimages, and another to Walsingham in Norfolk. Nor was he alone in making such arrangements; Canterbury remained a destination for Scottish pilgrims, along with other shrines in England, albeit on a fairly small scale. One such pilgrim was Alexander, son of Stephen, from Aberdeen, whose deformed feet were miraculously cured by the intervention of St Thomas Becket, when he came to his shrine in 1445.[17] English pilgrims are recorded visiting the shrine of St Margaret in Dunfermline, including soldiers from the army which besieged Loch Leven castle in 1334 – though Margaret did have strong English connections, being descended from the English royal family. Nor were these the only Englishmen to take a break from war to pay their respects to Scottish saints. Edward, prince of Wales (the future Edward II) visited the shrine of St Ninian at Whithorn in Galloway in 1301. St Ninian's cult flourished in northern England until the Reformation, and James V extended his protection to English pilgrims going to Whithorn. Other Englishmen made the journey to St Andrews, some of them buying pilgrim badges as a souvenir; seventeen of these badges have been found in England, most of them in London, and all of them south of the Trent.

One saint whose popularity was affected by the outbreak of war was St Cuthbert of Lindisfarne. Revered equally in northern England and southern Scotland, he was nevertheless co-opted by the English to aid their military efforts against the Scots. In 1296, the saint's banner was borne into Scotland at the head of a contingent of soldiers led by Antony Bek, one of the more militant bishops of Durham. Thereafter, until the Reformation, the banner frequently accompanied English armies across the border, and was reputed to bring victory over the Scots in battle. Certainly, it proved efficacious at Neville's Cross in 1346 and Flodden in 1513.[18] It is therefore perhaps not surprising that Scottish pilgrimage to his shrine at Durham fell off markedly. Nevertheless, Cuthbert retained a following in Scotland, and indeed, there appears to have been something of a revival of interest in the saint north of the border from the mid-fifteenth century, perhaps inspired by the efforts of Durham monks to revive interest in the cult in northern England.[19] As this suggests, Durham priory maintained a degree of influence across the border, in part through its dependent cell at Coldingham, Berwickshire, which it managed to hold on to until the 1470s (Chapter 9, Section i). It is a measure of this influence that the Scottish chronicler Walter Bower, Abbot of Inchcolm, writing in the 1440s, recorded that St Cuthbert had appeared to David II in a dream, just before Neville's Cross, 'bringing the mild request that the Scots should not invade or damage his lands', but the king ignored the vision, 'just as a snake foolishly closes his ears in response to a charmer'.[20] However, in the earlier part of his history, Bower had claimed Cuthbert for a Scot, for he had first become a monk at Melrose (though at the time, Melrose was under the rule of the Anglian kings of Northumbria).

Generally, religion was not a major issue between England and Scotland, until the English Reformation of the 1530s. Both Edward I and Edward II attempted to control appointments to Scottish bishoprics, and both were assiduous in their efforts to secure papal condemnation of recalcitrant Scottish bishops. The archbishops of York also claimed jurisdiction over the bishopric of Galloway, though this was effectively nullified from 1359, when the pope began to appoint Galloway's bishops directly. However, these disputes were essentially political, rather than doctrinal. Even after the outbreak of the Anglo-Scottish wars, the Scottish church continued to follow customary English rituals for church services. The only doctrinal dispute between the two countries before the Reformation was during the Papal Schism of 1378, which saw the election of two rival popes, Urban VI and Clement VII. This led to a split across Western Christendom along national lines, as the French recognized Clement, while the English backed Urban. The Scots followed the

French lead, with the result that the English and Scottish governments recognized different popes until 1418. However, this had little impact on Anglo-Scottish relations; the adherence to rival popes was a symptom of national hostilities, not a cause of it. When Dryburgh, Melrose and Newbattle abbeys were burned down by Richard II's invading army in 1385, one English chronicler reported that this was because of their allegiance to Clement VII. But this was probably just a *post facto* attempt to justify an act which violated the customs of war, for monasteries were supposed to enjoy immunity.[21]

Following the English Reformation, a small number of Catholic rebels fled to Scotland after the failure of the Pilgrimage of Grace of 1536–7. James V's refusal to bow to Henry's demands that they be handed over was a contributory factor to the outbreak of war in 1542. Conversely, following the Scottish Reformation (given effect with the Reformation Parliament of 1560), English hard-line Protestants could find shelter north of the border. One such was John Penry; fleeing England in 1589 after publishing scurrilous attacks on the clergy, he was welcomed by Presbyterian ministers in Edinburgh. The traffic was by no means all one way; England had also provided sanctuary for Scottish religious dissidents, such as John Knox, who sought refuge there in 1549, and married the daughter of the captain of Norham castle. When the Catholic Mary succeeded to the throne of England in 1553, he fled abroad; and for much of the next decade, he was as concerned with the English Protestant cause as the Scottish. Accordingly, his notorious *First Blast of the Trumpet against the Monstrous Regiment of Women* (1558) was directed as much at Mary Tudor, Queen of England, as at Marie de Guise, Regent of Scotland, who was moving against Protestantism in his native land. As Knox's concerns demonstrate, religious reform in both realms created a new dynamic in Anglo-Scottish relations. English and Scottish Protestants had a common interest which could transcend national hostilities, defined against the perceived threat from Catholic Europe. Thus, John Foxe's *Acts and Monuments* (better known as the *Book of Martyrs*), published in England in 1563, contained accounts of recently martyred Scottish Protestants.

Contacts between Englishmen and Scots were facilitated by the fact that Lowland Scots spoke a form of English. Whether Scots English should be regarded as a dialect, or as a separate language in its own right, is now a matter of some debate – but for most of this period, lowlanders were unequivocal in describing what they spoke as 'Inglis'; it was not until 1494 that it is first recorded as 'Scottis'. Before then,

'Scots' was used in a linguistic context exclusively to refer to the Gaelic spoken in the Highlands (although in terms of nationality, all inhabitants of Scotland were referred to as 'Scots'). Lowlanders expected their language to be readily understandable south of the border. Thus, when George, Earl of March, wrote to Henry IV in 1400, he wrote in a decidedly Scottish form of English, ending by apologizing for writing in 'Englishe', 'for that is more clear to mine understanding than Latin or French'.[22] Indeed, although for much of this period, the English were at war with the French while the Scots were allied with them, the French language (in its Anglo-Norman dialect) remained in much wider use, and for longer, in England than in Scotland. It has even been suggested that French came to be tainted in Scottish minds by association with the French habitually spoken by the kings of England and their servants.[23]

Hostilities notwithstanding, there was a degree of literary exchange between the two realms. The *Polychronicon* was a hugely influential history of England written by Ranulph Higden, the first version of which was finished in 1327; and in the 1360s it was used by the Scottish chronicler John of Fordun as a model for his *Chronica Gentis Scotorum* (Chronicles of the Scottish People). Geoffrey Chaucer was read and admired in Scotland. In a poem written around 1500, William Dunbar referred to 'the noble Chaucer, of makers [the] flower', describing him in another poem as 'rose of rhetoric all';[24] and a sumptuously illuminated manuscript of Chaucer's *Troilus and Criseyde* was produced in Scotland for Henry, Lord Sinclair, who was subsequently killed fighting the English at Flodden.[25] Other English poets were also known in Scotland. Alongside 'the reverend Chaucer', Dunbar refers to John Lydgate 'laureate' (*d.c.*1450) and 'the moral Gower' (John Gower, *d.*1408);[26] and similar allusions to this illustrious trio are made by the Scottish poets Gavin Douglas (the bishop of Dunkeld, *d.*1522) and Sir David Lyndsay (*d.*1555).

The Scottish poet Robert Henryson, who wrote at the end of the fifteenth century, found a posthumous audience in England. An anglicized text of his *The Testament of Cresseid* was printed in London in 1532; and his *Moral Fables* was printed there in 1577, with a note on the title page stating that it was 'compiled most eloquently in Scottish metre by Master Robert Henrison, and now lately Englished'.[27] Gavin Douglas died in exile in London in 1522, while attempting to secure English support for his nephew the earl of Angus (Margaret Tudor's second husband). During this time, he struck up a friendship with the Italian scholar Polydore Vergil, author of the *Anglica historia*, with whom he discussed Scottish history.

There were, however, limits to this cross-border diffusion of literature; for instance, while Lydgate was known north of the border by repute, it is less clear how widely his poetry was actually read there. Scottish manuscripts of John Lydgate's poems do survive, but most of these date from the first half of the sixteenth century, more than half a century after his death. It seems that his work took a long while to filter across the border, and was circulated in only a small number of copies.[28] As for Henryson, the 1532 edition of his *Testament of Cresseid* was attributed to Chaucer by its London printers.

It was with the advent of Protestantism in both countries that a common Anglo-Scottish literary culture truly began to emerge, built on shared religious assumptions. The dissemination of English Protestant books had a huge impact on written culture in Scotland; in particular, as English books began to be printed north of the border, so they increasingly influenced the spelling of vernacular Scottish books.[29] Before 1560, distinctively English forms of words were not used in Scottish printing; but by 1603, three-quarters of Scottish books printed in the vernacular used English forms. Initially, most of these books were simply editions of English theological writers; but anglicized editions of works written in Scots soon started to appear. Thus, the first edition of James VI's *Basilikon Doron*, printed in Edinburgh in 1598–9, appeared in an anglicized form (although James's manuscript contained many Scots word-forms).

This was partly due to the influence of the Huguenot Thomas Vautrollier and the Englishman Robert Waldegrave, London printers who both established printing presses in Scotland after falling foul of the English authorities, during Elizabeth's reign. But it was also an issue of prestige; books which aspired to academic standing were more likely to appear in anglicized form, suggesting that English was considered a higher-status language than Scots. These changes are illustrated by John Davidson's *Memorial of the Life and Death of Two Worthy Christians*. Originally written in Scots in 1574, it was first printed in 1595, in an only partially anglicized form, and Davidson felt it necessary to apologize for 'the baseness of the form of writing, which yet at the time of the making thereof, I thought most familiar according to the old manner of our country'.[30]

At the end of the thirteenth century, there were strong cultural and economic links between England and Scotland. The outbreak of war in 1296 undoubtedly interrupted these links, but it did not entirely sever them. The capture of David II in 1346 led to a degree of renewal, and these new ties survived the conflicts of the 1370s and 1380s. Proximity made England and Scotland natural trading partners, and intermittent hostilities could not long prevent merchants on both sides of the border from accessing such attractive and long-established markets. Similarly, a shared language facilitated both trade and cultural exchanges. But it was the imposition of Protestantism in both countries which established a common Anglo-Scottish Protestant culture, one of the factors which made the succession of the Scottish James VI to the kingship of England palatable to the English.

Chapter 11: National Identity and Propaganda: The Appeal to History and Contemporary Views of the 'Other'

i. National Identities

'There is nothing the Scots like better to hear than abuse of the English'.[1] So commented the Italian Aeneas Sylvius Piccolomini (the future Pope Pius II) after visiting Scotland on a diplomatic mission in 1435. His comments were echoed by the English physician Andrew Borde, who wrote from Glasgow in 1536, complaining of Scottish Anglophobia. The English were no better: the start of the Scottish wars had unleashed a torrent of abuse from south of the border. Typical was the chronicler Walter of Guisborough, writing at the end of Edward I's reign, who considered that the Scots deserved the yoke of servitude, describing them as 'restless, inconstant and unstable', and 'treacherous'. Such views hardened during Edward II's reign, when the Scots attacked England on a regular basis; another chronicle described the Scottish invasion of 1318 in almost apocalyptic terms, comparing the Scots to 'Saracens or pagans'.[2] Later English commentators repeated the scurrilous story that the infant David II had defecated in the altar when he was baptized; and so the 'Lanercost' chronicler referred to him with infantile glee as *cacator* ('shitter').[3]

Such mutual hostility was itself a driving force towards Anglo-Scottish conflict. One factor prompting Scottish invasions of England, particularly during the fourteenth century, was simply that many Scots hated the English as aggressors and invaders; according to Froissart, a party of French knights who visited Scotland in 1384 to arrange a military alliance reported that 'through Scotland, the French could have an easy way into England, for it is the nature of the Scots that they cannot love the English'.[4] Combined with the fact that raids on England could be very profitable, offering copious plunder and ransoms, this created a powerful incentive towards war. This hostility was harnessed and encouraged by Scottish magnates such as the Douglases, who owed their political prominence to the wars (at least, until political expediency dictated a more pro-English stance).

Many English borderers had also made successful and profitable careers out of fighting the Scots; and continuing border incidents and raiding created an atmosphere of mistrust and hostility in the Marches, even during times of truce (see Chapter 9). The Northumbrian John Hardyng, who had fought against the Scots under Hotspur, harboured a virulently bellicose antipathy towards them. His chronicle, written over the 1450s and 1460s, strongly advocated English invasion, and included advice as to how such an invasion might best be pursued.[5] Anglo-Scottish antagonism could erupt even in a neutral foreign setting. In 1391, during an Anglo-Scottish truce, the English marcher Thomas, Lord Clifford, and the Scot Sir William Douglas both went on crusade to the Baltic. When they ran across each other at Königsberg in Prussia, a brawl broke out, and Douglas was killed.

English hostility to the Scots was not, however, unbending; and it gradually became less pointed, as the Scottish wars declined in their impact after the fourteenth century, merging into the background level of generalized xenophobia that was an everyday part of English society. The 'Lanercost' chronicle was compiled by Franciscans in northern England, and the portions of it written after 1296 are marked by violent antipathy to the Scots. Nevertheless, on occasion, this antipathy could be outweighed by sympathy for fellow Franciscans in Scotland. For instance, describing how seamen from Newcastle burned Dundee in 1335, the chronicler related that they had burned the Franciscan friary, killing a friar 'who formerly had been a knight, a man of wholly pure and holy life' (an encomium which overlooked the probability that as a Scottish knight, he would have fought against the English). He also lamented that the friary's great bell had been plundered, and sold to the Dominicans of Carlisle, commenting disapprovingly that the seamen had no right to sell it nor the Dominicans any right to buy it.[6] The Northumbrian chronicler Sir Thomas Gray, who started his chronicle while a prisoner at Edinburgh castle in 1355–6, was greatly interested in Scottish affairs, and took a more balanced view than most of his compatriots. For instance, although his account of the 'Great Cause' follows the English line, it is preceded by an account of the descent of the line of Scottish kings, following the Scottish tradition from its foundation by the Greek Gaidel.[7]

English hostility to the Scots was further tempered by the fact that lowland Scots shared a common culture and language with their southern neighbours (see Introduction, Section ii and Chapter 10). English commentators recognized these cultural links, however patronizingly; thus, Higden's *Polychronicon* (written in the mid-fourteenth century) started with a description of Britain, which described the Scots as 'light of spirit, barbarous enough and wild, but in part amended through being mixed with the English'.[8] It was the Gaelic-speaking Scots who were regarded as truly beyond the pale – a view succinctly summed up in Polydore Vergil's *Anglica historia*, first published in 1534: 'The other part [of Scotland], being much under the north and full of hills, a most hardy and rough kind of men doth possess, which are not without good cause called wild and savage'.[9] And this was a prejudice which had been shared by lowland Scottish writers since the fourteenth century. For some Scots, however, the distinctiveness of Highland culture could be highlighted as a virtue; Hector Boece's Latin *History of the Scots*, published in 1527, drew on classical models to depict a Gaelic society which retained many of the virtues lost by lowlanders, corrupted by contact with the decadent and perfidious English.[10]

Scottish hostility towards the English was, in part, shaped by the demands of Scottish politics. Robert Bruce had to overcome the inconvenient fact that he had seized the kingship and imposed his authority by force, and was considered to be a usurper by many of his fellow countrymen. His response was to write John Balliol's reign out of existence, and to justify his kingship through his defence of Scottish liberty against the English. Conversely, King David's efforts to impose a settlement with Edward III on his subjects was accompanied by a more favourable – or at least, less overtly hostile – portrayal of the English in the writings of his supporters.[11] Faced with these attempts to disinherit him, Robert Stewart responded by presenting himself as the staunch defender of Scotland's independence against the continuing threat from an aggressive England (Chapter 3, Section i). Thus, the founders of both the Bruce and Stewart dynasties adopted an overtly anti-English stance as a means of strengthening their political position within Scotland, deliberately linking Scottish identity with hostility to England. And such views resonated with the nobility, many of whom had built up powerful local followings, as leaders of the war against the English, and against the English-backed regime of Edward Balliol. These views were unwittingly echoed by contemporary English commentators, who tended to describe Balliol's forces, and other Scots in the English allegiance, as 'the English', thus denying them their Scottish identity. This only served to reinforce perceptions of the wars of the 1330s as a struggle between nations, rather than an English intervention in a Scottish civil war.

Chivalry was also harnessed in the Scottish cause. Amongst the political classes, chivalric culture could act as a counter to international antagonisms, by emphasizing the admiration of bravery and prowess irrespective of nationality or allegiance. However, Scottish writers such as John Barbour, whose epic verse biography of Robert Bruce was written in the 1370s, equated chivalry with successful war against the English (though Barbour's work was nevertheless not marked by anti-English prejudice). Similar themes were echoed by sixteenth-century writers, such as Boece.[12]

The concept of a Scottish nation was already well established before 1296, but war with England served to strengthen a sense of national identity, in the face of an existential threat – embodied in Edward I's treatment of Scotland as a 'land', rather than a kingdom. An ideal of Scottish nationhood was articulated with great eloquence in the famous Declaration of Arbroath of 1320 (hailed in modern times as 'the definitive exposition of our Scottish identity').[13] But the degree to which the Declaration reflected common contemporary Scottish perceptions is debatable. It was composed as a response to a series of papal bulls excommunicating Robert I for his failure to observe a papally sponsored truce (Chapter 2, Section i); and it was directed specifically towards the curia, to explain why Robert was regretfully unable to comply with the pope's demands. Accordingly, it was artfully crafted to appeal to a highly educated ecclesiastical audience, steeped in classical learning, and the latest legal and political theory. Its most famous passage, 'we fight not for glory nor riches nor honours, but for freedom alone, which no good man gives up except with his life', was adapted from the Roman historian Sallust. The document was sealed by the foremost of Scotland's magnates; but in order to obtain these seals, Bruce found it necessary to employ a degree of coercion that may have helped to trigger the Soules conspiracy, aimed at dethroning him (Chapter 2, Section i).[14] This dissension revealed the very political divisions which the Declaration was intended to gloss over.

Perhaps more representative of popular opinion in Scotland is the comment of Sir William Oliphant, who held Stirling castle against Edward I in 1304. In the absence of his king, John Balliol, who had retired to exile in France, Oliphant claimed 'that he held of the Lion',[15] the emblem of Scotland's heraldic banner. The Scots had managed without a king from 1286 to 1292, and so the idea of loyalty to the Scottish nation, independent of its king, had already emerged. Nevertheless, this sense of nationhood did not encompass the entire realm to a uniform degree. The Western Isles had become part of the kingdom of Scotland only in 1266, and the process of bringing the area under the control of Scottish royal government was very far from complete by the outbreak of war in 1296. John MacDonald, the first to style himself Lord of the Isles, in 1336, was descended from a line of rulers who had once ranked themselves as kings.[16] John and his successors therefore had no long tradition of allegiance to the kings of Scots. In 1296, many Anglo-Scottish magnates had preferred the limited government of the kings of Scots to the far more pervasive government of the kings of England; but by the same token, for semi-detached Scottish magnates such as the Lords of the Isles, a loose allegiance to a far-distant Westminster often seemed preferable to the interference and intrusion of Scottish royal government closer at hand.

Equally, the exigencies of Scottish politics could override hostility to the English at an individual level. Thus, rebels such as James III's brother, Alexander, Duke of Albany, and various Dunbars and Douglases, looked to the English for support against their king. They would have justified themselves on the grounds that adherence to the English was preferable to the rule of a Scottish tyrant. Thus, one of the arguments advanced in favour of accepting Edward III as David II's heir in 1364 suggested it was better to live under such a king 'than to endure anyone ... as tyrant and plunderer', which appears to have been a veiled criticism of the regime of Robert Stewart during David's captivity (Chapter 3, Section i). And even such a stalwart warrior in the Bruce cause as William Douglas of Liddesdale was prepared to enter Edward III's allegiance, to secure his quick release from captivity and so preserve his position in Scotland. Conversely, English rebels or political factions sometimes sought the assistance of the Scots, such as Thomas of Lancaster in 1321–2, the earl of Northumberland in 1405, the Lancastrians in the 1460s or the northern rebels of 1569.

Ideas of nationhood, and the claims and perceived rights that were part and parcel of such ideas, were backed up by appeals to the authority of history. There had long been a tendency for English chroniclers to exaggerate the historical evidence for claims to the overlordship of Scotland, and after 1291, these inflated accounts were marshalled by the English Crown as proof of its rights. For example, the *Anglo-Saxon*

Chronicle included a description of a meeting in Chester in 973, where six anonymous British kings had pledged to ally themselves with Edgar, King of England. This account had already been considerably amplified by the twelfth century, when the chronicler John of Worcester claimed that Edgar had been met by eight kings, who rowed him down the river Dee as a token of his authority – one of them being identified as Kenneth, King of Scots.[17] Worcester's account was one of those cited by Edward I in 1291 to justify his claims to overlordship (Chapter 1, Section i).

Such precedents were sought right back into the realms of what would now be considered legend, but was then regarded as history, albeit history open to rival interpretations. In 1301, Edward I sent a letter to the pope in answer to a papal bull (Chapter 1, Section ii), which detailed English claims to overlordship right back to the first settlement of Britain. The case was laid out starting with 'a certain illustrious man of the Trojan race called Brutus', great-grandson of the Trojan Aeneas (the eponymous hero of Virgil's *Aeneid*). After the fall of Troy, Brutus came to the island of Albion. He defeated the giants who then inhabited it, and settled there, renaming it Britain after himself, and his people Britons. Subsequently, he divided the realm between his three sons; the eldest, Locrine, got the part which became known as England; the second son, Albanact, got Albany, later called Scotland; and the third, Camber, got Cambria, later called Wales. However, Albanact and Camber were explicitly made subordinate, 'the royal dignity being reserved for Locrine, the eldest'.[18] 'English' overlordship of 'Scotland' and 'Wales' was thus presented as being as longstanding as man's occupation of the British Isles.

This account rested ultimately on the authority of Geoffrey of Monmouth, whose vastly influential *History of the Kings of Britain* (written in the mid-twelfth century) provided the basis for the *Brut* chronicles, by far the most widely read histories in late medieval England. There had always been doubts about the veracity of Geoffrey's work, and by the sixteenth century many scholars were rejecting the tale of Brutus as fabulous; nevertheless, it was still forcibly put forward by Henry VIII in 1542, as justification for England's title to overlordship. From this viewpoint, the concept of Scotland as a fully sovereign realm was an historical aberration, for Scotland had always been subordinate to the kings of Britain, and so in turn to their political heirs, the kings of England. Thus, in demanding that the Scots accept their overlordship, the English were simply insisting on the recognition of their ancient historical rights.

The Scots, however, were able to counter this with a carefully constructed appeal to their own historiographical tradition, claiming that their kings were descended from Gaidel (otherwise known as Gaythelos) a Greek who had married Scota, the daughter of a Pharaoh; their descendants had settled in Ireland, before crossing to Scotland, where they drove the Britons out of Albany and took it for themselves. This tradition emphasized the long unbroken line of kings of Scots (113 of them, according to the Declaration of Arbroath), who were not descended from Albanact, and had never been subjected by anyone save Arthur – and then only briefly.

The Scots also made much of the fact that their royal line was descended from Queen Margaret, wife of Malcolm III (see Introduction, Section ii). Margaret had been canonized in 1250, providing a sainted ancestor for the kings of Scots (*de rigueur* for any self-respecting royal dynasty of the period). Margaret was descended from the pre-Conquest English royal family. The Norman kings of England and their successors could also claim descent from Margaret, through the marriage of her daughter to Henry I; but the Scottish dynasty descended from her son, David I. It could therefore be argued that the kings of Scots were the rightful heirs to the kingship of England. And indeed, it was so argued by Scottish envoys during peace negotiations with England in 1321.

From 1296, the ideologies which drove Anglo-Scottish relations were shaped largely by mutual hostility, stemming from the attempts by the English to impose their claims to overlordship. Religious issues played a negligible role, the Papal Schism notwithstanding (see Chapter 10). This was to change with the advent of Protestantism. Religious divides across Christendom now had the potential to create new national alliances overriding existing national enmities. And it was the need to accommodate new religious alignments that led to growing interest in the concept of a Britain united by the Protestant faith.

ii. England, Scotland and 'Britain'

On 20 August 1604, in London, King James issued a proclamation that considering:

> the blessed union, or rather reuniting of these two mighty, famous, and ancient kingdoms of England and Scotland, under one imperial

crown ... we have thought good to discontinue the divided names of England and Scotland out of our regal style, and do intend and resolve to take and assume unto us ... the name and style of King of Great Britain, including therein according to the truth, the whole island.

The same proclamation was made in Edinburgh on 15 November. This new title did not, however, prove popular in either England or Scotland.[19]

The problem was that the very term 'Britain' had carried different meanings for different people at different times – and indeed, not infrequently, different meanings for the same people at the same time. The Latin 'Britannia' was derived from the Greek name for the British Isles; but even here, there was ambiguity, because it was also used for the name of the Roman province, which encompassed only modern England and Wales. The term 'Great Britain' had first been coined in the twelfth century, but merely to distinguish the island of Britain from the Duchy of Brittany in France.[20] At the same time, the idea of Britain as a political construct was given an enormous boost by Geoffrey of Monmouth's *History of the Kings of Britain*.

Most English commentators, however, used the term very loosely, and frequently conflated 'Britain' with 'England'. For instance, Higden's *Polychronicon* starts with a description of 'Britannia Major [i.e., Great Britain], now called Anglia [i.e., England]'. The more populist and enormously influential *Brut* chronicle commented, 'Brut had conquered Albion, and named the land after his own name Britain, that now is called England'.[21] The tendency was only reinforced by the sixteenth-century revival of classical learning; English writers now preferred to parade their erudition by using the classical term 'Britannia' instead of the medieval term 'Anglia'. In vain did Scottish commentators claim that 'Britannia' referred only to the Roman province, south of Hadrian's wall, and that it was only this province which Brutus had conquered, and not the entire island. By the 1590s, the English identification of England with Britain was so ingrained that Shakespeare's audience could take for granted that 'this England' was a 'sceptred isle'.[22]

James was not, in fact, the first king of England to lay claim to the title of king of Britain; Athelstan, for instance, had coins minted proclaiming him 'King of all Britain' after 927. But the title fell out of use after 1066, as the Norman incomers came to identify themselves with England, rather than Britain, notwithstanding the fitfully continuing efforts of kings of England to extend their authority across the entire British Isles.

Edward I managed to realize this ambition (albeit only briefly), and he was lauded by several contemporary chroniclers as ruler of England, Scotland, Wales and Ireland, and celebrated as another Arthur, that most famous king of Britain. But though the Bury St Edmunds chronicler might comment that he had 'obtained the former monarchy of the whole of Britain, for so long torn and truncated',[23] Edward wielded his authority as king of England, and not king of Britain. Indeed, by this stage, Arthur himself had long been co-opted as a king of England (his record of heroic resistance to the Saxons notwithstanding). By this reckoning, the kingdom of England was the sovereign power in Britain, a view which found explicit expression in a tract published in 1547 that calling on the Scots to stop fighting against 'the mother of their own nation ... this realm now called England the only supreme seat of the empire of Great Britain'.[24]

The Scots, too, made political use of the concept of Britain. In 1307, an English official in Scotland reported that 'false preachers' were spreading a prophecy of Merlin, that 'after the death of the "Covetous King", the Scottish people and the Britons, by which should be understood the Welsh, shall league together and have the sovereign hand and their will'.[25] This was an obvious reference to Edward I, who was known to be in poor health. Robert and Edward Bruce subsequently sent letters to the Irish and the Welsh, emphasizing their common ancestry with the Scots, and urging them to an alliance against the English as the common enemy. However, rivalries between the various Irish kin-groups precluded any united front with the Scots (Chapter 2, Section i), and Wales remained securely under English rule. In 1316, the Welshman Sir Gruffydd Llwyd, a prominent official in the English administration of Wales, sent a reply, couched in the same terms of common descent and mutual animosity to the English, and offering support if the Scots were to invade; but the only upshot of this was his imprisonment by the English authorities.

Nevertheless, the Scots remained sympathetic to those they perceived as fellow victims of English aggression. One of the arguments put forward for rejecting the proposal for Edward III's succession to David II in 1364 was the way the English had treated the Welsh and Irish, 'so inhumanely and so like slaves that now the name and nobility of the Welsh has altogether vanished ... and they do the same to the Irish as far as they are able'.[26] Describing Owain Glyn Dŵr's revolt of 1401–*c*.1409 (Chapter 3, Section ii), the *Scotichronicon* quoted a version of Merlin's prophecy, including the lines:

> The Scots with the Britons will scatter the English in battle ...
> The island then ought to use the name of Brutus.[27]

However, such sympathy did not extend to any great practical assistance. Glyn Dŵr wrote to Robert III seeking his support, but after their catastrophic defeat at Humbleton Hill in 1402, the Scots were hardly in a position to offer much help.

While both sides adopted competing antagonistic concepts of Britain, a more neutral concept of an overarching and inclusive British identity was also current. The agreement drawn up in 1474, for the marriage of James III's son to Edward IV's daughter (Chapter 4, Section i), consciously evoked this idea, promoting the match on the grounds that:

> this noble isle called Great Britain cannot be kept and maintained better in wealth and prosperity than such things be practised and concluded between the kings of both the realms of Scotland and England, whereby they and their subjects might be assured to live in peace, love and tenderness.[28]

Notwithstanding the co-option of Arthurian history by the English, the Scots generally embraced stories of Arthur and the 'Matter of Britain' with great enthusiasm. Indeed, both James IV and James V named sons Arthur, surely indicative of a desire for them to emulate that most illustrious of the kings of Britain (though in the event, neither survived childhood). At an individual level, the inscription on the tomb of George, Earl of March (d.1422–3), apparently named him as 'Earl George the Briton', and noted his kinship to the kings of Scotland, England and Denmark.[29] This description was perhaps particularly appropriate for a border magnate who had spent several years in the English allegiance before reverting to the Scottish. More strikingly, because he had no connections with Scotland, or indeed Wales or Ireland, the English humanist and diplomat Sir Thomas Elyot described himself as an Anglo-British knight in a letter of 1538 – a dual identifier which contrasted with the common equation of Britain with England. The internationally celebrated Scottish philosopher John Mair went even further in his *History of Greater Britain* (1521). He had no time for the *Brut* tradition which he described as 'partly fabulous ... partly ridiculous', but nevertheless he argued that, on an historical basis, 'all men born in Britain are Britons'. And although he strenuously denied the historical validity of England's claims to overlordship, he equally strenuously advocated a union of the Crowns of England and Scotland, on the grounds that Scotland's nobility was overly powerful, and only a king who ruled both realms would have sufficient power to subdue them.[30]

The English Reformation, and the growth of Protestantism in Scotland, led to renewed interest in concepts of 'British' identity. This would find expression in works such as Foxe's *Book of Martyrs* (1563), which included Scottish as well as English martyrs; indeed, the title page referred specifically to 'this realm of England and Scotland'. In the late 1540s, Edward Seymour, Duke of Somerset, and Lord Protector of England, had attempted to win the support of Scottish Protestants for the marriage of Edward VI and Mary Stewart with a propaganda campaign stressing the joint British heritage of England and Scotland.

One of Somerset's chief propagandists was the Edinburgh merchant James Henrisoun (or Harryson), a Protestant who had offered his services to the English army which sacked his home town in 1544. Like John Mair, he argued that most of the population of both England and Scotland were descended from Britons anyway, so he proposed that 'the hateful terms of Scots and Englishman shall be abolished, and blotted out forever and we shall all agree in the only title and name of Britons'. Appealing to currently influential eschatological concepts of an emperor, who would emerge to oppose the Antichrist in the end days of the world (widely held to be close at hand), he pointed to the example of the emperor Constantius, who – according to Henrisoun's account – had subjected all Britain and married Helen, daughter of Coel, King of the Britons. Their son, Constantine the Great, 'being begotten in Britain, son of her that was the heir of Britain, born in Britain, and created emperor in Britain', was therefore a British emperor. Clearly, Henrisoun regarded him as a precedent and role-model for a king of Britain, who would unite the two realms, and restore the liberty of the (Protestant) Church.[31] Another tract, purportedly penned by Somerset himself, pointed out that by God's 'infinite mercy and most inscrutable providence', there were two heirs, an English prince and a Scottish queen, of matching age, offering an unparalleled opportunity for union. Like Henrisoun, the tract advocated taking 'the indifferent [i.e., neutral] old name of Britons again'.[32]

Written a decade later, John Knox's *First Blast of the Trumpet Against the Monstrous Regiment of Women* was addressed to 'Great Brittany', and castigated the Scots, 'unconstant and fickle of promise', and the English, 'proud and cruel', for missing the opportunity offered by providence to be 'joined together forever in godly concord'.[33] And Knox's sentiments were echoed by many of his fellow Scottish Protestants. The Scots commissioners who negotiated with the English in 1559 pointed out that England and Scotland shared a common language and religion, and even suggested that Scottish law was 'taken out of England and therefore both ... realms are ruled by one fashion'.[34] And the idea of a unified kingdom of Britain would have an obvious appeal to James VI.

However, the message that a union of the English and Scottish Crowns would be mutually beneficial was rather undermined by the aggressive stance of the English government. For many Scots, the attempts to secure the marriage of Mary appeared to be no more than yet another attempt to impose English overlordship by force – an opinion evidently shared by the Scottish supporters of English intervention who advised that if Henry VIII wanted the 'government and obedience' of Scotland, he should 'make ready force, for there was none other way but to get it with the sword'.[35] And of course, for Scottish Catholics, the English were now not only aggressors, but heretics to boot.

The concept of a united Britain did garner a certain amount of support in England. One notable proponent was William Cecil, secretary to Elizabeth I, who felt that Protestant England's security would best be served by union with, or dominion over, Scotland (Chapter 7). Elizabeth, however, had no interest in playing the part of a female, Protestant Constantine, as emperor of Britain.[36] Equally, other English Protestant commentators remained hostile to the Scots; in a work published in 1587 – the year that Mary, Queen of Scots, was executed – the polemical historian William Harrison dismissed the Scots as late arrivals in Britain, having crossed from Ireland (any association with Ireland being damning in itself from the perspective of Elizabethan England). These ancient Scots he described as barbarians, 'who used to feed on the buttocks of boys and women's paps, as delicate dishes'.[37] The astrologer and antiquarian John Dee went even further, trying to revive the issue of overlordship by advising Elizabeth to extract an oath of homage from James VI, as the 'noble and superior lady of the kingdom of Scotland'.[38]

Perhaps, paradoxically, 'Great Britain' had some appeal as a political concept to Scottish sensibilities, because it was seen in Scotland as offering an equal place to England within a wider British framework; while conversely, it was acceptable to the English – however grudgingly – because in England it was identified with the English realm writ large.

Nevertheless, this was not of itself sufficient to overcome the deep-seated distrust and hostility between Englishman and Scot. It would take more than a century from the accession of James VI of Scotland as James I of England for the idea of Britain as a unified polity to be finally realized.

Conclusion

When Alexander III died in 1286, England and Scotland had enjoyed some 70 years of largely peaceable relations. At the time, no one could have expected that war would break out within a decade, and that it would continue, on and off, for most of the next 250 years. Despite frequent and protracted negotiations, a lasting peace settlement proved elusive; the peace treaties agreed in 1328 and 1502 both broke down within a few years. Why did this hostility last so long? And how did it then abate to the point that a king of Scots was able to succeed, unopposed, to the English throne in 1603?

In the first place, it should be remembered that Anglo-Scottish relations in this period were by no means unremittingly hostile. While it is true that England and Scotland were formally at war between 1296 and 1551 – apart from the brief interludes of the 'Shameful Peace' of 1328, and the equally short-lived Perpetual Peace of 1502 – open war was far less common than this might suggest; truces (albeit often ill-kept) were in force for by far the majority of this period. During the fourteenth century, there were prolonged bouts of full-scale open war in 1296–1304, 1306–22, 1332–46 and 1377–89, but even these periods saw numerous short truces, and some more prolonged ones such as those of 1319–21, and 1385–8. Thereafter, open wars tended to be less frequent and shorter.[1] Dramatic events such as wars inevitably leave a greater trace in the historical record than more day-to-day activities; nevertheless, trade and cultural contacts flourished despite – and indeed, sometimes even because of – war.

The cause of the war in 1296 was England's longstanding claim to the overlordship of Scotland, and in particular, Edward I's determination to take advantage of the Scottish succession crisis to transform that claim into a closely defined legal reality. John Balliol's oath of fealty for the kingdom of Scotland in 1292 constituted an unequivocal statement of England's right to that overlordship. From the English point of view, when the legitimate exercise of that overlordship was subsequently resisted, Edward acted lawfully in resorting to force of arms to uphold his rights, leading to John's deposition, and the imposition of direct English rule. From this perspective, Robert Bruce's *coup* in 1306 was a treasonous act of rebellion against his lawful king.

The homage of 1292 created a definite precedent which Edward's successors could not simply ignore. One of the primary duties of a medieval monarch was to defend and maintain his or her kingdom, with all the rights and claims that went with it, so that it would be handed down to successors undiminished. For example, Edward III argued that his right to the French throne was God-given, and it was therefore his Christian duty to fight for it, and this was accepted and endorsed by many of his English subjects.[2] And no monarch could lightly give up such claims. This was spelled out in relation to Scotland in Henry VIII's Subsidy Act of 1543:

> And albeit that the enterprise and actual exercise of his highness' said title and right hath been spared and forborne, as well by his majesty as by the late noble king his highness' father ... yet that surcease and forbearing, nor any other things suffered by any of his majesty's most noble progenitors, can nor ought in any wise impair, prejudice or hurt the just, right, title and interest of our sovereign lord.[3]

In the same vein, on his accession to the English throne, James VI/I took the title 'King of Great Britain, France and Ireland' – some 150 years after the English had lost all of their French lands save Calais, and 45 years after Calais itself had fallen. And this despite the fact that his own Scottish ancestors had spent much of the previous three centuries allied with the French against English attempts to put this claim into effect. The determination to maintain the Crown's perceived rights reflected contemporary expectations of kingship. Thus, one of the charges laid against Edward II to justify his deposition in 1327 was that 'by want of good governance, he had lost the realm of Scotland'.[4] While the Crown might be criticized for its conduct of war against Scotland, the necessity of waging it was rarely questioned.

From the viewpoint of most Scots (though by no means all Scots at all times), for all the close links between the two realms before 1296, English overlordship was an unwarranted infringement of Scotland's independence and sovereignty – particularly as practised by the ruthlessly assertive Edward I. As for direct English rule, this was regarded as an intolerable foreign imposition. These views had found expression in the provisions of the treaty of Birgham, 1290 (Chapter 1, Section i), designed to protect Scottish laws and customs. In the event, the concerns raised proved fully justified by Edward's treatment of Scotland in 1296; his initial triumphalist settlement, after an easy conquest, made no allowance for Scottish sensibilities, and gave no place to the Scots in the administration of their own country. Nor were these concerns resolved by the settlement of 1305, although this did offer greater concessions (Chapter 1, Section ii); nor by Edward III's administration of Scottish lands in the 1330s and later (Chapter 2, Section ii and Chapter 9, i). Indeed, the same fears were still finding similar expression in the treaty of Greenwich, some 250 years on (Chapter 6, Section ii). So long as the English continued to press their perceived rights to overlordship, there would be Scots determined to resist them.

By the 1350s, Scotland's political community was dominated by a nobility who had acquired their power and status through war against the English, and against those Scots who were prepared to admit English overlordship. Anti-English sentiment remained widespread, and could easily be whipped up by the political opponents of any Scottish regime which could be portrayed as overly favourable to the English. Thus, Robert Stewart appealed to such sentiments to help maintain his position against David II (Chapter 3, Section i); and first Alexander, Duke of Albany, and then the young Prince James used them to attack James III (Chapter 4, Sections i and ii). Many Scots were able to gain considerable power and status as war leaders, and considerable profits from plundering England. By the same token, there were plenty of magnates and gentry in northern England who derived much of their power and status, as well as considerable Crown patronage, fees and wages, from the institution of war with Scotland. Indeed, the social structures of the Anglo-Scottish Marches were – to a considerable extent – shaped by war (Chapter 9, Section i). There was therefore a certain degree of vested interest on both sides of the borders in the endurance of this institution. And so, when the English offered to restore Berwick and Roxburgh in 1433, their offer was turned down, possibly against the wishes of James I. His subjects preferred to try to regain them by war (Chapter 3, Section iii).

The English occupation of parts of southern Scotland remained a standing *casus belli* – even after 1409, when English cross-border holdings were reduced to just Roxburgh and Berwick. Nor was this issue resolved when both towns were regained by the Scots (in 1460 and 1461 respectively), for Edward IV used Berwick as a justification for going to war in 1482, and took it back into English hands. Thereafter, the Scots made no further attempts to recapture it by force of arms, and its continued occupation did not prevent James IV from agreeing to the Perpetual Peace of 1502. Nevertheless, the treaty left the question of Berwick open, and the English continued to maintain a hugely expensive garrison there until well into Elizabeth's reign.

England had a far larger population than Scotland, and its economy generated a great deal more wealth; the doggedly determined English royal administration was able to extract a much greater proportion of that wealth, and divert it into the king's coffers. This disparity of resources did not, however, give the English enough of an advantage to enable it easily to fund the invasion and permanent occupation of Scotland – particularly as English soldiers generally expected to be paid, whereas Scots generally did not. By way of comparison, it had taken Edward I three wars and colossal expenditure to finally establish English lordship over Wales, over the period 1276 to 1295; and Wales was much smaller than Scotland, nor was it a unified and long-established kingdom.

Nevertheless, by dint of stubborn, ruthless determination, and by ignoring domestic opposition, Edward did manage to impose direct English rule over the whole of Scotland by 1304; and if Robert Bruce had been killed or captured in the early stages of his rebellion – as he very nearly was – then it would have collapsed, and English rule might perhaps have been maintained. Whether it could have been maintained in the long term is, of course, unknowable; certainly, the factional struggles of Edward II's reign would have offered ample opportunity for Scots discontented with English rule to reassert Scotland's independence. But it is worth noting that it took Robert Bruce as long to impose his authority over all of Scotland after 1306, as it had taken Edward I to do the same before 1304; and that until the end of the 1330s, large parts of the

Scottish political community remained willing to accept – or at least, could be coerced into accepting – English overlordship as an alternative to the Bruce dynasty. Even after this, there were Scottish rebels who were prepared to accept English overlordship as the price of English support for their particular agendas; and magnates such as the Lords of the Isles might prefer allegiance to a far-distant English government over the interference of a much nearer Scottish one.

After the death of Edward I, however, no English king was able, or willing, to dedicate the necessary resources sustainedly over a period long enough to re-establish English authority over Scotland. Edward III had considerable success, by backing Edward Balliol in 1333–6 in what was essentially a Scottish civil war; but from 1337, he turned his attention to war with France. England simply lacked the resources to impose and maintain its overlordship on Scotland by military force in the face of continuing resistance, at the same time as fighting France. And France now occupied a higher priority than Scotland. Henceforth, English interventions in Scotland were largely confined to defending their existing holdings; and punitive raiding (albeit sometimes on a grand scale) aimed at deterrence rather than conquest. After 1400, no reigning English monarch would cross the Anglo-Scottish border until James I/VI came south in 1603. In 1547, the Protector Somerset did make a determined effort to impose an Anglo-Scottish union by force, and initially met with some degree of success. However, after Mary's betrothal to the Dauphin and departure for France, and the consequent entry of the French into the war, the English found themselves once again fighting both France and Scotland; and once again, they lacked the resources to do so. The war degenerated into a dogged rearguard action by English forces, whose goal was now supposedly to impose English overlordship, but who had no realistic prospect of achieving this.

Conversely, the Scots were never able to pose a real threat to more than a part of England, and that not the wealthiest or most populous part. In terms of a direct military impact, Anglo-Scottish warfare was confined almost entirely to the north. Even in the years after Bannockburn, when England was in a state of dire political and military disarray, no Scottish army ever penetrated further south than the Humber – remaining safely far remote from the centres of English government. Thereafter, Scottish raiding was confined mainly to the borders. And while parts of the Marches were effectively overrun during Edward II's reign, the Scots never attempted to establish any lasting occupation of English lands. Robert I was able to impose a peace on England in 1328 only because of the acute political difficulties facing the unstable regime of Isabella and Mortimer. Under Robert, the Scots did mount a serious challenge to English hegemony over the British Isles. However, their invasion of Ireland failed, and attempts to stir up anti-English sentiment in Wales never amounted to much; the Scots proved unable to marshal the Irish and the Welsh into a broad alliance against England. It was only in conjunction with the French that Scotland could present a real threat to England, such as the plan for the combined invasions of 1385 (Chapter 3, Section ii).

Indeed, for much of this period, relations between England and Scotland can only be understood in the context of their relations with France. Anglo-Scottish relations were in large part shaped by Anglo-French hostility, which was itself exacerbated by the French alliance with Scotland. Indeed, the Franco-Scottish alliance of 1295 was one of the factors that decided Edward I on war the following year. In 1334, Philippe VI helped to save David Bruce's kingship when he offered him a base in France to establish a court in exile. In turn, this was one of the factors which sparked war between England and France three years later, which served to re-direct the main English military effort away from Scotland (Chapter 3, Section i).

For the Scots, alliance with France offered protection against English aggression; but there were other factors which sustained and reinforced it. For a small kingdom on the periphery of Europe, alliance with France offered enormous prestige, and the chance to participate in wider European affairs. In the fifteenth century, marriage alliances with the French royal family raised the standing of the Scottish monarchy, and confirmed its sovereign status. A number of Scots received generous patronage from the French Crown, and some settled in France, including nobles, and soldiers from the Scottish armies which served there in the 1420s. The alliance also protected Scottish trade with Flanders, which was under French rule for much of this period.[5]

For the English, however, the same alliance was a standing impediment to their ambitions in France; 1346, 1355, 1417 and 1513 all saw Scottish invasions of England launched at the instigation of the French, while English armies were invading France – 'the old pranks of the Scots, which is ever to invade England when the king is out' (as the Tudor chronicler Edward Hall put it).[6] In the 1520s and 1540s, Henry VIII's determination to make war on France once again entailed war with Scotland. And the 1420s had seen large Scottish armies fighting the

English in France, while the alliance also presented the threat of joint Franco-Scottish aggression.

With the end of the Hundred Years War, the French had less need of the Scots as an ally against England, offering the prospect of better Anglo-Scottish relations. Nevertheless, English fear of Franco-Scottish alliance remained in itself sufficient to undermine Anglo-Scottish peace. The improved relations painstakingly forged by James III broke down in large part due to Edward IV's fear of the spectre of the Auld Alliance. The same fear haunted Henry VII's Perpetual Peace. And post-Flodden relations were dominated by Henry VIII's refusal to accept the regency of the French-born duke of Albany, effectively an agent of François I. From the late fifteenth century, however, Anglo-Scottish relations were also increasingly entangled with the ongoing rivalry between the French royal house of Valois, and the Habsburg Empire. England was no longer the main threat to France, and Anglo-Scottish relations were increasingly determined by the rivalry between France and the Empire, and their need for allies against each other.

The Franco-Scottish alliance effectively ended in the 1550s. With Mary Stewart's betrothal to the Dauphin, the Auld Alliance, which had served to preserve Scottish independence, was transformed into a French domination of Scotland. When Mary returned to Scotland after the death of her husband, the French king, her nobility was united in rejecting French proposals for a resumption of the alliance. With the death of this 250-year-old alliance, a substantial cause of Anglo-Scottish hostility was eliminated.

One of the principal factors which undermined the Auld Alliance was religion; the increasingly powerful Scottish Protestant Congregation was determined to oust the French-dominated Catholic governing faction. With the succession of a Protestant queen in England, and a religious settlement which established the protestant Kirk in Scotland, the two regimes now had shared religion, and increasingly, a shared culture based on that religion. Elizabeth had been instrumental in ensuring the victory of the Congregation in 1560, and Mary Stewart's subsequent captivity in England gave Elizabeth huge influence over James's minority government; indeed, in the 1570s, English armies intervened to preserve James's kingship – and then left again. By 1603, the image of England as defender of the Scottish Kirk was nearly half a century old, offering a convincing alternative to the more traditional image of the Auld Enemy who sought to conquer the realm.

James's claim to the English throne came to him through dynastic accident. But the fact that a Scottish king was able to accede to the English throne unopposed – indeed, with his succession stage-managed by the English Secretary of State and the privy council – was due in large part to a shared Protestantism, and English fears of Catholic Counter-Reformation. By the time Elizabeth's reign was drawing to a close, England had seen the re-creation of the Protestant Church, and the establishment of a secure Protestant regime, which had survived numerous Catholic plots. A disputed succession could jeopardize this. To preserve the peace, the Protestant Church, and their own positions, Elizabeth's council needed the smooth succession of a suitable Protestant candidate.

James clearly had every intention of succeeding. He had begun to build up his own party within England, and had the resources of a kingdom to back up his claim against any potential rival. From the Scottish point of view, there may have been fears that the union of the Crowns would lead to the loss of their laws, liberties and autonomy, concern for which had featured so prominently in past negotiations with England. However, James VI was a king, and it was the divine duty of kings to pursue their rights. And, after all, it was a Scottish king taking an English throne.

From the English viewpoint, however, the prospect of a Scottish succession offered little threat to English liberty, since, as Henry VII had reputedly reasoned, 'England would not be absorbed by Scotland, but rather Scotland by England'.[7] The concept of a union of England and Scotland was by now thoroughly familiarized. It had been presented by Somerset's propaganda, on both sides of the border, as a prescription for strengthening Protestantism; and in the 1560s, William Cecil had seen a league with Protestant Scotland as the best English defence against the forces of Catholicism massing on the Continent – a proposal which was finally realized in the Anglo-Scottish amity of 1585. James was an adult, male Protestant, whose legitimate birth was not in question, and who already had two sons to succeed him. In the England of 1603, this was enough to ensure his acceptance. And so, three centuries of Anglo-Scottish hostility which arose out of dynastic accident was finally resolved by – dynastic accident.

Notes

Introduction

1. T. Craig, *De unione regnorum Britanniae tractatus*, ed. C.S. Terry (Scottish History Society, 1909), p. 468.
2. See, for instance, Barrow, *Robert Bruce*.
3. The term was used by Merriman, 'Assured Scots', writing in 1968.
4. See J. Wormald, *Mary Queen of Scots: A Study in Failure* (London, 1988), pp. 11–19. For Mary's subsequent reputation and literary treatment, see J.E. Lewis, *Mary Queen of Scots: Romance and Nation* (London, 1998).
5. Mason, *Kingship and the Commonweal*, ch. 2.
6. Quoted in Pittock, *Scottish Nationality*, p. 75.
7. Quoted by C. Kidd, 'Race, Empire, and the Limits of Nineteenth-Century Scottish Nationhood', *Historical Journal* xlvi (2003), p. 886; see also M.H. Hammond, 'Ethnicity and the Writing of Medieval Scottish History', *SHR* lxxxv (2006), pp. 1–27.
8. A. Bryant, *A History of Britain and the British People, Volume I: Set in a Silver Sea* (London, 1984), p. 206.
9. *BBC History Magazine* xii.10 (October, 2011), p. 31.
10. See, for instance, Davies, *Domination and Conquest*; Davies, *First English Empire*; Frame, *Political Development of the British Isles*; Brown, *Disunited Kingdoms*; Dawson, 'Two Kingdoms or Three?'; Ellis, *Tudor Frontiers*; Dawson, *Politics and Religion*.
11. E.M. Barron, *The Scottish War of Independence: A Critical Study* (London, 1914), p. viii.
12. For a penetrating analysis, see C. McArthur, *Brigadoon, Braveheart, and the Scots: Distortions of Scotland in Hollywood Cinema* (London, 2003).
13. Quoted in Pittock, *Scottish Nationality*, p. 91.
14. *The Herald*, 2 Jan. 2012 (www.heraldscotland.com/news/home-news/bannockburn-date-mooted-for-referendum.16330813; accessed: 31 December 2013).
15. *The Anglo-Saxon Chronicle*, tr. G.N. Garmonsway (London, 1972), p. 24 (A version, *sub anno* 924).

16. Barrow, 'Anglo-Scottish Border'.
17. *Early Scottish charters prior to AD 1153*, ed. A.C. Lawrie (Glasgow, 1905), no. 15.
18. Duncan, *Kingship of the Scots*, pp. 72–3.
19. *ASR*, no. 1.
20. *ASR*, no. 2. And see *ASR*, nos. 30 (pp. 203–7), and 31 (p. 231) respectively for the English claims and Scottish counter-claims in *c*.1301.
21. A.A.M. Duncan, 'John King of England and the Kings of Scots', in *King John: New Interpretations*, ed. S.D. Church (Woodbridge, 1999), pp. 247–71.
22. J. Gillingham, *The English in the Twelfth Century: Imperialism, National Identity and Political Values* (Woodbridge, 2000); R. Bartlett, *The Making of Europe: Conquest, Colonization and Cultural Change, 950–1350* (Harmondsworth, 1993).
23. For the process of 'anglicization', see Davies, *First English Empire*.
24. K.J. Stringer, *Earl David of Huntingdon 1152–1219: A Study in Anglo-Scottish History* (Edinburgh, 1985), ch. 9.
25. See R.M. Blakely, *The Brus Family in England and Scotland 1100–1295* (Woodbridge, 2005), and Beam, *Balliol Dynasty*.
26. *Annales monastici*, ed. H.R. Luard, RS (5 vols, 1864–9), iv, 277.

Chapter 1: Hammer of the Scots? Edward I and Scotland, 1286–1306

1. Fordun, p. 313.
2. For an upbeat assessment of the guardians' government, see Duncan, *Kingship of the Scots*, pp. 179–81; for a contrasting view, see Young, *Robert the Bruce's Rivals*, pp. 98–104.
3. A translation is provided by G.W.S. Barrow, 'A Kingdom in Crisis: Scotland and the Maid of Norway', *SHR* lxix (1990), pp. 120–41; see also W.B. Stevenson, 'The Treaty of Northampton (1290): A Scottish Charter of Liberties?', *SHR* lxxxvi (2007), pp. 1–15.
4. G.G. Simpson, 'The Claim of Florence, Count of Holland, to the Scottish Throne, 1291–2', *SHR* xxxvi (1957), pp. 111–24; Barrow, *Bruce*, pp. 52–64.
5. E.L.G. Stones, 'The Appeal to History in Anglo-Scottish Relations Between 1291 and 1401. Part I', *Archives* ix (1969–70), pp. 11–21.
6. *ASR*, no. 15.
7. *ASR*, no. 16; *Edward I and the Throne of Scotland*, eds. Stones and Simpson, D.10, pp. 30–1.
8. The most detailed analysis of the 'Great Cause' is Duncan, *Kingship of the Scots*, chs. 12–13.
9. *William Rishanger, cronica et annales*, ed. H.T. Riley, RS (1865), p. 371.
10. *ASR*, no. 24.
11. M. Strickland, '"All Brought to Nought and Thy State Undone": Treason, Disinvestiture and the Disgracing of Arms under Edward II', in *Soldiers, Nobles and Gentlemen*, eds. P. Coss and C. Tyerman (Woodbridge, 2009), pp. 288–96.
12. Fordun, p. 319.
13. *Scalacronica*, p. 39. Edward's government in Scotland is analysed by Watson, *Under the Hammer*, pp. 30–6.

14. *Documents Illustrative of the History of Scotland, 1286–1306*, ed. J. Stevenson (2 vols, London, 1870), ii, 203.
15. For the campaign and battle, see M. Prestwich, 'The Battle of Stirling Bridge: An English Perspective', in *The Wallace Book*, ed. E.J. Cowan (Edinburgh, 2007), pp. 64–76; A.M. Spencer, 'John de Warenne, Guardian of Scotland, and the Battle of Stirling Bridge', in *England and Scotland*, eds. King and Simpkin, pp. 39–51.
16. C.J. McNamee, 'William Wallace's Invasion of Northern England in 1297', *NH* xxvi (1990).
17. *Rishanger*, ed. Riley, p. 385.
18. N. Reid, 'The Kingless Kingdom: The Scottish Guardianships of 1286–1306', *SHR* lxi (1982), pp. 112–13.
19. E.L.G. Stones, 'The Submission of Robert Bruce to Edward I, c.1301–2', *SHR* xxxiv (1955). For the terms, see *ASR*, no. 32.
20. For the campaign and settlement, see M. Haskell, 'Breaking the Stalemate: The Scottish Campaign of Edward I, 1303–4', in *Thirteenth-Century England VII*, eds. M. Prestwich, et al. (Woodbridge, 1999), pp. 223–42; F.J. Watson, 'Settling the Stalemate: Edward I's Peace in Scotland, 1303–1305', in *Thirteenth-Century England VI*, eds. M. Prestwich, et al. (Woodbridge, 1997), pp. 127–44.
21. *ASR*, no. 33.
22. Davies, *Domination and Conquest*; Davies, *First English Empire*; Frame, *Political Development of the British Isles*.

Chapter 2: Scottish Civil Wars, 1306–37

1. A. Young, 'The Comyns and Anglo-Scottish Relations (1286–1314)', in *Thirteenth-Century England VII*, eds. M. Prestwich, et al. (Woodbridge, 1999), pp. 218–22.
2. *The Chronicle of Lanercost, 1272–1346*, trs. H. Maxwell (Glasgow, 1913), p. 178; M. Strickland, 'Treason, Feud and the Growth of State Violence: Edward I and the "War of the Earl of Carrick", 1306–7', in *War, Government and Aristocracy in the British Isles, c.1150–1500*, eds. C. Given-Wilson, et al. (Woodbridge, 2008), pp. 84–113.
3. *CDS*, ii, no. 1913.
4. For the campaign, see D. Simpkin, 'The English Army and the Scottish Campaign of 1310–1311', in *England and Scotland*, eds. King and Penman, pp. 14–39.
5. *CDS*, iii, no. 337.
6. See Duncan 'War of the Scots', pp. 149–50, which revises the previously accepted chronology of these events.
7. Bannockburn has given rise to a veritable plethora of studies – some eminently scholarly, others less so. The best recent discussions are the commentary in *The Bruce*, ed. A.A.M. Duncan (Edinburgh, 1997), pp. 440–519; and Brown, *Bannockburn*.
8. The most convincing analysis of the invasion remains R. Frame, 'The Bruces in Ireland, 1315–18', in Frame, *Ireland and Britain, 1170–1450* (London, 1998), pp. 71–98. See also McNamee, *Wars of the Bruces*, pp. 166–86 (which offers an alternative view of Edward Bruce's Irish kingship); S. Duffy, 'The Bruce Brothers

and the Irish Sea World, 1306–29', *Cambridge Medieval Celtic Studies* xxi (1991), pp. 55–86.
9. For Harclay, see H.R.T. Summerson, *Medieval Carlisle* (Kendal, 2 vols, 1993), ii, 230–56.
10. The campaign is detailed in R. Nicholson, 'The Last Campaign of Robert Bruce', *EHR* lxxvii (1962), pp. 233–46; Nicholson, *Edward III and the Scots*, ch. 3; and Rogers, *War Cruel and Sharp*, pp. 13–24.
11. *ASR*, nos. 40–1. Note that the treaty is also referred to as the treaty of Northampton, where it was ratified in May.
12. For the negotiations, see S. Cameron and A. Ross, 'The Treaty of Edinburgh and the Disinherited (1328–1332)', *History* lxxxiv (1999), pp. 237–56.
13. See Rogers, *War, Cruel and Sharp*, p. 31n.
14. *Foedera, Conventiones, Litteræ, et Cujuscunque Generis Public Acta*, ed. T. Rymer (4 vols in 7 parts, Record Commission edn, 1816–69), II, ii, 847–8.
15. *Scalacronica*, pp. 113–15; *ASR*, no. 41 (p. 335).
16. The best accounts of the siege and battle are Nicholson, *Edward III and the Scots*, ch. 9; and Rogers, *War Cruel and Sharp*, ch. 4.
17. *Calendar of Close Rolls* 1333–7, p. 129.
18. *Chronica A. Murimuth et R. de Avesbury*, ed. E.M. Thompson, RS (1889), p. 301.
19. For an alternative interpretation, see A. Ross, 'Men for All Seasons? The Strathbogie Earls of Atholl and the Wars of Independence, *c.*1290–*c.*1335. Part 2: Earl David IV (1307–35)', *Northern Scotland, 1st ser.,* xxi (2001), pp. 1–16.
20. A different interpretation is offered by I. MacInnes, '"To Subject the North of the Country to his Rule": Edward III and the "Lochindorb Chevauchée" of 1336', *Northern Scotland, 2nd ser.,* iii (2012), pp. 183–201.

Chapter 3: The Hundred Years War: War on Two Fronts, 1337–1453

1. *The Original Chronicle of Andrew of Wyntoun*, ed. F.J. Amours, Scottish Text Society (6 vols, 1903–14), vi, 90.
2. *The Anonimalle Chronicle, 1333–81*, ed. V.H. Galbraith (Manchester, 1927), p. 13.
3. Fordun, i, 366 (translation from *Scotichronicon*, vii, 155).
4. *Scotichronicon*, vii, 253.
5. For detailed accounts of the invasion and battle, see C.J. Rogers, 'The Scottish Invasion of 1346', *NH* xxxiv (1998), pp. 51–69; Rollason and Prestwich (eds.), *Neville's Cross*.
6. Differing interpretations of these negotiations are offered by A.A.M. Duncan, '*Honi soit qui mal y pense*: David II and Edward III, 1346–52', *SHR* lxvii (1988), pp. 113–41; and Penman, *David II*, pp. 153–74.
7. Fordun, p. 361.
8. *Rot. Scot.*, i, 811–14. For the negotiations, see Penman, *David II*, pp. 185–8.
9. The best accounts of Anglo-Scottish affairs in this period are Macdonald, *Border Bloodshed*, and Boardman, *Early Stewart Kings*.

10. For this interpretation, see Macdonald, *Border Bloodshed*, pp. 22–44.
11. For Gaunt's involvement in Anglo-Scottish affairs, see A. Goodman, *John of Gaunt: The Exercise of Princely Power in Fourteenth-Century Europe* (Harlow, 1992).
12. J.J.N. Palmer, *England, France and Christendom, 1377–99* (London, 1972), p. 60. For a more positive assessment, see C. Fletcher, *Richard II: Manhood, Youth and Politics 1377–99* (Oxford, 2008), pp. 128–31.
13. The battle and its background are discussed in Tuck and Goodman, *War and Border Societies*; Macdonald, *Border Bloodshed*, pp. 107–12.
14. See the essays by Goodman and Grant in *War and Border Societies*, eds. Tuck and Goodman; Grant offers a more upbeat assessment of the results of the battle for the Scots.
15. For the campaign, see A.L. Brown, 'The English Campaign in Scotland, 1400', in *British Government and Administration*, eds. H. Hearder and H.R. Loyn (Cardiff, 1974), pp. 40–54; A. Curry, et al., 'New Regime, New Army? Henry IV's Scottish Expedition of 1400', *EHR* cxxv (2010), pp. 1382–413.
16. *Scotichronicon*, viii, 37. Henry's maternal grandmother was Alice Comyn, heiress to the Comyn earls of Buchan.
17. A fascinating English report on these negotiations is translated in *ASR*, pp. 346–65.
18. The 'Mammet' is discussed by P. McNiven, 'Rebellion, Sedition and the Legend of Richard II's Survival in the Reigns of Henry IV and Henry V', *Bulletin of the John Rylands Library* lxxvi (1994), pp. 93–117; P. Morgan, 'Henry IV and the Shadow of Richard II', in *Crown, Government and People in the Fifteenth Century*, ed. R.E. Archer (Stroud, 1995), pp. 1–31; S. Walker, 'Rumour, Sedition and Popular Protest in the Reign of Henry IV', *Past and Present* clxvi (2000), pp. 31–65.
19. The most detailed analysis of Anglo-Scottish relations in this period is Hunt, 'Governorship of the First Duke of Albany', pp. 71–204.
20. *Scotichronicon*, viii, 87.
21. MacDougall, *Antidote to the English*, p. 60. For the service of Scots in France, see B.G.H. Ditcham, 'The Employment of Foreign Mercenary Troops in the French Royal Armies 1415–1470', Ph.D. thesis (University of Edinburgh, 1978).
22. For an alternative – rather more generous – interpretation, see P.J. Bradley, 'Henry V's Scottish Policy: A Study in Realpolitik', in *Documenting the Past: Essays in Medieval History Presented to George Peddy Cuttino*, eds. J.S. Hamilton and P.J. Bradley (Woodbridge, 1989), pp. 177–95.
23. Good accounts of England's relations with Scotland in this period are provided by Griffiths, *Henry VI*, pp. 154–62, 402–11; and Downie, *She is but a Woman*, pp. 32–49.
24. For the negotiations, see C. Macrae, 'The English Council and Scotland in 1430', *EHR* liv (1939), pp. 415–26.
25. *Proceedings and Ordinances of the Privy Council of England*, ed. N.H. Nicolas (7 vols, Record Commission, 1834–7), iv, 75.
26. For this interpretation, see Brown, 'French Alliance or English Peace?', pp. 92–4.
27. Cited by R. Welford, *History of Newcastle and Gateshead* (3 vols, London, 1884–7), i, p. 319.

Chapter 4: The Wars of the Roses, 1453–1502

1. For James's relations with the Douglases, see Brown, *Black Douglases*, pp. 285–308. Anglo-Scottish relations in this period are covered by Pollard, *North-Eastern England*, ch. 9; McGladdery, *James II*; Macdougall, *James III*; and Macdougall, *James IV*.
2. 'Auchinleck Chronicle', in McGladdery, *James II*, p. 164; *Rot. Scot.*, ii, 358; *CDS*, iv, no. 1245.
3. For Exeter's rebellion, and James's possible involvement, see B. Wolffe, *Henry VI* (London, 1981), pp. 282–4; R.A. Griffiths, 'Local Rivalries and National Politics: The Percies, the Nevilles and the Duke of Exeter, 1452–4', *Speculum* xliii (1968), p. 615.
4. *RPS*, 1455/6/6.
5. *Letters and Papers Illustrative of the Wars of the English in France during the Reign of Henry VI*, ed. J. Stevenson, RS (2 vols in 3 parts, 1861–4), i, 324.
6. *Memorials of the Reign of King Henry VI: Official Correspondence of Thomas Bekynton*, ed. G. Williams, RS (2 vols, 1872), ii, 141–4.
7. For the Franco-Burgundian context, see C.S.L. Davies, 'The Wars of the Roses in European Context', in *The Wars of the Roses*, ed. A.J. Pollard (2nd edn, Basingstoke, 1995), pp. 162–85.
8. 'Auchinleck Chronicle', in McGladdery, *James II*, p. 169.
9. Waurin, *Anchiennes cronicques d'Engleterre* (3 vols, Paris, 1858–63), iii, 166.
10. For the invasion, see Goodman, *Wars of the Roses*, pp. 60–3; Gillingham, *Wars of the Roses*, pp. 141–5.
11. For Henry's short-lived restoration, see M. Hicks, *The Wars of the Roses* (New Haven, 2010), pp. 196–205.
12. *CSP, Milan*, no. 249.
13. Neville, *Violence, Custom and Law*, p. 157.
14. For the 1480–82 war and its origins, see Cunningham, 'The Yorkists at War'; Macdougall, 'Richard III and James III'.
15. *CDS*, iv, app., no. 28 (p. 414); Macdougall, *James III*, p. 160.
16. *CDS*, iv, app., no. 28 (p. 414).
17. *CSP Venice*, i, no. 475.
18. *RPS*, 1482/3/44.
19. J.W. Armstrong, 'Local Society and the Defence of the English Frontier in Fifteenth-Century Scotland: The War Measures of 1482', *Florilegium* xxv (2008), pp. 127–49.
20. *RPS*, A1482/3/3.
21. *CSP, Venice*, i, no. 483.
22. *Fœdera*, xii, 175.
23. Grant, 'Richard III and Scotland', pp. 115, 125.
24. *Letters and Papers Illustrative of the Reigns of Richard III and Henry VII*, ed. J. Gairdner, RS (2 vols, 1861–3), i, 53.
25. *British Library Harleian MSS. 433*, ed. R. Horrox and P.W. Hammond (4 vols, Stroud, 1979–83), iii, 68.
26. The sermon is translated in Pollard (ed.), *North of England*, pp. 193–200.

27. *Rot. Scot.*, ii, 480.
28. *Rot. Scot.*, ii, 481.
29. *RPS*, A1488/10/1.
30. *RPS*, 1488/10/51.
31. *CSP, Venice*, i, no. 647.
32. *The* Anglica Historia *of Polydore Vergil, A.D. 1485–1537*, ed. D. Hay, Camden Soc. (1950), p. 87.
33. *CSP, Spain*, i, no. 130.
34. For accounts of the war, see Arthurson, 'The King's Voyage into Scotland'; and S. Cunningham, 'National War and Dynastic Politics: Henry VII's Capacity to Wage War in the Scottish Campaigns of 1496–7', in *England and Scotland*, eds. King and Simpkin, pp. 297–328.

Chapter 5: Auld Alliance, New Europe, 1503–37

1. The most useful general works are: for the Scottish perspective, Macdougall, *James IV*; Emond, 'Minority of James V'; and for the English perspective, Head, 'Henry VIII's Scottish Policy' (see also Eaves, *Henry VIII's Scottish Diplomacy* and *Henry VIII and James V's Regency*, but the analysis is dated). For the period of the Perpetual Peace, Dunlop, 'The Politics of Peace-Keeping', offers a slightly more upbeat assessment than Macdougall, *James IV*. For a more military approach, Phillips, *Anglo-Scottish Wars*; and for the French context, Macdougall, *Antidote to the English*.
2. Polydore Vergil, *Anglica Historia* (1555 version), tr. D.F. Sutton (http://www.philological.bham.ac.uk/polverg/), bk xxvi. ch. 41.
3. *CSP, Spain*, i, no. 210.
4. Buchanan, *History* (1582), ii, pp. 246–7.
5. *CDS*, iv, app. 1, no. 37; *Fœdera*, xiii, 12.
6. For the Italian Wars, see M. Mallett and C. Shaw, *The Italian Wars 1494–1559: War, State and Society in Early Modern Europe* (Harlow, 2012).
7. *Statutes of the Realm*, eds. A. Luders, et al. (11 vols, 1810–28)., iii, 43.
8. See K. Stevenson, 'Chivalry, British Sovereignty and Dynastic Politics: Undercurrents of Antagonism in Tudor–Stewart Relations, *c.*1490–*c.*1513', *Historical Research* lxxxvi (2013), pp. 601–18.
9. For accounts of the battle, see Barr, *Flodden*, which includes a useful appendix of contemporary accounts; and Phillips, *Anglo-Scottish Wars*, pp. 117–33.
10. *LP*, III.i, p. 457.
11. *The Letters of James V*, eds. R.K. Hannay and D. Hay (Edinburgh, 1954), p. 79.
12. *Letters of James V*, p. 76.
13. *LP*, III.ii, p. 742.
14. *LP*, III.ii, p. 994.
15. *Registrum Magni Sigilii Regum Scotorum*, eds. P.J. Balfour and J.M. Thomson (11 vols, Edinburgh, 1883), iii, p. 61.

Chapter 6: Reformations and Rough Wooing, 1537–60

1. For an overview of the reformations in England and Scotland, and their impact on Anglo-Scottish relations, see Ryrie, *Age of Reformation*.
2. *State Papers: King Henry the Eighth*, eds. A. Strachan, et al. (11 vols, 1830–52), v, 80.
3. *State Papers: King Henry the Eighth*, v, 212.
4. *LP*, XVIII.i, p. 8.
5. *Hamilton Papers*, ii, no. 207 (p. 326).
6. The fullest accounts of Somerset's campaigns are Merriman, *Rough Wooings*, chs. 10–13; and Phillips, *Anglo-Scottish Wars*, ch. 6.
7. For Pinkie, see D.H. Caldwell, 'The Battle of Pinkie', in *Scotland and War, AD 79–1918*, ed. N. Macdougall (Edinburgh, 1991), pp. 61–94; and Phillips, *Anglo-Scottish Wars*, pp. 190–200.
8. *Original Letters Illustrative of English History*, ed. H. Ellis, 3rd ser., iii (1846), pp. 295–6.
9. *The Scottish Correspondence of Mary of Lorraine*, ed. A.I. Cameron (Edinburgh, 1927) p. 282.
10. *RPS*, 1548/7/1.
11. M. Wood, 'Instructions to the French Ambassador, 30 March 1550', *SHR* xxvi 1947, pp. 154–67.
12. For Mary of Guise's regency, see Ritchie, *Mary of Guise*.
13. *RPS*, A1555/6/40.
14. *CSP, Scot*, i, no. 416, p. 198.
15. For the wider context of Ireland in Anglo-Scottish relations in the mid- to late sixteenth century, see Dawson, 'Two Kingdoms or Three?'; Dawson, *Politics of Religion*.
16. *Scottish Correspondence of Mary of Lorraine*, p. 427.
17. British Library, Cotton MS Caligula B.X, f. 28 (calendared in *CSP, Foreign Eliz.*, i, 519).
18. Cited in Alford, 'William Cecil', 74–5.
19. Cited in Dawson, 'Two Kingdoms or Three?', 121.
20. Lord Stewart to Robert Dudley, cited in Adams, 'The Release of Lord Darnley', p. 135.

Chapter 7: Better Together? 1561–1603

1. For Anglo-Scottish relations after Mary's return, see Adams, 'The Release of Lord Darnley', and Dawson, 'Mary Queen of Scots, Lord Darnley, and Anglo-Scottish Relations'.
2. *Register of the Privy Council of Scotland* (14 vols, Edinburgh, 1877–98), i, 266.
3. *CSP, Foreign Series*, 1562, no. 170.
4. 'A Declaration of the Lords Proclaimed at Dumfries, 1565', printed in D. Calderwood, *The History of the Kirk of Scotland* (8 vols, Edinburgh, 1842–9), ii, p. 573.
5. For Cecil's perspective and the negotiations that followed, see Alford, 'William Cecil', pp. 186–217; Alford, *Early Elizabethan Polity*, pp. 158–81.

6. 'Instructions by Queen Elizabeth to her Commissioners', printed in *The Love Letters of Mary Queen of Scots to James Earl of Bothwell*, ed. H. Campbell (2nd edn, London 1825), app., p. 12.
7. 'The form of the answer gevin to the Erle of Murray, and his complices', printed in W. Goodall, *An Examination of the Letters, said to be written by Mary Queen of Scots, to James Earl of Bothwell* (2 vols, Edinburgh, 1754), ii, p. 305.
8. For the Rising, Mary's part in it, and Elizabeth's response, see Pollitt, 'Defeat of the Northern Rebellion', and Holmes, 'Mary Stewart in England', pp. 200–202. For the Scottish civil war, and English involvement, see Dawson, *Politics of Religion*, pp. 171–99.
9. *CSP, Spain (Simancas)*, iii, no. 158.
10. *CSP, Scotland*, vi, 538.
11. *CSP, Scotland*, viii, 45–6; 414.
12. For the negotiations and treaty, see Grant, 'Making of the Anglo-Scottish Alliance'.
13. For the effect on Anglo-Scottish relations, see Doran, 'Revenge her Foul and Most Unnatural Murder?'.
14. *Statutes of the Realm*, iv, 705.
15. *CSP, Scotland*, ix, 495–502.
16. For Scottish Catholic plotting with Spain, and James's response see Grant, 'Brig o' Dee Affair'. For an alternative interpretation, with a more religious emphasis, see K.M. Brown, *Bloodfeud in Scotland, 1573–1625* (Edinburgh, 1986), pp. 144–9.
17. *CSP, Spain (Simancas)*, iii, no. 439.
18. *CSP, Scotland*, ix, 684–5.
19. D. Calderwood, *The History of the Kirk of Scotland*, eds. T. Thomson and D. Laing (8 vols, 1842–9), v, p. 8.
20. *Letters of James VI and I*, ed. G.P.V. Akrigg (Berkeley, 1984), p. 91; *CSP, Scotland*, vi, 523.
21. For Anglo-Scottish relations in the final years of Elizabeth's reign, see Doran, 'Loving and Affectionate Cousins?'.
22. *Letters of James VI and I*, ed. Akrigg, pp. 170–71.
23. *Letters of James VI and I*, ed. Akrigg, p. 181.

Chapter 8: Armies and Warfare

1. 'A Question about the Succession, 1364', ed. A.A.M. Duncan, in *Scottish History Society Miscellany XII* (1994), p. 31.
2. For his career, see M.H. Brown, 'Douglas, Archibald, fourth earl of Douglas (c.1369–1424)', *ODNB*. Note that Douglas was fighting for Henry Percy at Shrewsbury, in 1403 (Chapter 3, Section ii).
3. *Scalacronica*, pp. xl–xli, 69, 141.
4. Phillips, *Anglo-Scottish Wars*, pp. 214–16.
5. R. Jones, 'Re-thinking the Origins of the "Irish" Hobelar', Cardiff Historical Papers (2008).

6. D.H. Caldwell, 'Scottish Spearmen, 1298–1314: An Answer to Cavalry', *War in History* xix (2012), pp. 267–89; K. DeVries, *Infantry Warfare in the Early Fourteenth Century* (Woodbridge, 1996).
7. *Scalacronica*, p. 75.
8. *Scalacronica*, pp. 81–3; *Lanercost*, trs. Maxwell, p. 232.
9. *RPS*, 1458/3/7.
10. 'Articules of the Bataille bitwix the kynge of Scottes and therle of Surrey', in Barr, *Flodden*, p. 150.
11. A.J. Macdonald, 'Triumph and Disaster: Scottish Military Leadership in the Later Middle Ages', in *England and Scotland*, eds. King and Simpkin, pp. 280–1. For a more positive assessment of the Scottish use of pikes, see G. Phillips, 'In the Shadow of Flodden: Tactics, Technology and Scottish Military Effectiveness, 1513–1550', *SHR* lxxvii (1998), p. 171.
12. Macdonald, 'Triumph and Disaster', pp. 276–7; Caldwell, 'Scottish Spearmen, 1298–1314', p. 275.
13. *Bruce*, ed. Duncan, XIX, ll. 170–82 (p. 706).
14. Armstrong, 'Local Society and the Defence of the Frontier'.
15. *CSP, Scotland*, i, no. 40.
16. For his career, see H.S. Lucas, 'John Crabbe, Flemish Pirate, Merchant and Adventurer', *Speculum* xx (1945), pp. 334–50; E.W.M. Balfour-Melville, 'Two John Crabbs', *SHR* xxxix (1960), pp. 31–4.
17. Cunningham, 'The Yorkists at War', pp. 188–9.
18. The letter is translated in *Scalacronica*, pp. 207–9 (and see also *Scalacronica*, p. 134).
19. D. Cornell, 'A Kingdom Cleared of Castles: The Role of the Castle in the Campaigns of Robert Bruce', *SHR* lxxxvii (2008), pp. 233–57.
20. *The Exchequer Rolls of Scotland*, eds. J. Stuart, et al. (23 vols, Edinburgh, 1878–1908), iii, 672. Guns in Anglo-Scottish warfare are discussed by D.H. Caldwell, 'The Scots and Guns', in *England and Scotland*, eds. King and Penman; D. Grummitt, 'A Military Revolution in the North? The Impact of Gunpowder Weaponry on the Anglo-Scottish Marches in the Fifteenth Century', in *England and Scotland*, eds. King and Simpkin, pp. 283–96; and Phillips, *Anglo-Scottish Wars*.
21. A. Saunders, *Norham Castle* (London, 1998); Grummitt, 'A Military Revolution in the North'.
22. M.H. Merriman, 'The Forts of Eyemouth: Anvils of British Union?', *SHR* lxvii (1988), pp. 142–55.
23. P. Pattison, *Berwick Barracks and Fortifications* (London, 2011), pp. 32–5.
24. *BP*, i, no. 581.
25. The National Archives, Kew, SP 1/5, f. 45 (calendared in *LP*, I.ii, no. 2284).
26. National Archives, SP 1/46, f. 207 (calendared in *LP*, IV.ii, no. 3914).
27. For Anglo-Scottish naval conflict, see N.A.M. Rodger, *The Safeguard of the Sea: A Naval History of Britain, I: 660–1649* (London, 1997); S. Murdoch, *The Terror of the Seas? Scottish Maritime Warfare, 1513–1713* (Leiden, 2010).
28. Macdougall, *James IV*, pp. 233–8.
29. Rodger, *The Safeguard of the Sea*, pp. 168–9; N. Macdougall, '"The Greatest Scheip that Ewer Saillit in Ingland or France": James IV's "Great Michael"', in *Scotland and War, AD 79–1918*, ed. N. Macdougall (Edinburgh, 1991), pp. 36–60.

30. Honoré Bonet, *The Tree of Battles*, ed. G.W. Coopland (Liverpool, 1949), p. 189.
31. *The Chronicle of John Hardyng*, ed. H. Ellis (London, 1812), p. 366.
32. *Hamilton Papers*, i, no. 245 (p. 313).
33. *Scotichronicon*, vii, 145; I.A. MacInnes, '"Shock and Awe": The Use of Terror as a Psychological Weapon during the Bruce–Balliol Civil War, 1332–8', in *England and Scotland*, eds. King and Penman, pp. 40–59.
34. For the purchase of truces, see McNamee, *Wars of the Bruces*, pp. 129–40.
35. *Hamilton Papers*, i, no. 245 (p. 313).
36. For the concept of 'military revolution', as applied to the Anglo-Scottish wars, see 'Introduction', in *England and Scotland*, eds. King and Simpkin, pp. 1–18; Phillips, *Anglo-Scottish Wars*.

Chapter 9: The Marches

1. *The Westminster Chronicle, 1381–1394*, eds. L.C. Hector and B.F. Harvey (Oxford, 1982), p. 348; King, 'Best of Enemies', p. 116.
2. Stringer, 'Identities in Thirteenth-Century England'; and the 'Breaking of Britain' project, at www.breakingofbritain.ac.uk.
3. For the Comyns, see Young, *Robert the Bruce's Rivals*.
4. W.M. MacKenzie, 'The Debatable Land', *SHR* xxx (1951), pp. 109–25; Barrow, 'Anglo-Scottish Border'.
5. For this expression, see, for instance, *Rot. Scot.*, ii, 611 (a writ of 1341).
6. R. Lomas, 'The Impact of Border Warfare: The Scots and South Tweedside, c.1290–c.1520', *SHR* lxxv (1996), pp. 148, 150.
7. *Calendar of Inquisitions Miscellaneous*, vi, no. 339, 597.
8. *Exchequer Rolls of Scotland*, ed. Stuart, v, 582, 645; vii, 495; A. Goodman, 'The Impact of Warfare on the Scottish Marches, c.1481–c.1513', in *The Fifteenth Century VII*, ed. L. Clark (Woodbridge, 2007), pp. 195–211.
9. J. Leslie, *The Historie of Scotland*, eds. E.G. Cody and W. Murison, Scottish Text Society (2 vols, 1888–95), i, p. 97. This is the 1596 Scots translation by James Dalrymple of Leslie's 1578 Latin work *De origine moribus, et rebus gestis Scotorum*.
10. 'MSS. of the Duke of Roxburghe', *Historical Manuscripts Commission, Fourteenth Report, Appendix*, iii (1894), no. 6.
11. Lomas, 'Impact of Border Warfare'; Goodman, 'Impact of Warfare'.
12. *Historiæ Dunelmensis scriptores tres*, ed. J. Raine, Surtees Society (1839), p. ccl.
13. King, 'Pur Salvation du Roiaume'; A. King, 'Fortresses and Fashion Statements: Gentry Castles in Fourteenth-Century Northumberland', *JMH* xxxiii (2007), pp. 372–97.
14. Brown, 'Development of Scottish Border Lordship'; Tuck, 'Emergence of a Northern Nobility'; Tuck, 'Northumbrian Society in the Fourteenth Century'.
15. For Ramsey, see Brown, 'Development of Scottish Border Lordship', p. 15; for Coupland, A. King, 'War, Politics and Landed Society in Northumberland, c.1296–c.1408', Ph.D. thesis (Durham University, 2001), pp. 154–73.
16. For an illuminating discussion of border magnates in the wider context, see Brown, *Disunited Kingdoms*.

17. Watson, *Under the Hammer*; B. Webster, 'The English Occupation of Dumfriesshire in the Fourteenth Century', *Transactions of the Dumfriesshire and Galloway Natural History and Antiquarian Society*, 3rd ser., xxxv (1956–7), pp. 64–80; I.A. MacInnes, '"To be Annexed Forever to the English Crown": The English Occupation of Southern Scotland, c.1334–37', in *England and Scotland*, eds. King and Simpkin, pp. 183–201.
18. See the essays by Brown, Ruddick and King in *England and Scotland*, eds. King and Penman.
19. Brown, 'War, Allegiance and Community'.
20. A.L. Brown, 'The Priory of Coldingham in the Late Fourteenth Century', *Innes Review* xxiii (1972), pp. 91–101; R.B. Dobson, 'The Last English Monks on Scottish Soil: The Severance of Coldingham Priory from the Monastery of Durham, 1461–78', *SHR* xlvi (1967), pp. 1–25.
21. *CDS*, iv, no. 397.
22. Richard Fawcett and Richard Oram, *Melrose Abbey* (Stroud, 2004), pp. 43–4.
23. *RPS*, 1455/10/5, 6, 9.
24. *Calendar of Patent Rolls 1485–94*, 322.
25. *BP*, i, no. 571.
26. R.L. Storey, *Thomas Langley and the Bishopric of Durham 1406–1437* (London, 1961), pp. 136–43; H. Summerson, 'Peacekeepers and Lawbreakers in Medieval Northumberland, c.1200–1500', in *Liberties and Identities in the Medieval British Isles*, ed. M. Prestwich (Woodbridge, 2007), pp. 69–74; Cameron, *James V*, p. 75.
27. *Calendar of Patent Rolls 1494–1509*, p. 160.
28. *RPS*, 1587/7/70.
29. J.R.M. Sizer, 'Armstrong, William, of Kinmont (fl.1569–1603)', *ODNB*.
30. J. Hodgson and J.H. Hinde, *A History of Northumberland* (7 vols in 3 parts, Newcastle upon Tyne, 1820–58), III, ii, p. 233.
31. 'Henry IV: Parliament of April 1414', *PROME*, item 20.
32. J. Hodgson, 'Musters for Northumberland in 1538', *Archaeologia Aeliana*, 1st ser., iv (1855), pp. 168–9, 181–3.
33. 'Edward IV: Parliament of November 1461', *PROME*, item 39.
34. A. King, 'The Anglo-Scottish Marches and the Perception of "the North" in Fifteenth-Century England', *NH* xlix (2012), pp. 37–50.
35. Leslie, *Historie of Scotland*, eds. Cody and Murison, i, 101–2.
36. *BP*, ii, no. 1066.
37. For a different view, stressing cross-border identities, see Meikle, *A British Frontier?*
38. Neville, *Violence, Custom and Law*, pp. 1–7; H. Summerson, 'The Early Development of the Laws of the Anglo-Scottish Marches, 1249-1448', in *Legal History in the Making*, eds. W.M. Gordon and T.D. Fergus (London, 1991), pp. 29–32; W.W. Scott, 'The March Laws Reconsidered', in *Medieval Scotland: Crown, Lordship and Community*, eds. A. Grant and K.J. Stringer (Edinburgh, 1993), pp. 114–30.
39. Neville, *Violence, Custom and Law*, pp. 9–11.
40. For the developments summarized here, see Neville, *Violence, Custom and Law*, pp. 27–45; Summerson, 'Laws of the Anglo-Scottish Marches'; Brown, 'Scottish March Wardenships'. Lists of wardens are provided by Storey, 'Wardens of the Marches' (English wardens, 1377–1489); Rae, *Administration*, pp. 237–49 (Scottish, 1513–1603); D.L.W. Tough, *The Last Years of A Frontier: A History of the*

Borders During the Reign of Elizabeth (Oxford, 1928), pp. 279–86 (English and Scottish, 1558–1603).
41. The National Archives, Kew, E 101/73/2, nos. 41, 42.
42. *Exchequer Rolls of Scotland*, ed. Stuart, iii, 691, 465.
43. Etty, 'A Tudor Solution to the "Problem of the North"?'; Etty, 'Neighbours from Hell?'.
44. *BP*, ii, no. 410.
45. K. McAlpine, 'Proude Armstrongs and Border Rogues: History in "Kinmont Willie", "Jock o the Side" and "Archie o Cawfield"', in *The Ballad in Scottish History*, ed. E.J. Cowan (East Linton, 2000), pp. 73–94.
46. *BP*, ii, no. 595.
47. *CSP, Scotland*, xiii/2, no. 828.
48. Printed in J. Nicolson and R. Burn, *The History and Antiquities of the Counties of Cumberland and Westmorland* (2 vols, London, 1777), i, p. lxxv.
49. *Historical Manuscripts Commission, Report on the Manuscripts of Colonel David Milne Home* (1902), p. 50; *Calendar of State Papers Relating to Scotland*, xi, no. 174; xii, no. 451.
50. Cited by Rae, *Administration*, p. 48.
51. *The Register of the Privy Council of Scotland, 1545–1625*, eds. J.H. Burton and D. Masson (14 vols, Edinburgh, 1877–98), ii, 523.
52. A summary of the March law as constituted in the late sixteenth century is provided by Tough, *Last Years of a Frontier*, pp. 100–111.
53. Northumberland Archives, Woodhorn, ZSW 1/101.
54. *BP*, ii, no. 283.
55. McAlpine, 'Proude Armstrongs and Border Rogues'.

Chapter 10: Relations between Peoples

1. *Calendar of Patent Rolls 1364–7*, p. 257; *Calendar of Patent Rolls 1370–4*, p. 457. Anglo-Scottish trade is discussed by Ditchburn, *Scotland and Europe*, ch. 4.
2. Cited by Ditchburn, *Scotland and Europe*, p. 149.
3. *RPS*, 1535/33, 34.
4. *Calendar of Close Rolls 1341–3*, p. 496.
5. For the relationship of English and Scottish money, and related economic issues, see D.M. Metcalf (ed.), *Coinage in Medieval Scotland (1100–1600)*, British Archaeological Reports (1977), particularly the essays by R. Nicholson and C.E. Challis; and E. Gemmill and N. Mayhew, *Changing Values in Medieval Scotland: A Study of Prices, Money, and Weights and Measures* (Cambridge, 1995).
6. For Scots serving in English armies, see A.R. Bell, et al., *The Soldier in Later Medieval England* (Oxford, 2013), pp. 242–3.
7. I.A. MacInnes, 'Who's Afraid of the Big Bad Bruce? Balliol Scots and "English Scots" during the Second Scottish War of Independence', in *The Soldier Experience in the Fourteenth Century*, eds. A.R. Bell, et al. (Woodbridge, 2011), p. 135.
8. *The Westminster Chronicle, 1381–1394*, eds. L.C. Hector and B.F. Harvey (Oxford, 1982), p. 143.
9. A.J. Macdonald, 'Swinton, Sir John (*c*.1350–1402)', *ODNB*.

10. *Actes de la chancellerie d'Henri VI concernant la Normandie sous la domination anglaise (1422–1435)*, ed. P. le Cacheux (2 vols, Rouen, 1908), ii, 143–5.
11. Cited by D. Grummitt, *The Calais Garrison: War and Military Service in England, 1436–1558* (Woodbridge, 2008), p. 116.
12. *ASR*, pp. 353–5.
13. A. Broadie, 'Mair, John (c.1467–1550)', *ODNB*.
14. 'Edward III: Parliament of June 1369', *PROME*, item 15.
15. 'How Dumbar was Desyrd to be ane Freir', *The Poems of William Dunbar*, ed. P. Bawcutt, Association for Scottish Literary Studies (2 vols, 1998), i, 249, ll. 33–4.
16. *Fœdera*, ed. Rymer, viii, 55.
17. M. Penman, 'The Bruce Dynasty, Becket and Scottish Pilgrimage to Canterbury, c.1178–c.1404', *JMH* xxxii (2006), pp. 346–70; S.C. Wilson, 'Scottish Canterbury Pilgrims', *SHR* xxiv (1926–7), pp. 258–64.
18. J.R.E. Bleise, 'St Cuthbert and War', *JMH* xxiv (1998), pp. 235–41.
19. T. Turpie, 'A Monk from Melrose? St Cuthbert and the Scots in the Later Middle Ages, c.1371–1560', *Innes Review* lxii (2011), pp. 47–69.
20. *Scotichronicon*, vii, 255–7.
21. R. Cox, 'A Law of War? English Protection and Destruction of Ecclesiastical Property during the Fourteenth Century', *EHR* cxxviii (2013), pp. 1393–4.
22. *Royal and Historical Letters during the Reign of Henry IV*, ed. F.C. Hingeston, RS (2 vols, 1860), i, 24.
23. S. Boardman, 'A People Divided? Language, History and Anglo-Scottish Conflict in the Work of Andrew of Wyntoun', in *Ireland and the English World in the Late Middle Ages*, ed. B. Smith (Basingstoke, 2009), pp. 112–29.
24. *Poems of William Dunbar*, ed. Bawcutt, i, 95, l. 50; p. 192, l. 253.
25. K. Murray, 'Passing the Book: The Scottish Shaping of Chaucer's Dream States in Bodleian Library, MS Arch. Selden, B.24', in *The Anglo-Scottish Border and the Shaping of Identity, 1300–1600*, eds. M.P. Bruce and K.H. Terrell (Basingstoke, 2012), pp. 121–40.
26. *Poems of William Dunbar*, ed. Bawcutt, 'The Golden Targe', i, 192, ll. 253, 262.
27. T.W. Machan, 'Robert Henryson and the Matter of Multilingualism', *Journal of English and Germanic Philology* cix (2010), pp. 52–70; J. MacQueen, 'Henryson, Robert (d.c.1490)', *ODNB*.
28. A.S.G. Edwards, 'Lydgate in Scotland', *Nottingham Medieval Studies* liv (2010), pp. 185–94.
29. M.A. Bald, 'The Anglicisation of Scottish Printing', *SHR* xxxiii (1926), pp. 107–15; Dawson, 'Anglo-Scottish Protestant Culture'; A.J. Devitt, *Standardizing Written English: Diffusion in the Case of Scotland 1520–1659* (Cambridge, 1989).
30. Quoted in Bald, 'The Anglicisation of Scottish Printing', p. 110.

Chapter 11: National Identity and Propaganda: The Appeal to History and Contemporary Views of the 'Other'

1. *Aeneas Sylvius Piccolomini, Memoirs of a Renaissance Pope*, ed. L.C. Gabel and trs. F.A. Gragg (London, 1960), p. 33.

2. *The Chronicle of Walter of Guisborough*, ed. H. Rothwell, Camden Society (1957), pp. 264, 294; *The Brut*, ed. F.W.D. Brie, Early English Text Society (2 vols, 1906–08), i, 210.
3. *Chronicon de Lanercost*, ed. J. Stevenson, Bannatyne Club lxv (Edinburgh, 1839), p. 346; and see J. Barnie, *War in Medieval Society: Social Values and the Hundred Years War, 1337–99* (London, 1974), pp. 49–52.
4. *Œuvres de Froissart*, ed. Kervyn de Lettenhove (25 vols, Brussels, 1867–77), x, 299; Macdonald, *Border Bloodshed*, pp. 185–92.
5. A.J. Macdonald, 'John Hardyng, Northumbrian Identity and the Scots', in *North-East England in the Later Middle Ages*, eds. C.D. Liddy and R.H. Britnell (Woodbridge, 2005), pp. 29–42.
6. *Lanercost*, trs. Maxwell, p. 291.
7. *Scalacronica*, pp. 17–31; King, 'Englishmen, Scots and Marchers', pp. 219–20; and see below.
8. *Polychronicon Ranulphi Higden monachi Cestrensis*, eds. C. Babington and J.R. Lumby, RS (9 vols, 1865–86), i, 386–8.
9. *Polydore Vergil's English History, from an Early Translation*, ed. H. Ellis, Camden Society (1846), p. 10.
10. See the essays in D. Broun and M. MacGregor (eds.), *Mìorun Mòr nan Gall, 'The Great Ill-Will of the Lowlander'? Lowland Perceptions of the Highlands, Medieval and Modern* (Glasgow, 2007), at: www.arts.gla.ac.uk/scottishstudies/ebooks/miorunmor.htm.
11. M.A. Penman, '*Anglici caudati*: Abuse of the English in Fourteenth-Century Scottish Chronicles, Literature and Records', in *England and Scotland*, eds. King and Penman, pp. 216–35.
12. C. Edington, 'Paragons and Patriots: National Identity and the Chivalric Ideal in Late-Medieval Scotland', in *Image and Identity*, eds. Broun, et al., pp. 69–81; Mason, *Kingship and the Commonweal*, ch. 3.
13. By the Conservative Scottish Secretary, speaking in 1997; quoted by T. Brotherstone and D. Ditchburn, '1320 and a' that: The Declaration of Arbroath and the Remaking of Scottish History', in *Freedom and Authority: Scotland c.1050–c.1650*, eds. Brotherstone and Ditchburn (East Linton, 2000), p. 14. Much ink has been spilled on the subject of the Declaration of Arbroath; particularly valuable are E.J. Cowan, 'Identity, Freedom and the Declaration of Arbroath', in *Image and Identity*, eds. Broun, et al., pp. 38–68; G. Simpson, 'The Declaration of Arbroath Revitalised', *SHR* lvi (1977), pp. 11–33; G.W.S. Barrow (ed.), *The Declaration of Arbroath: History, Significance, Setting* (Edinburgh, 2003); and Tebbit, 'Papal Pronouncements'. For a translation of the Declaration, see *The Bruce*, ed. A.A.M. Duncan (Edinburgh, 1997), pp. 779–82.
14. Duncan, 'War of the Scots', p. 129–31.
15. *Scalacronica*, p. 47.
16. R.A. McDonald, *The Kingdom of the Isles: Scotland's Western Seaboard, c.1100–c.1336* (East Linton, 1997).
17. S. Matthews, 'King Edgar and the Dee: The Ceremony of 973 in Popular History Writing', *NH* xlvi (2009), pp. 63–4, 74.
18. *ASR*, no. 30.

19. *Stuart Royal Proclamations*, eds. J.F. Larkin and P.L. Hughes (2 vols, Oxford, 1973–83), i, pp. 95–6; B. Galloway, *The Union of England and Scotland 1603–08* (Edinburgh, 1986), pp. 59–62.
20. D. Hay, 'The Use of the Term "Great Britain" in the Middle Ages', *Proceedings of the Society of Antiquaries of Scotland* lxxxix (1955–6), pp. 55–66.
21. *Polychronicon*, eds. Babington and Lumby, ii, 1; *Brut*, ed. Brie, i, 256.
22. William Shakespeare, *Richard II*, act 2, scene 1.
23. *The Chronicle of Bury St Edmunds, 1212–1301*, ed. A. Gransden (London, 1964), p. 133 (my translation).
24. Cited by R.A. Mason, 'Scotching the *Brut*: Politics, History and National Myth in Sixteenth-Century Britain', in *Scotland and England*, ed. Mason, p. 68.
25. *CDS*, ii, no. 1926.
26. 'A Question about the Succession', ed. Duncan, p. 39.
27. *Scotichronicon*, viii, 111.
28. *Rot. Scot.*, ii, 446.
29. *Scotichronicon*, viii, 201.
30. *A History of Greater Britain, by John Major*, trs. A. Constable, Scottish History Society (1892), pp. 2, 18; Mason, *Kingship and the Commonweal*, ch. 2.
31. *The Complaynt of Scotlande*, ed. J.A.H. Murray, Early English Text Society (1872), app. II, pp. 218, 230; Williamson, 'Scotland, Antichrist'; M. Merriman, 'Henrisoun, James (d. before 1570)', *ODNB*.
32. *Complaynt of Scotlande*, ed. Murray, app. III, pp. 239, 240.
33. Knox, *Works*, ed. D. Laing (6 vols, Edinburgh, 1846–52), iv, p. 394.
34. Cited by Williamson, 'Scotland, Antichrist', p. 41.
35. *Hamilton Papers*, i, no. 350 (p. 506).
36. R.A. Mason, 'Scotland, Elizabethan England and the Idea of Britain', *Transactions of the Royal Historical Society*, 6th ser., xiv (2004), pp. 279–93.
37. Cited by MacColl, 'The Construction of England', p. 602.
38. Cited by Wormald, 'The Union of 1603', p. 23.

Conclusion

1. 'Introduction', in *England and Scotland at War*, eds. King and Simpson, pp. 3–4.
2. A. King, 'War and Peace: A Knight's Tale. The Ethics of War in Sir Thomas Gray's *Scalacronica*', in *War, Government and Aristocracy in the British Isles, c.1150–1500*, eds. C. Given-Wilson, et al. (Woodbridge, 2008), pp. 148–62.
3. *Statutes of the Realm*, iii, 938.
4. *Fœdera,*, ed. Rymer II, i, 650.
5. A maximalist case for Scottish trade with Flanders as a factor in the Franco-Scottish alliance is made by A. Stevenson, 'The Flemish Dimension of the Auld Alliance', in *Scotland and the Low Countries, 1124–1994*, ed. G.G. Simpson (East Linton, 1996), pp. 28–42.
6. *Hall's Chronicle*, ed. H. Ellis (London, 1809), p. 555.
7. Polydore Vergil, *Anglica Historia*, tr. Sutton (http://www.philological.bham.ac.uk/polverg/), bk xxvi. ch. 41.

Select Bibliography

It is impossible in a work of this nature to attempt to list all the relevant works which have helped to shape this book. Below is a selection of some of the most useful.

At the time of publication, the Ph.D. theses referred to in the endnotes and below are available for free download, from EThOS (Electronic Theses Online Service), at the British Library website (http://ethos.bl.uk/Home.do).

Many of the English and Scottish government records referred to in the notes can be accessed on British History Online, Medieval and Early Modern Sources Online, and (for the sixteenth century) State Papers Online.

General

Brown, M., *Disunited Kingdoms: Peoples and Politics in the British Isles, 1280–1460* (Harlow, 2013).
Ferguson, W., *Scotland's Relations with England: A Survey to 1707* (Edinburgh, 1977).
King, A., and Penman, M. (eds.), *England and Scotland in the Fourteenth Century: New Perspectives* (Woodbridge, 2007).
King, A., and Simpkin, D. (eds.), *England and Scotland at War, c.1296–c.1513* (Leiden, 2012).
Macdougall, N., *An Antidote to the English: The Auld Alliance, 1295–1560* (East Linton, 2001).
Mason, R. (ed.), *Scotland and England, 1286–1815* (Edinburgh, 1987).
Ryrie, A., *The Age of Reformation: The Tudor and Stewart Realms, 1485–1603* (Harlow, 2009).

See also the *ODNB*, which includes entries on many of the individuals who played a role in Anglo-Scottish relations.

Introduction

Barrow, G.W.S., 'The Anglo-Scottish Border', *NH* i (1966), pp. 21–42.
Davies, R.R. (ed.), *The British Isles, 1100–1500: Comparisons, Contrasts and Connections* (Edinburgh, 1988).

Davies, R.R., *Domination and Conquest: The Experience of Ireland, Scotland and Wales, 1100–1300* (Cambridge, 1990).
Davies, R.R., *The First English Empire: Power and Identities in the British Isles, 1093–1343* (Oxford, 2000).
Duncan, A.A.M., *The Kingship of the Scots, 842–1292: Succession and Independence* (Edinburgh, 2002).
Frame, R., *The Political Development of the British Isles, 1100–1400* (Oxford, 1990).
Green, J., 'Anglo-Scottish Relations, 1066–1174', in *England and her Neighbours, 1066–1453*, eds. M.C.E. Jones and M.G.A. Vale (London, 1989), pp. 53–72.
Pittock, M.G.H., *Scottish Nationality* (Basingstoke, 2001).
Stringer, K.J., 'Identities in Thirteenth-Century England: Frontier Society in the Far North', in *Social and Political Identities in Western History*, eds. C. Bjørn, A. Grant and K.J. Stringer (Copenhagen, 1994), pp. 28–66.

1. Edward I: Hammer of the Scots?

Barrow, G.W.S., *Robert Bruce and the Community of the Realm of Scotland* (4th edn, Edinburgh, 2005).
Beam, A., *The Balliol Dynasty 1210–1364* (Edinburgh, 2008).
Prestwich, M., *Edward I* (2nd edn, London, 1997).
Stones, E.L.G., and Simpson, G.G. (eds.), *Edward I and the Throne of Scotland, 1290–1296: An Edition of the Record Sources for the Great Cause* (2 vols, Oxford, 1978).
Watson, F., *Under the Hammer: Edward I and Scotland, 1296–1306* (East Linton, 1998).
Watson, F., 'The Demonisation of King John', in *Scottish History: The Power of the Past*, eds. E.J. Cowan and R.J. Finlay (Edinburgh, 2002), pp. 29–45.
Young, A., *Robert the Bruce's Rivals: The Comyns, 1212–1314* (East Linton, 1997).

2. Scottish Civil Wars – 1306–37

Barrow, *Bruce*.
Beam, *Balliol Dynasty*.
Brown, M., *Bannockburn: The Scottish War and the British Isles, 1307–23* (Edinburgh, 2008).
Duncan, A.A.M., 'The War of the Scots, 1306–23', *Transactions of the Royal Historical Society*, 6th ser., ii (1992), pp. 125–51.
Haines, R.M., *King Edward II: His Life, His Reign and its Aftermath, 1284–1330* (Montreal, 2003).
McNamee, C., *The Wars of the Bruces: Scotland, England and Ireland, 1306–28* (East Linton, 1997).
Nicholson, R., *Edward III and the Scots: The Formative Years of a Military Career, 1327–35* (Oxford, 1965).
Ormrod, W.M., *Edward III* (London, 2011).
Penman, M., *Robert the Bruce: King of the Scots* (London, 2014).
Phillips, S., *Edward II* (London, 2010).
Rogers, C.J., *War Cruel and Sharp: English Strategy under Edward III, 1327–60* (Woodbridge, 2000).

3. The Hundred Years War, 1337–1453

Boardman, S., *The Early Stewart Kings: Robert II and Robert III, 1371–1406* (Edinburgh, 1996).
Brown, M., *James I* (East Linton, 1994).
Brown, M., 'French Alliance or English Peace? Scotland and the Last Phase of the Hundred Years War, 1415–53', in *The Fifteenth Century VII*, ed. L. Clark (Woodbridge, 2007), pp. 81–99.
Campbell, J., 'England, Scotland and the Hundred Years War in the Fourteenth Century', in *Europe in the Late Middle Ages*, eds. J.R. Hale, et al. (London, 1965), pp. 184–216.
Downie, F., *She is but a Woman: Queenship in Scotland 1424–1463* (Edinburgh, 2006).
Griffiths, R.A., *The Reign of King Henry VI: The Exercise of Royal Authority, 1422–61* (London, 1981).
Hunt, K.J., 'The Governorship of the First Duke of Albany, 1406–20', Ph.D. thesis (University of Edinburgh, 1998).
King, A., 'A Good Chance for the Scots? The Recruitment of English Armies for Scotland and the Marches, 1337–47', in *England and Scotland*, eds. King and Simpkin, pp. 119–56.
Macdonald, A.J. *Border Bloodshed: Scotland, England and France at War, 1369–1403* (East Linton, 2000).
Penman, M., *David II, 1329–71* (East Linton, 2004).
Rollason, D., and Prestwich, M. (eds.), *The Battle of Neville's Cross, 1346* (Stamford, 1998).
Tuck, A., and Goodman, A. (eds.), *War and Border Societies in the Middle Ages* (London, 1992).

4. The Wars of the Roses, 1453–1502

Arthurson, I., 'The King's Voyage into Scotland: The War that Never Was', in *England in the Fifteenth Century*, ed. D. Williams (Woodbridge, 1987), pp. 1–22.
Cunningham, S., 'The Yorkists at War: Military Leadership in the English War with Scotland 1480–82', in *The Yorkist Age*, eds. H. Kleineke and C. Steer (Donington, 2013), pp. 175–94.
Downie, *She is but a Woman*.
Grant, A., 'Richard III and Scotland', in *The North of England*, ed. Pollard.
Macdougall, N., 'Richard III and James III: Contemporary Monarchs, Parallel Mythologies', in *Richard III: Loyalty, Lordship and Law*, ed. P.W. Hammond (London, 1986), pp. 148–71.
Macdougall, N., *James IV* (Edinburgh, 1989).
Macdougall, N., *James III* (Edinburgh, 2009).
McGladdery, C., *James II* (Edinburgh, 1990).
Pollard, A.J., *North-Eastern England during the Wars of the Roses: Lay Society, War and Politics, 1450–1500* (Oxford, 1990).
Pollard, A.J. (ed.), *The North of England in the Age of Richard III*, ed. A.J. Pollard (Stroud, 1996).

5. Auld Alliance, New Europe, 1503–37

Barr, N., *Flodden 1513* (Stroud, 2001).
Cameron, J., James V: The Personal Rule, 1528–1542, ed. N. Macdougall (East Linton, 1998).
Dunlop, D., 'The Politics of Peace-Keeping: Anglo-Scottish Relations from 1503 to 1511', *Renaissance Studies* viii (1994), pp. 138–61.
Eaves, R.G., *Henry VIII's Scottish Diplomacy, 1513–1524* (New York, 1971).
Eaves, R.G., *Henry VIII and James V's Regency 1524–1528* (Lanham, MD, 1987).
Emond, W.K., 'The Minority of King James V 1513–1528', Ph.D. thesis (University of St Andrews, 1988).
Emond, W.K., 'The Parliament of 1525', in *The History of the Scottish Parliament: Parliament and Politics in Scotland, 1235–1560*, eds. K.M. Brown and R.J. Tanner (Edinburgh, 2004), pp. 160–78.
Head, D.M., 'Henry VIII's Scottish Policy: A Reassessment', *SHR* lxi (1982), pp. 1–24.
Macdougall, *James IV*.
Phillips, G., *The Anglo-Scottish Wars, 1513–50: A Military History* (Woodbridge, 1999).

6. Reformations and Rough Wooing, 1537–60

Adams, S., 'The Release of Lord Darnley and the Failure of the Amity', *Innes Review* xxxviii (1987), pp. 123–53.
Bonner, E.A., 'The Genesis of Henry VIII's "Rough Wooing" of the Scots', *NH* xxxiii (1997), pp. 36–53.
Cameron, James V. Head, 'Henry VIII's Scottish Policy'.
Merriman, M., 'The Assured Scots: Scottish Collaborators with England during the Rough Wooing', *SHR* xlvii (1968), pp. 10–34.
Merriman, M., *The Rough Wooings: Mary Queen of Scots 1542–1551* (East Linton, 2000).
Phillips, *Anglo-Scottish Wars*.
Ritchie, P.E., 'Marie de Guise and the Three Estates, 1554–1558', in *History of the Scottish Parliament*, eds. Brown and Tanner, pp. 179–202.
Ritchie, P.E., *Mary of Guise in Scotland, 1548–1560: A Political Career* (East Linton, 2002).

7. Better Together? 1561–1603

Adams, 'The Release of Lord Darnley'.
Alford, S., 'William Cecil and the British Succession Crisis of the 1560s', Ph.D. thesis (University of St Andrews, 1996).
Alford, S., 'Knox, Cecil and the British Dimension of the Scottish Reformation', in *John Knox and the British Reformations*, ed. R.A. Mason (Aldershot, 1998), pp. 201–19.
Alford, S., *The Early Elizabethan Polity: William Cecil and the British Succession Crisis, 1558–1569* (Cambridge, 1998).
Dawson, J.E.A., 'Mary Queen of Scots, Lord Darnley, and Anglo-Scottish Relations in 1565', *International History Review* viii (1986), pp. 1–24.
Dawson, J.E.A., *The Politics of Religion in the Age of Mary, Queen of Scots: The Earl of Argyll and the Struggle for Britain and Ireland* (Cambridge, 2002).

Dawson, J.E.A., 'Two Kingdoms or Three? Ireland in Anglo-Scottish Relations in the Middle of the Sixteenth Century', in *Scotland and England*, ed. Mason, pp. 113–38.
Donaldson, G., *Scotland: James V–James VII* (1978).
Doran, S., 'Revenge her Foul and Most Unnatural Murder? The Impact of Mary Stewart's Execution on Anglo-Scottish Relations', *History* lxxxv (2000), pp. 589–612.
Doran, S., 'Loving and Affectionate Cousins? The Relationship between Elizabeth I and James VI of Scotland 1586–1603', in *Tudor England and its Neighbours*, eds. S. Doran and G. Richardson (Basingstoke, 2005), pp. 203–34.
Grant, R., 'The Brig o' Dee Affair, the Sixth Earl of Huntly and the Politics of the Counter-Reformation', in *The Reign of James VI*, eds. J. Goodare and M. Lynch (East Linton, 2000), pp. 93–109.
Grant, R., 'The Making of the Anglo-Scottish Alliance of 1586', in *Sixteenth-Century Scotland*, eds. J. Goodare and A.A. MacDonald (Leiden, 2008), pp. 211–36.
Holmes, P.J., 'Mary Stewart in England', *Innes Review* xxxviii (1987), pp. 195–218.
Pollitt, R., 'The Defeat of the Northern Rebellion and the Shaping of Anglo-Scottish Relations', *SHR* lxiv (1985), pp. 1–21.
Wormald, J., 'The Union of 1603', in Scots and Britons: Scottish Political Thought and the Union of 1603, ed. R.A. Mason (Cambridge, 1994).

8. Armies and Warfare

Brown, *Bannockburn*.
King, 'A Good Chance for the Scots?'.
Macdonald, *Border Bloodshed*.
McNamee, *Wars of the Bruces*.
Phillips, *Anglo-Scottish Wars*.
Prestwich, M., *Armies and Warfare in the Middle Ages: The English Experience* (New Haven and London, 1996).
Rogers, *War Cruel and Sharp*.
Spiers, E.M., et al. (eds.), *A Military History of Scotland* (Edinburgh, 2012).
Watson, *Under the Hammer*.

9. The Marches

Becker, J.M., 'Armed Conflict and Border Society: The East and Middle Marches, 1536–60', Ph.D. thesis (Durham University, 2006).
Brown, M., 'The Development of Scottish Border Lordship, 1332–58', *Historical Research* lxx (1997), pp. 1–22.
Brown, M., *The Black Douglases: War and Lordship in Late Medieval Scotland, 1300–1455* (East Linton, 1998).
Brown, M., 'The Scottish March Wardenships (*c*.1340–*c*.1480)', in *England and Scotland*, eds. King and Simpkin, pp. 203–29.
Brown, M., 'War, Allegiance and Community in the Anglo-Scottish Marches: Teviotdale in the Fourteenth Century', *NH* xli (2004), pp. 219–38.
Ellis, S.G., *Tudor Frontiers and Noble Power: The Making of the British State* (Oxford, 1995).

Etty, C., 'A Tudor Solution to the "Problem of the North"? Government and the Marches Towards Scotland 1509–1529', *NH* xxix (2002), pp. 209–26.

Etty, C., 'Tudor Revolution? Royal Control of the Anglo-Scottish Border, 1483–1530', Ph.D. thesis (Durham University, 2005).

Etty, C., 'Neighbours from Hell? Living with Tynedale and Redesdale, 1489–1547', in *Liberties and Identities in the Medieval British Isles*, ed. M. Prestwich (Woodbridge, 2008), pp. 120–40.

Etty, C., '"Noo man indented for the keping of the Borders": Royal Administration of the Marches, 1483–1509', in *England and Scotland*, eds. King and Simpkin, pp. 329–53.

Goodman, A., 'The Anglo-Scottish Marches in the Fifteenth Century: A Frontier Society?', in *Scotland and England*, ed. Mason, pp. 18–33.

Groundwater, A., *The Scottish Middle March, 1573–1625: Power, Kinship, Allegiance* (Woodbridge, 2010).

King, A., 'Englishmen, Scots and Marchers: National and Local Identities in Thomas Gray's *Scalacronica*', *NH* xxxvi (2000), pp. 217–31.

King, A., '"Pur Salvation du Roiaume": Military Service and Obligation in Fourteenth-Century Northumberland', in *Fourteenth Century England II*, ed. C. Given-Wilson (Woodbridge, 2002), pp. 13–31.

King, A., 'Best of Enemies: Were the Fourteenth-Century Anglo-Scottish Marches a "Frontier Society"?', in *England and Scotland*, eds. King and Penman, pp. 116–35.

Meikle, M.M., *A British Frontier? Lairds and Gentlemen in the Eastern Borders, 1540–1603* (East Linton, 2004).

Neville, C.J., *Violence, Custom and Law: The Anglo-Scottish Border Lands in the Later Middle Ages* (Edinburgh, 1998).

Rae, T.I., *The Administration of the Scottish Frontier, 1513–1603* (Edinburgh, 1966).

Storey, R.L., 'The Wardens of the Marches towards Scotland, 1377–1489', *EHR* lxxii (1957), pp. 593–615.

Tuck, J.A., 'Richard II and the Border Magnates', *NH* iii (1968), pp. 27–52.

Tuck, J.A., 'Northumbrian Society in the Fourteenth Century', *NH* vi (1971), pp. 22–39.

Tuck, J.A., 'War and Society in the Medieval North', *NH* xxi (1985), pp. 33–52.

Tuck, J.A., 'The Emergence of a Northern Nobility, 1250–1400', *NH* xxii (1986), pp. 1–17.

Tuck and Goodman, *War and Border Societies*.

10. Relations between Peoples

Dawson, J., 'Anglo-Scottish Protestant Culture and Integration in Sixteenth-Century Britain', in *Conquest and Union: Fashioning a British State, 1485–1725*, eds. S.G. Ellis and S. Barber (London, 1995).

Ditchburn, D., *Scotland and Europe: The Medieval Kingdom and its Contacts with Christendom, c.1214–1560* (East Linton, 2001).

Galloway, J.A., and Murray, I., 'Scottish Migration to England, 1400–1560', *Scottish Geographical Magazine* cxii (1996), pp. 29–38.

Thomson, J.A.F., 'Scots in England in the Fifteenth Century', *SHR* lxxix (2000), pp. 1–16.
Thrupp, S.L., 'A Survey of the Alien Population of England in 1440', *Speculum* xxxii (1957), pp. 528–40.

11. National Identity and Propaganda: The Appeal to History and Contemporary Views of the 'Other'

Boardman, S., 'Chronicle Propaganda in Fourteenth-Century Scotland: Robert the Steward, John of Fordun and the "Anonymous Chronicle"', *SHR* lxxvi (1997), pp. 23–43.
Boardman, S., 'Late Medieval Scotland and the Matter of Britain', in *Scottish History: The Power of the Past*, eds. E.J. Cowan and R.J. Finlay (Edinburgh, 2002), pp. 47–72.
Broun, D., *The Irish Identity of the Kingdom of Scots in the Twelfth and Thirteenth Centuries* (Woodbridge, 1999).
Broun, D., et al. (eds.), *Image and Identity: The Making and Re-making of Scotland through the Ages* (Edinburgh, 1998).
MacColl, A., 'The Construction of England as a Protestant "British" Nation in the Sixteenth Century', *Renaissance Studies* xviii (2004), pp. 582–608.
MacColl, A., 'The Meaning of "Britain" in Medieval and Early Modern England', *Journal of British Studies* xl (2006), pp. 248–69.
Mason, R., *Kingship and the Commonweal: Political Thought in Renaissance and Reformation Scotland* (East Linton, 1998).
Tebbit, S., 'Papal Pronouncements on Legitimate Lordship and the Formulation of Nationhood in Early Fourteenth-Century Scottish Writings', *Journal of Medieval History* xl (2014), pp. 44–62.
Watson, F., 'The Enigmatic Lion: Scotland, Kingship and National Identity in the Wars of Independence', in *Image and Identity*, eds. Broun, et al., pp. 18–37.
Williamson, A.H., 'Scotland, Antichrist and the Invention of Great Britain', in *New Perspectives on the Politics and Culture of Early Modern Scotland*, eds. J. Dwyer, et al. (Edinburgh, 1982), pp. 34–58.

Glossary

appanage A landed estate granted to the brother or younger son of a king.

arquebus Early type of firearm, forerunner of the musket.

arquebusier A foot soldier armed with an **arquebus**.

assurance Sixteenth-century term for a formal pledge of allegiance made by Scots to the king of England.

assured Scots Scots who had given **assurance**, and so were in the English allegiance.

attainder Legal process by which a person convicted of treason forfeits his lands and titles, and any right to pass them on to his heirs.

Auld Alliance Scots term, first recorded in the sixteenth century, for the 'old alliance' between Scotland and France.

canon law Body of international ecclesiastical law governing the Catholic Church, influenced by principles of **Roman law**.

chevauchée A fast-moving mounted raid deep into enemy territory, aimed at causing maximum destruction by burning and plundering.

commission of array A small body of local magnates and gentry, appointed by the English Crown to conscript specified numbers of men within a particular locality to serve as soldiers. March wardens exercised these powers as part of their office.

common law Law common to the entire realm, administered by the king's courts. England and Scotland had their own separate common laws, though the early development of Scottish common law was heavily influenced by English practice.

Congregation, the A mid-sixteenth-century Scottish party which favoured the establishment of a reformed church in Scotland.

Counter-Reformation The movement in the Catholic Church, launched at the Council of Trent (1545–63), to combat the Protestant Reformation.

curia The papal court.

customary law Any body of law based on custom, precedent and practice rather than on written statutes.

Debatable Lands An area of Liddesdale, about ten miles by four, known as the Debatable Lands after it became the subject of a long-running border dispute from the mid-fifteenth century.

denizen A foreigner permitted to reside permanently in another realm.

Disinherited, the A faction of Scottish and English nobles who had forfeited lands in Scotland to Robert Bruce, and who supported Edward Balliol's expedition in 1332, in the hope of regaining them (Chapter 2, Section ii).

Emperor, the Ruler of the 'Holy Roman Empire', which in the sixteenth century encompassed what is now Germany, Austria, Belgium and the Netherlands.

franchise See **liberty**.

'Great Cause' Term coined by historians for the hearings before Edward I in 1291–2 to decide the succession to the Scottish kingship (Chapter 1, Section i).

King's party The Scottish faction supporting James VI's kingship, against the rule of his mother, Mary (see **Queen's party**).

Kirk, the The reformed, Protestant, Church of Scotland.

Landsknechte Professional mercenary foot soldiers from Germany, usually armed with **pikes** or **arquebuses**.

law of arms, laws of war Body of international **customary law** which governed the conduct of warfare, and disputes between soldiers.

liberty A lordship where many of the usual functions of royal government were exercised by the lord's own officials, rather than by officers of the Crown. Such lordships were therefore separate from the Crown's legal system. Also called a **franchise**.

livery Distinctive insignia or uniform given to a lord's retainers to identify them as such.

Lords of the Congregation The Scottish magnates who led the **Congregation**.

man-at-arms A man equipped with full armour and a warhorse (though men-at-arms frequently fought on foot).

March day Formal meeting between the **March wardens** from both sides of the border, at specified meeting places, fixed by custom (Chapter 9, Section ii).

March law Body of laws dealing with cross-border disputes between Englishmen and Scots (Chapter 9, Section ii).

March warden, warden of the Marches Officer appointed by the Crown with responsibility for the defence of the March, and for administering **March law** (Chapter 9, Section ii).

notary Official scribe licensed by the Catholic Church to make authoritative legal records of public transactions.

papal bull Official decree or instruction issued by the pope, so-called from the lead seal or 'bull' used to authenticate it.

pike A long spear, sixteen to twenty feet in length, widely used on the Continent from the end of the fifteenth century. They were very unwieldy, and troops needed to be trained and drilled in how to use them effectively.

primogeniture   Principle of inheritance, practised in English and Scottish **common law**, whereby the eldest son inherited his father's entire estate. Where no sons survived, the estate would be divided equally between surviving daughters.

prince   In **Roman law**, an independent sovereign ruler.

Queen's party   The Scottish faction supporting the queenship of Mary, Queen of Scots, after the coronation of her son, James VI, in 1567 (see **King's party**).

Roman law   International body of law derived from the legal principles of the Roman Empire.

schiltrom   Scots term for a large body of foot soldiers, formed up in close formation.

seisin   Legal possession, usually of land; so **to take seisin** is to gain possession.

surnames   Kin-groups on the borders, banded together for protection and maintenance (Chapter 9, Section i).

truce   An agreement temporarily suspending hostilities; while a truce was in force, the parties remained legally at a state of war.

wappinshaw   Scots term for a muster or review of all those obliged to bear arms in a particular lordship.

Currency

England and Scotland both used currencies based on the Carolingian French denominations of pounds, shillings and pence. At the beginning of the period, there was parity between English and Scottish currency, but the exchange rates started to vary from 1355 (see Chapter 10). Most coinage was minted as silver pennies.

1 pound (£) = 20 shillings (s.) = 240 pennies (d.)
1 s. = 12d.

The Mark (or 'Merk' in Scots), used as a unit of account, equalled two-thirds of a pound.

1 mark = 13s. 4d.

It is difficult to make meaningful comparisons with modern prices, but for most of this period, £5 was considered a reasonable annual salary for a clerk; an annual income of £10 was considered the minimum necessary to maintain the estate of a gentleman; and an annual income of £1,000 was considered sufficient to maintain the estate of an earl.

Index

d. = died; *da.* = daughter; *ex.* = executed; *k.* = killed
Abp = Archbishop; Bp = Bishop; Cts = Countess; D. = Duke; E. = Earl; K. = King; Q. = Queen
Dates of reigns are given for rulers

Aberdeen, 45, 133, 174, 176
Aberdeen, William Elphinstone, Bp of (*d.*1514), 88
Agincourt, battle of (1415), 3, 66, 140
Albany, D. of, *see* Stewart, Robert; Stuart, John
Alexander II, K. of Scots (1214–49), 8, 15, 17
Alexander III, K. of Scots (1249–86), 8, 10, 13, 14, 15, 29, 40
Alnwick, 7, 71; abbey, 150; castle, 38, 77, 146
Ancrum Moor, battle of (1545), 113
Angus, E. of, *see* Douglas; Stewart; Umfraville
Arbroath, Declaration of (1320), 185, 188
Argyll, Archibald Campbell, E. of (*d.*1558), 110, 111
Argyll, Archibald Campbell, E. of (*d.*1573), 120, 122, 125, 126, 128–9; as Archibald Campbell, 119
Armstrong surnames, 105, 158
Armstrong, Willie, *see* Kinmont Willie
Arran, James Hamilton, E. of (*d.*1529), 93, 94, 96, 98, 101
Arran, James Hamilton, E. of (*d.*1575), 109–13, 114, 115, 116, 118, 142; as D. of Châtelherault, 118, 119, 121–2
Arran, James Hamilton, E. of (*d.*1609), 121, 123; as father's heir, 111
Arran, E. of, *see also* Stewart, James
Arundel, Edmund Fitzalan, E. of (*ex.*1327), 34
Arundel, Richard Fitzalan, E. of (*d.*1376), 47
Atholl, John Strathbogie, E. of (*ex.*1306), 29, 30
Atholl, David Strathbogie, E. of (*d.*1326), 33, 39
Atholl, David Strathbogie, E. of (*k.*1335), 39, 44–5
Atholl, Catherine Beaumont, Cts of, 45
Arthur, K. of the Britons, 188, 190, 191
assurance, 113, 115, 116, 226 (*see also* Scots, assured)

Balliol family, 9–10
Balliol, Edward, *see* Edward (Balliol), K. of Scots
Balliol, John, *see* John (Balliol), K. of Scots
Bamburgh castle, 77, 79
Bannockburn, battle of (1314), 5, 32, 33, 34, 35, 41, 42, 60, 138, 139; anniversary of, 5, 87
Baugé, battle of (1421), 67, 138
Beaton, David, *see* St Andrews, David Beaton, Abp of
Beaumont, Henry (*d.*1340), 39–40, 44
Beaufort, Edmund, *see* Somerset
Beaufort, Henry, Bp of Winchester, cardinal (*d.*1447), 68, 69
Beaufort, Joan, *see* Joan (Beaufort), Q. of Scots
belt, reputedly made of human skin, 24
Berwick, 18, 19, 23, 31, 41, 48, 54, 60, 64, 68, 69, 71, 74, 75, 79, 81, 84, 85–6, 88, 89, 90, 96, 100, 102, 104, 106, 109, 112, 118, 119, 122, 138, 144, 145, 146, 150, 151, 155, 175, 198; attacked by English (1319), 35; attacked

229

Berwick – *continued*
by Scots (1297), 24; attacked by Scots (1355), 53, 56; attacked by Scots (1384), 58; attacked by Scots (1417), 66; captain of, 53, 75; captured by English (1296), 21; captured by English (1333), 42, 43; captured by English (1482), 82–3; captured by Scots (1318), 35; castle, 24, 56, 57, 83, 144, 154, 156; garrison, 32, 63, 87, 156; sheriffdom of (Berwickshire), 42, 43, 51, 154, 155, 161, 173; taken by Scots (1461), 76–7
Black Death, the, 51, 152, 175
Boece, Hector, historian (*d*.1536), 184, 185
Boniface VIII, *see* Pope Boniface
border, Anglo-Scottish, 6, 7, 43, 150, 156, 161
Boroughbridge, battle of (1322), 36, 139
Bothwell, Patrick Hepburn, E. of (*d*.1508), 87
Bothwell, James Hepburn, E. of, 2nd consort of Mary Q. of Scots (*d*.1578), 110, 111, 126
Bothwell, E. of, *see also* Stewart, Francis
Brittany, 49, 93, 172, 189
Broughty Craig, 114, 115, 116, 117, 145, 146
Bruce family, 9–10, 34
Bruce, Edward (*k*.1318), 4, 32, 33–4, 36, 190
Bruce, Edward (*d*.1611), 133
Bruce, Mary, 30
Bruce, Robert, the 'Competitor' (*d*.1295), 10, 13–14, 15, 16, 17, 18–19
Bruce, Robert, E. of Carrick (*d*.1304), 10, 14, 19, 21, 22
Bruce, Robert, E. of Carrick (*d*.1329), *see* Robert I
Bruce, Robert (*k*.1332), 40–1
Brut chronicle, 187, 189, 191
Brutus (*or* Brut), K. of the Britons, 5, 187, 189, 191
Burgundy, Philip 'the Good', D. of (*d*.1467), 71, 75, 76
Burgundy, Charles 'the Bold', D. of (*k*.1477), 78, 79
Byland, battle of (1322), 36, 138

Calais, 49, 70, 73, 74, 120, 173, 175, 196
Cambridge university, 18, 173–4
cannibalism, 33, 147–8, 193
Carlisle, 33, 42, 58, 71, 74, 76, 77, 157
Carlisle, castle, 35, 100, 165, 168
Carlisle, bishops of, 162
Carlisle, Dominicans of, 183
Carrick, John, E. of, *see* Robert III
Carrickfergus castle, 33, 94, 146
Castile, 57, 173
Cecil, William (*d*.1598), 121, 122, 123–4, 126–7, 133, 193, 202
Cecil, Robert (*d*.1612), 133–4
Cecilia, da. of Edward IV (*d*.1507), 79, 81, 82, 83, 84

Charles V, Emperor (1519–56, *d*.1558), 99, 101, 105, 107, 108, 111, 118, 119
Charles VI, K. of France (1380–1422), 59, 65, 67
Charles VII, K. of France (1422–61), 69, 71, 74, 76, 77; as Dauphin, 67, 68
Charles VIII, K. of France (1483–98), 84, 85, 87, 88
Charles IX, K. of France (1560-74), Châtelherault, D. of, *see* Arran
Chaucer, Geoffrey (*d*.1400), 179, 180
chivalry, 14, 45, 48, 52, 55, 185
Clifford family, 153, 154
Clifford, Robert, Lord (*k*.1314), 24
Clifford, Henry, E. of Cumberland (*d*.1542), 104
Clifford, Thomas, Lord (*d*.1391), 183
Coldingham, 90
Coldingham, priory, 97, 112, 150, 155–6, 177
Comyn family, 13, 15, 19, 20, 24, 27, 29, 30, 33, 34, 36, 39, 61
Comyn, Alexander, E. of Buchan (*d*.1289), 21
Comyn, Alice, Cts of Buchan (*d*.1349), 207, n.16
Comyn, John, of Badenoch (*d.c*.1302), 14, 17
Comyn, John (*k*.1306), 27, 28, 29, 33
Comyn, John, E. of Buchan (*d*.1308), 31
Comyn, John (*k*.1314), 33
Congregation, the, 120–2, 123, 126, 201, 226
Courtrai, battle of (1302), 27, 139
Craig, Thomas (lawyer, *d*.1608), 1, 2
Cravant, battle of (1423), 138
Crécy, battle of (1346), 3, 49, 140
Cressingham, Hugh (*k*.1297), 23, 24
cross-border landholding, 8, 9–10, 14, 17, 21, 33, 38, 39, 52, 63, 84, 87, 102, 113, 130, 149–50, 152–3, 155–6, 177
crusades, 7, 43, 45, 183
Culblean, battle of (1335), 45
Cuthbert, St, 71, 176–7

Dacre, Hugh (*d*.1383), 167
Dacre, Leonard (*d*.1573), 128
Dacre, Thomas, Lord (*d*.1525), 96, 97, 99, 100, 101, 164
Dacre, William, Lord (*d*.1563), 146, 166
Darnley, Henry Stewart, Lord, consort of Mary, Q. of Scots (*k*.1567), 124, 125, 126, 127, 129
Dauphin, *see* Charles VII; François II
Debatable Lands, 104, 109, 150, 161, 166, 185, 227 (*see also* Liddesdale)
David I, K. of Scots (1124–53), 6–7, 9, 28, 150, 188
David II, K. of Scots (1329–71), 49, 55, 69, 137, 138, 147, 153, 154, 155, 162, 172, 173, 176, 177, 182, 184, 190, 197; captivity, 50–4, 55, 137, 154, 170, 180, 186; exile,

INDEX 231

43–5, 47, 48, 200; heir to Robert I, 37, 38; ransom, 51–2, 53, 54, 55, 56, 57, 60, 172; rule as a minor, 40–3
Dee, John, astrologer, (d.1609), 193
Dervorguilla of Galloway (d.1290), 10, 18
Disinherited, the, 39–43, 51, 52, 54, 146, 227
Douglas family, 60, 153, 154, 163, 164, 182, 186
Douglas, Archibald (k.1333), 42
Douglas, Archibald, E. of (d.1400), 61
Douglas, Archibald, E. of (k.1424), 62–3, 64, 66, 68, 165; grievous wounds, 63, 138
Douglas, Archibald, E. of Angus (d.1513), 81, 87
Douglas, Archibald, E. of Angus (d.1557), 96–7, 98, 99, 100, 102–6, 110, 111, 112, 113, 115, 179
Douglas, Archibald, E. of Angus (d.1588), 129, 130
Douglas, James (k.1330), 39
Douglas, James, E. of (k.1388), 59, 64, 164
Douglas, James, E. of (d.1443), as James Douglas, 64
Douglas, James, E. of (d.1491), 73–4, 75, 76, 77, 81, 84, 85
Douglas, James, E. of Morton (ex.1581), 125, 129
Douglas, Gavin, Bp of Dunkeld (d.1522), 179
Douglas, George, E. of Angus (d.c.1403), 63
Douglas, George, E. of Angus (d.1463), 77
Douglas, George (d.1552), 105, 110
Douglas, William, of Liddesdale (k.1353), 43, 45, 47, 49, 50, 52, 153–4, 186
Douglas, William, E. of (d.1384), 56, 167, 168; as William, Lord Douglas, 53–4, 154
Douglas, William (k.1391), 183
Douglas, William, E. of Angus (d.1437), 70, 156, 163
Douglas, William, E. of (k.1452), 73–4
Drumlanrig, battle of (1548), 115, 138
Dryburgh abbey, 58, 150, 178
Dudley, Andrew (d.1559), 114, 115
Dudley, Robert, E. of Leicester (d.1588), 122, 124
Dumbarton castle, 42, 128
Dumfries, 29, 57, 66, 71, 76, 77, 82, 114; sheriffdom of (Dumfriesshire), 43, 51, 115, 154
Dunbar, 71, 85, 86; castle, 21, 22, 31, 47, 73, 84, 90, 117
Dunbar, battle of (1296), 22, 23, 24
Dunbar family, 149, 153, 154, 163, 186
Dunbar, Agnes, Cts of March (d.1369), 47
Dunbar, George, E. of March (d.1416x23), 56, 61, 62–3, 64, 65, 156, 163, 164, 165, 168
Dunbar, George, E. of March (d.1455x7), 70, 151, 163–4
Dunbar, Marjory, Cts of, 21, 22
Dunbar, Patrick, E. of March (d.1308), 21

Dunbar, Patrick, E. of March (d.1369), 33, 44, 47, 50, 53
Dunbar, Thomas, E. of Moray (d. by 1422), 63
Dunbar, William, poet (d.1513x30), 175, 179
Dundee, 114, 115, 146, 174, 183
Dunstanburgh castle, 77
Durham, 50, 71, 157; bishops of, 162; bishopric of, 148, 153, 163; priory, 10, 150, 151, 152, 155–6, 177;
Durham, Antony Bek, Bp of (d.1311), 22, 177
Durham, Thomas Ruthall, Bp of (d.1523), 146

Edinburgh, 23, 45, 48, 57, 58, 83, 109, 112, 114, 115, 116, 119, 128, 151, 174, 176, 178, 180, 189, 192; castle, 22, 32, 83, 112, 118, 129, 144, 145, 183; Holyrood, 57, 58, 112; sheriffdom of, 43
Edward I, K. of England (1272–1307), 7, 8, 10, 13–30, 33, 39, 41, 51, 61, 109, 113, 139, 142, 151, 152, 154, 161, 174, 177, 185, 187, 190, 195–6, 197, 198, 199, 200; government of Scotland, 22–4, 28; historical reputation, 4; and John, K. of Scots, 19–22; and Robert I, 29–31; and Scottish succession, 14–18; the 'Great Cause', 18–19; war with Scotland (1297–1304), 24–27
Edward II, K. of England (1307–27), 30–7, 40, 42, 139, 140, 142, 148, 150, 154, 177, 182, 196, 199; betrothal to Margaret of Norway, 14–16; deposition, 35, 37; opposition in England, 30–2, 35, 36, 198; as Prince of Wales, 26, 176; war with Scotland (1307–22), 30–3, 35–7, 51
Edward III, K. of England (1327–77), 37–56, 137, 142, 143, 144, 184, 186, 193, 197, 199; and Disinherited, 39–42; under Mortimer, 37–8; war with France, 46–9, 52–4, 55–6, 162, 172–3, 196; war with Scotland, 42–9, 54
Edward IV, K. of England (1461–83), 76–84, 86, 87, 113, 142, 146, 160, 173, 191, 198, 201; opposition in England, 76, 77, 78; war with Scotland, 80–4
Edward VI, K. of England (1547–53), 113, 192; as Prince of Wales, 110
Edward (Balliol), K. of Scots (1332–56, d.1364), 41–5, 48, 50, 51, 53, 54, 60, 154, 199; and disinherited, 39–41
Elgin, 22
Elizabeth, Q. of England (1558–1603), 120–34, 145, 180, 193, 198, 201, 202; and Mary, Q. of Scots, 123–6; Mary's captivity, 126–9; as princess, 111; and succession of James VI, 130–4; support for Scottish 'King's Party', 3, 128–30

Elizabeth (Woodville), Q. of England, consort of Edward IV (*d*.1492), 78, 79, 86
Eric II, K. of Norway (1280–99), 13, 15
Eure, Ralph (*d*.1617), 164–5
Eure, William (*d*.1548), 113
Eyemouth fort, 114, 119, 145

Falkirk, battle of (1298), 25, 139, 140
Faughart, battle of (1318), 34
Ferdinand II, K. of Aragon (1479–1516), 88–9, 91, 94, 95
Flanders, 23, 24, 25, 43, 47, 55, 58, 80, 140, 200
Flodden, battle of (1513), 3, 95, 138, 140, 146, 171, 177, 179, 201
Florence, Ct of Holland (*k*.1296), 16, 17, 18
François I, K. of France (1515–47), 96, 97–102, 103, 105, 107, 108, 110, 113, 201
François II, K. of France (1559–60), 120–2, 123; as Dauphin, 115, 117, 120, 199, 201
French soldiers in Scotland, 47, 52, 53, 57, 58–9, 60, 62, 81, 101, 115, 116, 117, 118–19, 120–1, 122, 142, 143, 144, 145, 148, 182
Froissart, Jean, chronicler (*d.c.*1404), 55, 173, 182

Gaidel (*or* Gaythelos), founder of Scottish line of kings, 183, 188
Galloway, 9, 14, 25, 51, 77, 151, 172; bishopric of, 177
Gascony, 8, 20, 37, 41, 43, 45, 49, 170
Gaunt, John of, *see* Lancaster
Gaveston, Piers, E. of Cornwall (*k*.1312), 30, 31
Glasgow, Robert Wishart, Bp of (*d*.1316), 24, 29
Gloucester, D. of, *see* Richard III
Gloucester, Gilbert Clare, E. of (*d*.1295), 10
Gloucester, Gilbert Clare, E. of (*k*.1314), 31, 32
Glyn Dŵr, Owain (*d.c.*1416), 63, 190–1
Gray, Patrick, Lord (*d*.1584), 114, 115
Gray, Thomas (*d*.1344), 138, 139
Gray, Thomas, chronicler (*d*.1369), 138, 139, 183
Grey, Catherine (*d*.1568), 124, 133
Grey, William, Baron (*d*.1562), 114, 115, 116, 117

Haddington fort, 115, 116, 117, 145
Haddon Rig, battle of (1542), 108, 109
Harclay, Andrew, E. of Carlisle (*ex*.1323), 33, 36–7, 139
Hardyng, John, chronicler (*d.c.*1464), 147, 183
Hastings, John (*d*.1313), 17, 19
Henri II, K. of France (1547–59), 117, 118–19, 120
Henri IV, K. of France (1589–1610), 132
Henry III, K. of England (1216–72), 8, 10, 14
Henry IV, K. of England (1399–1413), 61–5, 71, 109, 144, 163, 165, 179

Henry V, K. of England (1413–22), 62, 65–7, 70, 73, 126; as Prince of Wales, 65
Henry VI, K. of England (1422–61), 67–76, 78, 173; conflict in England, 73, 74, 75–6; exile, 71, 76, 77, 78; minority, 67, 68, 69, 165
Henry VII, K. of England (1485–1509), 85–93, 94, 163, 164, 175, 201, 202; as Henry Tudor, 84, 85; war with Scotland, 90–1 (*see also* Warbeck, Perkin)
Henry VIII, K. of England (1509–47), 93–113, 114, 124, 133, 146, 187, 193, 196, 200, 201; reformation, 106, 107, 110; war with France and Scotland, 94–5, 99–102, 111–13
Hertford, E. of, *see* Seymour
Higden, Ranulph, chronicler (*d*.1364), 179, 184, 198
Highlands, the, 4, 9, 119, 158, 160, 179
Holy League (1495), 88, 89
Holy League (1511), 94
Holyrood, *see* Edinburgh
Home castle, 96, 114, 115
Home family, 99, 100
Home, Alexander Lord (*d*.1506), 87
Home, Alexander Lord (*ex*.1516), 96–7
Home, David, of Wedderburn, 98
Howard, John, Lord (*k*.1485), 82, 112
Howard, Thomas, *see* Norfolk; Surrey
Humbleton Hill, battle of (1402), 63, 64, 65, 72, 138, 165, 173, 191
Huntingdon, David, E. of (*d*.1219), 14, 17, 18
Huntly, George Gordon, E. of (*d*.1562), 108, 110, 111, 114, 123
Huntly, George Gordon, E. of (*d*.1576), 125, 126, 128, 129
Huntly, George Gordon, E. of (*d*.1636), 131–2

Inchcolm Island, 114, 115; abbey, 177
Ireland, 4, 9, 10, 28, 30, 88, 91, 94, 107, 108, 119, 120, 122, 126, 147, 161, 188, 190, 191, 193, 196; Anglo-Irish, serving in English armies, 21, 31, 32, 142; Gaelic Irish, 4, 5, 9, 30, 34, 190, 200; Scottish invasion, 33–4, 200
Isabella, Q. of Castile (1474-1504), 88–9, 91
Isabella, Q. of England, consort of Edward II (*d*.1358), 37, 38, 39, 200
Isles, the, *see* Western Isles, the
Isles, Lords of the, *see* MacDonald, 186, 199

James I, K. of Scots (1406–37), 69–70, 144, 165, 173, 198; captivity, 64–8, 147; as Robert III's heir, 62, 64
James II, K. of Scots (1437–60), 73–6, 144, 156; as minor, 70

INDEX

James III, K. of Scots (1460–88), 78–86, 87, 89, 90, 137, 186, 191, 197, 203; as minor, 76, 77; war with England, 80–4
James IV, K. of Scots (1488–1513), 6, 87–95, 100, 138, 140, 143, 145, 171, 191, 198; alliance with France, 94–5; as D. of Rothesay, 79, 81, 85, 86, 197; minority rule, 87–8; negotiations with Spain, 88–90; shipbuilding, 146–7; war with England, 90–1, 95
James V, K. of Scots (1513–42), 104–9, 111, 120, 176, 178, 191; governed by Angus, 103–4; minority rule, 95, 96, 97, 98, 100, 102
James VI and I, K. of Scots (1567–1625), K. of England (1603–25), 1, 3, 15, 28, 126–34, 130, 160, 166, 180, 181, 188, 191, 193, 194, 196, 199, 202; and English succession, 130–4; king's party, 128, 227; minority rule, 126, 127, 128, 129
Jean II, K. of France (1350-64), 52, 53–4
Jedburgh, 48, 54, 57, 60, 65, 169; lordship of, 56
Joan, Q. of Scots, consort of David II (*d*.1362), 38, 41
Joan (Beaufort), Q. of Scots, consort of James I (*d*.1445), 68, 70
John (Balliol), K. of Scots (1292–6, *d*.1314), 10, 19–22, 41, 60; as claimant, 14, 15, 16, 17, 18–19, 184; after deposition, 24, 26; 'Toom Tabard', 22
John XXII, *see* Pope John

Kerr family, 155
Kerr, Andrew (*c*.1481), 152
Kerr, Andrew (*d*.1526), 145
Kerr, George, 132
Kerr, Robert (*k*.1508), 92–3
Kerr, Robert (*d*.1650), 165
Kerr, William (*d*.1600), 166
king's party, *see* James VI and I
Kinmont Willie, 158, 165, 168–9
Knox, John, theologian (*d*.1572), 174, 178, 192–3

Lancaster, John of Gaunt, D. of (*d*.1399), 57–8, 61, 68, 173; David II's heir, 52, 54
Lancaster, Thomas, E. of (*ex*.1322), 31, 32, 35, 36, 37, 139, 186
Landsknechte, 101, 116, 142–3, 227
laws and customs of war, 21, 30, 40, 42, 143–4, 148, 169, 178, 227
Leith, 82, 112, 114, 117, 121, 122, 146
Lennox, D. of , *see* Stuart, Esmé
Lennox, Malcolm, E. of (*k*.1333), 29
Lennox, E. of , *see also* Stewart, Matthew
Leslie, John, Bp of Ross, historian (*d*.1596), 151, 160

Liddesdale, 79, 82, 87, 104, 105, 116, 150, 154, 158, 168, 227
Lisle family, 104, 105
Lisle, Robert (*k*.1479), 80
Lochmaben, 48, 54, 57, 58, 82, 154
London, 27, 31, 38, 50, 51, 60, 105, 114, 170, 171, 174, 176, 179, 180, 188; Tower of, 22, 65, 137, 144
Lothian, 4, 6, 31, 36, 47, 53, 114, 115, 150, 173
Loudon Hill, battle of (1307), 30
Louis XI, K. of France (1461-83), 77, 78, 79, 80, 81, 82, 84; as heir to the Dauphin Charles, 68
Louis XII, K. of France (1498–1515), 93, 94, 95
Luttrell, John (*d*.1551), 114, 115, 116, 117

MacDonald, John, Lord of the Isles (*d.c*.1387), 44, 186
MacDonald, John, E. of Ross and Lord of the Isles (*d*.1503), 76, 81
MacDonald, Alexander (*d.c*.1536), 105
MacDougall family, 30
MacDougall, John (*d*.1316), 34
Macduff of Fife, 20, 21
Macduff, Isabel, Cts of Buchan (*d.c*.1313), 30
Mair (Major), John, historian (*d*.1550), 2, 174, 191, 192
Maitland, William (*d*.1573), 122, 123, 124, 125
Malcolm III, K. of Scots (1058–93), 6, 9, 17, 188
'Mammet', Richard II imposter (*d.c*.1417), 62, 65
Mar, Donald, E. of (*d.c*.1297), 21–2
Mar, Donald, E. of (*k*.1332), 40–1
Mar, John Erskine, E. of (*d*.1634), 133
March, E. of, *see* Dunbar
Marches, the, 55, 67, 70, 72, 144, 149–69, 173, 176, 183, 197
Marches, English, 24, 35, 36, 37, 48, 50, 57, 59, 61, 65, 66, 118, 132, 139, 172, 199; West March, 82, 109
Marches, Scottish, 41, 57, 82; East March, 78, 91, 96, 105; Middle March, 74, 150; West March, 77, 113, 150
March days, 56, 57, 80, 81, 92, 162, 164, 167, 168, 169, 227
March laws, 56, 92, 161–9, 227
Marches, lieutenant of, English, 57; Scottish, 57, 108
March wardens, 56, 164–9, 227; English, 53, 59, 63, 66, 71, 78, 80, 81, 84, 96, 104, 105, 108, 109, 113, 117, 141, 146, 157, 160, 162–3, 164, 226; Scottish, 56, 80, 84, 87, 92, 96, 104, 105, 115, 162, 163–4
Margaret, 'Maid of Norway', 8, 13, 14–16
Margaret (of Anjou), Q. of England, consort of Henry VI (*d*.1482), 71, 75–6, 77, 78

Margaret, St, Q. of Scots, consort of Malcolm III (d.1093), 6, 188
Margaret (Tudor), Q. of Scots, consort of James IV (d.1541), 6, 89, 91, 92, 94, 124, 133, 172, 179; as regent for James V, 95–6; exile, 97, 98; returns to Scotland, 101, 102–3
Mary, Q. of England (1553–8), 118, 119–20, 145, 178; as Henry VIII's heir, 100, 102, 103
Mary, Q. of Scots (1542–67, ex.1587), 120–6; betrothal to Prince Edward, 110–11, 112, 192, 193; captivity, 126–9, 130, 201; Dauphin, 115, 116, 117, 120, 199, 201; execution, 131, 193; historical reputation, 2; marriage to François, queen's party, 127, 128–9, 228; minority, 109, 110, 111, 118
Mary (of Guelders), Q. of Scots, consort of James II, 71; regent for James III, 76–7
Marie (de Guise), Q. of Scots, consort of James V (d.1560), 107, 110, 111, 118–19, 120, 121, 122, 178
Matilda, Q. of England, consort of Henry I (d.1118), 6, 17
Maximilian, Emperor (1486-1519), 80, 81, 88, 94, 95
Melrose abbey (Rox.), 58, 150, 156, 176, 177, 178
Menteith, Alan, E. of (d. bef. 1309), 29
Menteith, Alexander, E. of (d. bef. 1306), 21–2
Menteith, John Graham, E. of (ex.1347), 50–1
mercenaries, 9, 83, 85, 114, 119, 142–3 (see also Landsknechte)
Methven, battle of (1306), 30
Monmouth, Geoffrey of, chronicler (d.1154/5), 187, 189
Moray, E. of, see Dunbar; Randolph; Stewart
Mortimer, Roger, E. of March (ex.1330), 37, 38, 39, 40, 41, 200
Morton, E. of, see Douglas, James
Mowbray family, 39
Mowbray, John (k.1332), 39, 42, 44
Murray, Andrew (d.1297), 23
Murray, Andrew (d.1338), 44–5
Myton, battle of (1319), 35

Neville family, 75, 153, 154, 163
Neville, Charles, E. of Westmorland (d.1601), 127–8
Neville, Henry, E. of Westmorland (d.1564), 119
Neville, John, Lord (d.1388), 59
Neville, John, Lord Montagu (k.1471), 76, 78; as John Neville, 74
Neville, Richard, E. of Salisbury (k.1460), 71
Neville, Richard, E. of Warwick 'the kingmaker' (k.1471), 74, 77, 78

Neville's Cross, battle of (1346), 3, 50, 51, 54, 137, 138, 154, 172, 176, 177
Newbattle abbey, 58, 178
Newcastle upon Tyne, 19, 21, 43, 44, 105, 122, 130, 151, 157, 171, 183; garrison, 45
Norfolk, Thomas Howard, D. of (d.1554), 108–9
Norfolk, Thomas Howard, D. of (ex.1572), 121, 127
Norham, 151; castle, 16, 87, 118, 119; castle, attacked by Scots, 35, 37, 38, 78, 91, 94, 145, 151; castle, captains of, 113, 138, 178
Northumberland, E. of, see Percy
Northumbria, kingdom of, 5–6

O'Donnell, Hugh, Lord of of Tyrconnell (d.1537), 88, 94
O'Donnell, Manus, Lord of of Tyrconnell (d.1537), 119
Orkney, Henry Sinclair, E. of (d.1420), 63, 64
Otterburn, battle of (1388), 59, 64, 149, 173
Oxford university, 10, 18, 60, 173–4

papacy, the, 109–10, 177
Papal Schism (1378), 177–8, 188
parliaments, English, 16, 41, 42, 61, 68, 76, 78, 90, 94, 101, 110, 159, 160, 175; Scottish, 13, 33, 40, 52, 54, 61, 64, 79, 80, 82, 84, 85, 96, 102, 110, 111, 113, 119, 120, 122, 127, 156, 171, 174, 178
Penrith, 57, 66, 150
Percy family, 65, 66, 153, 154, 162–3
Percy, Henry, Lord (d.1314), 24
Percy, Henry, Lord (d.1352), 39
Percy, Henry, E. of Northumberland (k.1408), 56, 63–4, 66, 168, 186; as Henry, Lord Percy, 56, 165, 167
Percy, Henry, 'Hotspur' (k.1403), 59, 63, 66, 163, 165, 183
Percy, Henry, E. of Northumberland (k.1455), as heir, 66
Percy, Henry, E. of Northumberland (k.1461), as Henry Percy, 71
Percy, Henry, 80
Percy, Henry, E. of Northumberland (d.1537), 104, 105, 146
Percy, Thomas, Lord Egremont, 74
Percy, Thomas, E. of Northumberland (ex.1572), 127–8
Perth, 30, 40, 45, 48, 120, 142; castle, 31
Philip II, K. of Spain (1556–98), 124, 125, 131–2; as K. of England, consort of Q. Mary (1554–8), 118, 119
Philippe IV, K of France (1285–1314), 20, 25, 26, 27
Philippe VI, K of France (1328–50), 43, 45, 47, 49–50, 52, 200

INDEX

Piccolomini, Aeneas Sylvius (d.1464), 182
pilgrimage, 55, 70, 71, 176, 177
Pilgrimage of Grace (1536–7), 106, 107, 178
Pinkie, battle of (1547), 3, 114, 146
Piperden, battle of (1435), 70
piracy, pirates, 56, 60, 64, 88, 121, 142, 147, 167, 170
Poitiers, battle of (1356), 3, 53–4
Pope Benedict XII (1334–42), 45
Pope Boniface VIII (1294–1303), 26, 27, 187
Pope Clement V (1305–14), 30
Pope Gregory XIII (1572–85), 130
Pope John XXII (1316–34), 34–5, 38, 185
Pope Julius II (1503–15), 94
Pope Paul III (1534–47), 107, 108
Pope Sixtus IV (1471–84), 83, 85

queen's party, *see* Mary, Q. of Scots

Ramsay, John (k.1513), 86, 87, 90
Ramsey, Alexander (k.1342), 49, 153–4
Randolph, John, E. of Moray (k.1346), 43, 45
Randolph, Thomas, E. of Moray (d.1332), 35, 40, 47
Redesdale, 79, 158–60, 164
Richard II, K. of England (1377–99), 56, 58–60, 61, 156, 163, 173, 178 (*see also* 'Mammet')
Richard III, K. of England (1483–5), 84–5; as D. of Gloucester, 81, 82–4, 113, 163
Robert I (Bruce), K. of Scots (1306–29), 4, 19, 40, 44, 49, 50, 138, 143, 146, 148, 185, 199; as E. of Carrick, 19, 21, 24, 26–7; expedition to Ireland, 34; heirs, 36, 37; historical reputation, 2, 3; peace negotiations, 36–8, 39; Scottish opposition to, 29–30, 33, 36, 198 (*see also* Soules conspiracy); seizes Scottish kingship, 2, 29–30, 41; war with England, 30–8
Robert II, K. of Scots (1371–90), 55–6, 57, 60; Robert I's heir, 36; David II's heir, 40, 49, 51–3, 197, as Robert, Lord Stewart, 43, 44, 50, 51–3, 55, 172, 186
Robert III, K. of Scots (1390–1406), 60–1, 62, 64, 143; as John, E. of Carrick, 57
Roslin, battle of (1303), 27
Ross, William, E. of (d.1323), 21–2
Ross, William, E. of (d.1372), 50
Rothesay, D. of, *see* Stewart, David; James IV
Roxburgh, 24, 25, 27, 45, 48, 49, 53, 54, 58–9, 60, 66, 68, 69, 70, 75–6, 79, 81, 168, 198; castle, 32, 44, 57, 114, 144, 154, 155, 158; English garrison, 74, 143, 156; English keeper of, 75, 156; sheriffdom of (Roxburghshire), 43, 49, 51, 153, 154
Rutland, Thomas Manners, E. of (d.1543), 108

Rutland, Henry Manners, E. of (d.1563), 117
St Andrews, 176; castle, 113; university, 173
St Andrews, William Lamberton, Bp of (d.1328), 29
St Andrews, James Kennedy, Bp of (d.1465), 78–9
St Andrews, David Beaton, Abp of, and Cardinal (d.1539), 107, 110, 111, 112, 113
Salisbury, William Montague, E. of (d.1344), 47
Sark, river, battle of (1448), 71, 95, 138
schiltroms, 32, 139, 140, 148, 228
Scota, da. of the Pharoah, consort of Gaidel, 5, 188
Scots, Gaelic-speaking, 9, 151, 160, 174, 179, 184; assured, 2, 113, 114, 115, 138, 155, 116, 226; service in English armies, 6, 7, 8, 14, 20, 21, 23, 51, 52, 57, 76, 81, 85, 127, 172–3; service in French armies, 53–4, 66–8, 69, 84–5, 118, 200–1
Scott, Walter, of Buccleuch (d.1611), 165, 168–9
Scone, 13, 19, 29, 41; Stone of, 22, 38
Selkirk, 27; Forrest, 155; sherrifdom of, 43
Seton, Alexander (d.c.1348), 32, 144
Seymour, Edward, E. of Hertford, D. of Somerset (ex.1552), as Protector, 113–17, 118, 142, 145, 146, 155, 192, 199, 202; as E. of Hertford, 112–3, 147
Seymour, Edward, Viscount Beauchamp (d.1612), 133, 134
Shakespeare, William (d.1616), 3, 4, 189
'Shameful Peace', the, *see* treaty of Edinburgh
Shrewsbury, battle of (1403), 63, 138
Shrewsbury, E. of, *see* Talbot, Francis
SNP, the, 5
Solway Moss, battle of (1542), 109, 110, 114
Somerset, D. of, *see* Seymour
Somerset, Edmund Beaufort, D. of (k.1455), 73, 74, 75
Soules conspiracy (1320), 36, 39, 185
Spain, 89, 94, 98, 108, 120, 125, 127, 128, 129, 131, 132, 173 (*see also* Castile)
Stewart, Alexander, D. of Albany (k.1485), 79, 80, 81, 82–4, 85, 88, 186, 197
Stewart, David, D. of Rothesay (k.1402), 61, 62, 164
Stewart, Francis, E. of Bothwell (d.1612), 132–3
Stewart, Henry, Lord Darnley, *see* Darnley
Stewart, James (d.1309), 24
Stewart, James, E. of Buchan (c.1500), 75, 89
Stewart, James, E. of Moray (d.1545), 105
Stewart, James, E. of Moray (k.1570), 125, 126–8; as James Sewart, 120, 122, 123, 124

Stewart, James, E. of Arran (k.1596), 130
Stewart, John, E. of Buchan (k.1424), 66, 67
Stewart, Matthew, E. of Lennox (k.1571), 110, 112, 114, 118, 124, 128, 129
Stewart, Murdoch (ex.1425), 62–3, 65, 66
Stewart, Robert, Lord, see Robert II
Stewart, Robert, D. of Albany (d.1420), 62, 64–6
Stewart, Thomas, E. of Angus (d.1362), 53, 173
Stuart, Esmé, D. of Lennox (d.1583), 129
Stuart, John, D. of Albany (d.1536), 95, 103; governor of Scotland, 96–7, 99–102, 201; visits France, 98–9
Stirling, 121; castle, 22, 25, 27, 32, 45, 48, 111, 130, 185
Stirling Bridge, battle of (1297), 24, 25, 138, 139
Suffolk, Charles Brandon, D. of (d.1545),
surnames, 104, 105, 158–60, 228 (see also Armstrong)
Surrey, Thomas Howard, E. of (later D. of Norfolk, d.1524), 95, 101

Talbot, Francis, E. of Shrewsbury (d.1560), 116
Talbot, Richard, Lord (d.1356), 39, 44
Teviotdale, 112, 113, 116, 155, 156, 161
treaties: Amiens (1302), 27; Asnières (1301), 26; Ayton (1497), 92; Berwick (1357), 54; Berwick (1560), 122, 124; Berwick (1586), 130, 132; Birgham-Northampton (1290), 15, 16, 20, 110, 197; Corbeil (1326), 37, 43; Edinburgh-Northampton (1328, the 'Shameful Peace'), 38, 39, 40, 41, 42, 52, 54, 195, 199; Edinburgh (1560), 122, 124, 127, 128; Fotheringay (1482), 82; Greenwich (1543), 111, 112, 116, 197; Haddington (1548), 115, 117; London (1518), 98; Norham (1551), 117, 119; Paris (1295), 20, 21, 22, 37, 47; Perpetual Peace (1502), 91, 93, 94, 198; Rouen (1518), 98, 99, 100, 101, 103; Vincennes (1371), 55, 137; Westminster-Ardtornish, 76; York (1237), 8, 150
Tudor, Henry, see Henry VII
Tudor, Margaret, see Margaret (Tudor), Q. of Scots
Tynedale, 79, 150, 158–60, 164, 168

Ulster, 33, 94, 105
Ulster, Richard Burgh, E. of (d.1326), 31, 34
Umfraville family, 39, 150, 153, 159
Umfraville, Gilbert, E. of Angus (d.1307), 21
Umfraville, Ingram (d.c.1321), 140, 153, 159
universities, see Cambridge, Oxford, St Andrews

Vergil, Polydore, chronicler (d.1555), 89, 179, 184
Verneuil, battle of (1424), 68, 138, 173

Wales, the Welsh, 4, 5, 6, 9, 10, 14, 20, 22, 23, 63, 65, 105, 187, 189, 190, 191, 198, 200; service in English armies, 21, 25, 32, 63; Welsh Marches, 39
Wales, Prince of, see Edward II; Edward VI; Henry V
Wallace, William (ex.1305), 23, 24–5, 27, 138; historical reputation, 3, 5
Warenne, John, E. of (d.1304), 22–3, 24, 31
Warbeck, Perkin, pretender (ex.1499), 87–91
Wark on Tweed, 149; castle, 21, 57, 58, 61, 76, 101, 113, 118, 119, 145
Warkworth castle, 38, 71, 144
'Warwolf', the, 27
Weardale campaign (1327), 38, 41, 142
Western Isles (the Isles), 30, 34, 41, 44, 62, 105, 108, 119, 146, 158, 186
Westminster, 10, 20, 23, 25, 54, 71, 111, 127, 150, 155, 175, 186; abbey, 22
Wharton, Thomas (d.1568), 109, 113, 114, 115
wife, fierce, 148
William 'the Lion', K. of Scots (1165–1214), 7–8, 13, 14, 16, 17
Wolsey, Thomas, cardinal (d.1530), 93, 98, 99, 102, 103, 174
Wyntoun, Andrew, chronicler (d.c.1422), 47, 53

York, 5, 8, 25, 38, 41, 100, 127
York, Abps of, 177
York, William Melton, Abp of (d.1340), 35
York, Richard, D. of (k.1460), 73–6
York, Richard, D. of (? k.1483), 87

www.ingramcontent.com/pod-product-compliance
Lightning Source LLC
Chambersburg PA
CBHW070029010526
44117CB00011B/1762